THE KLONDIKE
DETECTIVE

Murder on King Solomon's Dome

BRUCE L. WILLIS

ISBN: 1546645187
ISBN 13: 9781546645184

CHAPTER 1

It was a fool's errand to wait for a man who might never appear and I was tired. The extreme cold and exhaustion induced a fiendish desire that if he crossed the frozen river, the ice would crack and he would disappear screaming into the icy depths. He had driven me to this frenzied wish and part of me was ashamed, but my conscience recently had drifted into a remote and strange territory. It was not hard to justify this, he and I were in a type of war, and the man was a monster who deserved it. I was the constant shield, dented and bent but now I wanted to be the sword, if only once to bring finality to this nightmare. The loss of a suspect would not matter since he would not talk, and we had the evidence, but it would stop his acts of terror. His maliciousness frightened our most hardened prisoners, who begged if I caught him, to put him in a separate cell under a heavy guard. If that ever happened I would pity any police who had to deal with him.

He had an uncanny ability to know our plans and survived, with knowledge from paid informants. These vermin were beyond our reach and his continued freedom made my job both difficult and deadly. If I was to wager which of us would survive, he had the much better odds. As a master criminal he had survival skills including choosing the most frigid day of travel, which meant he would not expect to be followed. As a top marksman, he normally hit his targets, but I was lucky and avoided his attempts to kill me, but it would only be a matter of time before he disposed of me, hopefully where someone would find me.

Only people from the Yukon Territory understand true cold, since if we ignore it, we die. Outside with the wind my skin would freeze in two or three minutes and this weather created a city of unknown strangers, with hats over foreheads, scarves over noses, you could not recognize a neighbor. You relied on voices unless the wind was too strong, then you asked.

This cold ate away at me. The shaking started at my back and continued through my body and into my hands to the point I could not feel my fingers and toes. I could not rely on my accuracy since my trembling hands would send shots in every direction and I hoped my eyelids would not freeze which would force me to abandon my lookout. I was in an abandoned warehouse overlooking the Yukon River in Lousetown, next to Dawson City. If a miner had money, and wicked tastes, he travelled to Lousetown, a place of saloons, gambling halls and hotels, all busy with short-term guests.

The disappearing sun was behind the building and anyone who looked at the window could not see me, since the window was dirty and parts of an old curtain hid my reflection. My pocket watch showed almost five as I still waited to see if he appeared. The snow had stopped, but gusts of wind blocked my view. My field glasses were useless since that degree of cold causes metal to burn and stick to my face. There was an unlit stove in the upstairs room, which was left that way, since the building was deserted and I trespassed and didn't want the smoke to draw attention.

It was early November 1901 and I had been in the Yukon Territory for almost six months. I was twenty-one, but with this cold, it felt like I was an old relic of forty-one. I wanted a drink and did not care if it was whisky or beer, but I needed something to stop this shivering and all I had was my frozen steel water bottle and my sandwich which were hard as ice. The North West Mounted Police were on the hunt for Searle and I was part of that chase.

I had a new and serious problem since my legs were now stiff and non-responsive and as I turned back to the window I saw a man in a bulky black coat and wool cap emerge from the evergreen trees on the far side of the river. When he arrived near the warehouse I could see it was my man. I headed towards the stairs but I almost collapsed and grabbed the banister as I slid backward down the stairs to end up sprawled on the floor but I could not feel pain since that part was frozen. I kicked open the door and stepped into a dark and empty street where swirling wood smoke enveloped me but I saw ahead that Searle handed a package to a man in a brown overcoat. My partner was at the end of this street and Frank and his brother watched on the next street so I was alone. If he ran they would pursue him, but they had to be cautious since he knew the streets, and expected to be followed.

The man with the package had my interest and would be dangerous so I withdrew my revolver. The absence of decent light meant I needed a fast pace and looked around for a constable but they were inside and not patrolling the streets. Ice fog rolled in from the river, which hid the man, but I kept walking then stopped to listen and heard the faint sound of a creaking gate, so I crept to that sound. I gently lifted it to prevent any noise and carefully closed it. Reflective lights from the buildings showed his footpath in the snow.

A warehouse came into view and the light revealed a short fat man with a scarf that covered his face. No weapon was revealed but I assumed he was armed and he had a strange behavior because he never looked back. This meant he was either careless or had associates in wait at the warehouse. Every time I did something alone it never went well, but if I ran back to the Detachment, it would be half an hour and he could remove any loot and disappear. I was so desperate to find Searle I continued my pursuit in the fog.

I needed to move or my legs would stop. The streets remained deserted since this cold front drove both civilized people and my enemies indoors. I was thankful that the snow silenced my steps as I quietly pulled out my revolver and looked. He was gone and I almost swore since I was so close to success. I had not heard any sound of a door but my senses warned me to jump, as he leaped at me with a knife. I moved left as he moved past.

"Drop it," I yelled as he ran and I fired near him.

"Stop or I will shoot again." I hate when they ignore me and this bloody fool changed directions as I fired over his head. He fell on some ice and I ran and kicked his arm and knocked away his knife. I had my revolver pointed at him when Jerome called out that he was behind me.

My partner, Constable Jerome Scott was now beside me and I told him I would cover him if he tied up the prisoner. Once he was restrained, I pulled down the scarf that covered his face and remembered him. Last summer he had followed me from the Royal Alexandria Hotel when I had dinner with a reporter. I searched him and found a package and inside was a key to a bank safety deposit box. To find that deposit box would be easy, since Dawson City had only two banks, the British North America Bank and the Commerce Bank.

I asked Jerome to take the prisoner to the Detachment and he said he would send a patrol for me. When they were gone I moved around the warehouse to discover a door, stood and listened, but could not hear a sound other than dogs barking in the street. The handle turned, I stepped in and moved slowly forward into the darkness. Something on the floor tripped me and I reached down to pick up a lantern. I struck a safety match, adjusted the wick and the flickering light showed a locked door. I fired at the lock, opened it and discovered a large storage area. The lantern's glow showed five large crates and about one hundred large sacks. I went back to the entrance to hear if my shot brought any unwanted visitors but the only sound was my racing heart.

Returning with my bayonet I opened the first crate to discover twenty Lee-Enfield rifles. In the remaining crates were at least one hundred more and ammunition. I assumed the sacks contained bullion since we still had not recovered all the stolen gold from the steamships. I ripped the first one with my bayonet and gold nuggets spilled out. This was enough gold to kill without a second thought and it was time to leave, but my perverse nature kept me there to protect the evidence.

Searle should have a watcher near the warehouse but if we maintained a chain of custody, this evidence could be entered at trial. His associate led me to this warehouse and Searle handed him the parcel so I had a factual connection to a gang that had carried out large numbers of gold robberies and I had stumbled on important evidence that could tie Searle to many years in jail.

Why had this gold not been sent out during the summer? This bothered me since Searle had used this warehouse to store the gold and he was a master of deviousness and quick response. I thought of another problem, whether his associates knew about this and was I know in a warehouse during a gang war? This evidence must be grabbed before it was moved since he could return at any time and the rifles were evidence to another part of a conspiracy. I shifted the lantern and then thought this was unwise so I moved out of the light. I had overstayed my time here and if someone entered, I was trapped with no exit. A voice yelled for me to drop my weapon. My revolver did not make a sound as it dropped and I raised my hands. I turned to see Bert, Jerome, and two constables.

"Caldwell, why could you not wait for the patrol? I do not know what to do with you since you appear to have such a death wish." I told them what I had found and we protected the gold and guns while a constable went to obtain a wagon. Searle had disappeared. Jerome told me that Frank tracked him to the end of Lousetown but lost him, helped by the darkness, ice fog and wood smoke. We had my statement to charge the suspect with assault and possession of stolen property. The package and bank deposit key were locked in the evidence locker while the gold sacks and boxes of rifles were put in the office under guard. I hoped this was the last unknown gang member since I was tired and this investigation was like a rotten tooth that never let up.

My walk home was aided by the dark, the wood smoke and ice fog that concealed me but also anyone in wait for me. I held my revolver since I did not want any more surprises. I had moved back to the rooming house for a few days, while work was done on my house, but as I neared Sixth Avenue, I heard a crack like a shot, dropped and lay on the ground for a couple of minutes. Then I heard the same sound again, looked and saw a tree that caused this noise. Extreme cold caused this.

One husky started to howl and soon the whole city enjoyed the concert. In far off hills, wolves completed the chorus, and then suddenly it stopped as if an orchestra leader lowered his baton. I looked at the sky and saw the outline of the moon and stars and wondered why did wolves and huskies howl at a moon. My dogs barked as I arrived and I spent a few minutes with them and entered the house, climbed to my room and closed the door. I looked out the window to see the city covered by smoke and fog. Sixth Avenue was further up the mountain where we were not obscured by smoke or fog. A combination of frustration and fear kept me awake since I was tired but could not sleep and thought of why I was here which was part of a long and strange journey. I remembered my friend Corporal Tupper who was home safe in the Detachment, which took me back to another dangerous time.

We had both fought in South Africa against the Boers, although we were not in the same unit. He served with the Royal Canadian Regiment while I was a trooper with the Strathcona's Horse Regiment. It was September 1900 and I had been in the war since May. Our regiment was part of the Third Mounted Brigade when fighting brought us close to the Modder River. The Boers captured a platoon of Canadians and our job was to carry out a rescue. We wandered into a trap where I was captured and brought by irregular soldiers to a camp where they tied me to a soldier from the Royal Canadian Regiment. After they left he started.

"Are you all idiots? What a useless rescue." His facial expression showed disdain and disgust in equal measures. I gritted my teeth and tried not to explode.

"My name is John Caldwell. We were two troops from the Strathcona's and we left our mounts and the rest of the squadron to maintain silence to walk slowly into an ambush. We dropped our weapons and raised our hands, but seeing you here, you know exactly what that is like." My explanation resulted in a long silence followed by a wild exclamation with such explosive power, complexity, and vigor, that I started to laugh, which did not help our introduction. After months in the army, I had learned a new appreciation for the English language.

"Grant Tupper, and I come from Nova Scotia." He was large and broad, about six feet tall, with a nose so large it would keep his lips dry if it rained. That protrusion partly covered his large moustache and his hair was brown and covered his large ears. You could not call him handsome, but he looked trustworthy. His uniform was worn and dirty since he had been in the camp for two months.

I am big, about six feet five inches and weigh about two hundred and fifty pounds. I have sandy hair, a big grin and an attitude that gets me into trouble. I had been told I am handsome, but I do not know because I am shy around girls. We were in a large barn and could hear sounds of a nearby river. The windows were covered and we were left alone. I never understood why they kept us apart from the other prisoners and over the next few weeks we became friends. I was surprised to discover a gentle soul beneath his rough face and size.

Grant told me stories of his uncle who had sailed around the world. He laughed about misadventures in his rural school and we discovered we had read many of the same books and discussed our love of *Dickens, Scott, and Stevenson*. We defended our favorite authors, *Wilkie Collins, Hart, and Henty* and recaptured those stories to drive away boredom.

It was difficult to tell my personal history since I was ashamed of my actions. We lived in a large house on Jarvis Street in Toronto where I was the third and youngest child. My oldest brother was involved in the family business while my sister married a partner in a prestigious law firm. I started at Upper Canada College in the first grade where my brother, father, and grandfather had attended. I was rebellious, loved practical jokes and resented our British headmaster. I heard him tell another teacher that his primary duty was to bring civilization to the backward sons of Toronto. Each summer I stayed at our stables in King City that was north of Toronto. One of the stable hands had raced horses in Dublin and told amusing stories of the tricks of Irish horse racing. Michael knew what food to give a horse and what not to feed them.

"If you want to cause mischief, feed a horse rich alfalfa." He stopped to cough.

"Boy," he said, "The gas will knock you over. And if it is a big horse, you will hear that at quite a distance and as a bonus, the droppings will make you sick." He added, that the horse would be fine and perhaps he should not have told me that, as it formed the basis for my secret rebellion against the head-master. This occurred in May for the school parade for the Queen's birthday. The school had our cadet corps, affiliated with the Queen's Own Rifles on parade where I was a cadet Captain. It was my last year of school and I was eighteen.

Early that morning I snuck into the stables to start my act of revenge. The headmaster rode his horse on parade and as he passed the first column, a rumbling began that increased in volume and timing. The horse became increasingly excited and started to jump. An explosion came from the rear of the horse and there was a parting of the way between headmaster and horse. He ascended a distance and came down, but alone. The horse trotted and dropped short and sharp eruptions. The headmaster was not hurt but was irate and the whole spectacle was greeted with a raucous cheer, but I stood shocked and silent.

I never intended that result as my experiment had gone out of control. All I wanted was enough flatulence for smelly gas but I was done in with an inspection of the school lockers. The headmaster discovered alfalfa in my locker and the school and I had a permanent separation. Which was a shame since I was the best student and a top sportsman in rugby, boxing, and hockey, and without my final exams, I could not attend Victoria College at the University of Toronto. That night my father did not want to hear my side of the story.

"Such a sordid affair and you have been sent down from the school." Father's solution was harsh and unforgiving. I was expelled from school, house, city, and province. Despite mother's pleas, I was sent west to work on my uncle's ranch, near Calgary in the District of Alberta, but I barely remembered my time on the Canadian Pacific train. My misery was so evident that other passengers avoided me and no one shared my seat or looked at me.

The ranch was huge as it produced grain and raised cattle. I went to the bunkhouse, lay down and decided my life was at an end. On the morning of the third day the manager marched me into an ice-cold shower, and after new clothes were thrown at me, I was ordered to dress and follow him. Inside the office, I noticed a fireplace, comfortable chairs, and a table.

"My name is Roderick McCallum and I am your boss. If you have problems, sort it out. Only bother me if it is a life or death dilemma, and end your self-pity. I read your father's letter but at least you have a family. My parents died when I was sixteen and I was left with nothing and my only solution was to leave the Highlands, and join the Hudson Bay Company. My life was a constant number of trading forts." My new boss stood and examined me. Staring back, he was about fifty, tall, with a dark tan and wrinkles on his face, a large moustache and enormous arms. He waited for a few minutes and continued.

"You will work with the cattle, to feed and protect them and study to learn how to kill marauding animals. Most of the ranch hands are from the Ukraine and Germany and teaching them English will be after dinner. Chess is a skill you will also master since I need a partner. The final correspondence exams for Ontario must be completed by June 30th. Your books are here and the exams will arrive soon and you will pass." He moved closer to glare into my eyes.

"In this world, you have two choices. You can be happy or miserable and I suggest the former since I made that choice and I think your uncle chose the latter because he disappeared on a drunk six months ago. It is a good thing the ranch is in your grandfather's name. One other thing, your grandfather's letter was sent to me, he believes in you and that you will succeed and make him proud and he loves you. We are done, the cook shed is to your right, so eat because you will be very busy."

I was very occupied and became an expert in weapons, passed my exams with top marks and taught the ranch hands English, both reading, and writing. I became an expert in chess and discovered the harder I worked, the happier I became. The mountains gave me a respect for the weather while the cattle and horses taught me patience. The newcomers to Canada taught me familiarity to men I normally would not be with. I read the collected works of *Shakespeare*, many major works of English, and history. Mr. McCallum was a great fan of *Robbie Burns* and *Rudyard Kipling*. During our games of chess, we took turns reciting our favorite poems and quotes.

Reading the Calgary paper, I discovered Canada's involvement in the South African War and a squadron of the Strathcona's Horse recruited me. I was twenty and ready for war, which offered an adventure. When he learned that, my father was irate but I did not care since I had not seen him for two years. It was hard to say farewell to the ranch hands and Mr. McCallum, as they were good friends and my introduction to a new and different life. As I finished telling Grant about my life before soldiering I was glad he never asked if I regretted my actions.

We were so tired of the barn and captivity. One day they took us to a farmhouse and I thought they were going to execute us. My Dutch was basic and I pleaded with them that we were Christians and not to kill us. They laughed and one said in English, that we were to act as servers since they had organized a dance. Late that night we rested in the kitchen and noticed there was only one Boer soldier on a chair to guard us. He seemed friendly but had a grip on a Mauser pistol on his lap. I yawned and looked at Grant, winked and closed my eyes. I checked twenty minutes later and saw him asleep as we moved to escape through the door.

A British patrol was found the next day and we rode with a company of soldiers to the rescue but the Boers were long gone when we arrived. Almost a year of fighting seemed like a lifetime. At the start, the Boers trounced the British forces in a series of skirmishes and the British, along with the other Empire soldiers, were bloodied or killed and we learned the skill of a well-organized retreat until the weight of the Empire and placing the wives and children in camps turned the tide.

The sergeant made me troop leader, as I could sense when the enemy was near and I was placed in the second last position in our troop. The last position was the getaway trooper so if something happened to the patrol, his job was to ride back and provide a report, if he still lived. My job was to tap the trooper in front, who would pass the message to the leader. I was on a reconnaissance patrol for a small brigade when I was shot. It was not the Boers, but a soldier in the Seventh Leicestershire Yeomanry Regiment. A cart jolted me on the way to a field hospital and each bump brought intense pain and my curses to be shot by our own side.

Grant learned of my injury and travelled to the hospital and it did not take him long to figure out my black mood. I told him to leave and said I was better off dead and then shouted that I lived a wasted life. He sat there, smiled, said nothing and waited and over the next few days, I started to take an interest in my surroundings and began to talk about books and started to walk and joke. Grant provided me with magazines, *Cassel's*, and the *Strand* and before he left he made me promise to look him up and to have a drink before we headed into our different worlds.

I never saw Grant again during that war. I was granted special leave so I decided that England needed my special charms and took a ship to London to reside at the Savoy. I wrote to my cousin, who studied at Cambridge, who came down to show me the city. He introduced me to his tailors, which meant formal suits, his interest in music, which included light operas and music halls, and entertainment including pantomimes and magic lantern shows. I was still too shy to talk to the ladies but discovered whisky, fine wine, and French cooking.

February was an eventful month. My trust fund began on February 8, 1901, when I turned twenty-one. My grandfather and Aunt Dorothy took pity on me and had created a generous fund. A week later at Buckingham Palace, the regiment received the Queen's South Africa Medal. The last night before leaving London, instead of a wild introduction to the bars of London, I went to the Savoy theatre for my last show of Gilbert and Sullivan.

We returned to Canada where I was discharged in Halifax and tried to find Grant but learned he had departed to the Yukon Territory. I returned to Toronto and stayed with my cousin. I intended to work until the fall when I would attend the University of Toronto. My skills were limited, expert horsemen, crack shot and the ability to fight but I had no interest in becoming a clerk or shopkeeper, and was at a loss to find something to keep me interested.

It did not take long before I took a job at a Queen Street Hotel saloon owned by David Miles. My job was the removal of bothersome clients and I had certain advantages that included my size and my knowledge of survival fighting. At school, I was on the boxing team and as part of army basic training I learned hand combat and I was helped by the fact I was sober and the patrons drunk. Mr. Miles had me walk with him as his guard to the bank. He was tall, friendly and had a wonderful grin and at the end of the day, his choice was light rum. We were on the square and had a mutual trust. In late March, he asked me why was I not doing something else.

"John, it was great having you, but move on." I started to read about the Yukon Territory and the gold rush became my dream. Articles from the *Globe's* correspondent in Dawson City kept me enthralled and the thought of travelling to the Klondike gold fields took hold of me. I was twenty-one and believed anything was possible and remembered I had promised Grant to have that drink. During visits with Grandfather, I learned he controlled the family business. Grandfather told me with a chuckle, he had also been removed from Upper Canada College. He thought my prank to be one of the best stories he had ever heard. He also had military service in the militia, fighting the Fenians in the 1860's and our relationship was close and comfortable. Often when I was a guest at his house and headed to bed I heard his call for one more scotch. I loved him and could never say no and when I told him of my thoughts of an adventure to the gold fields, he thought that was just dandy. It was hard to say goodbye to my family and there was no reconciliation with my father as I started my adventure to the Yukon Territory on May 15th, 1901.

CHAPTER 2

It was Saturday, June 1, 1901, and the sun and cloudless sky created a perfect day. As we rounded the last bend on the Yukon River, the paddlewheel steamer the *Canadian* blew its whistle, and Dawson City came into in view. Steep bluffs descended from the mountains to the Klondike and Yukon Rivers. Thousands of people on the dock cheered, shouted and waved since this was the reunification of families and friends and the first boat to arrive in seven months.

A huge and noisy welcome welcomed us. Posters, banners, and flags fluttered on buildings near the river and bandsmen, dressed in blue and white, played Dixie and other popular songs. Dressed in white, the orchestra leader wore a tall blue hat and danced to the music and bowed at our boat. Passengers on the deck waved and danced as we neared shore and the ship's whistle kept time to the brass band, which was a jamboree to remember.

Front Street was filled with hotels, saloons, gambling houses, and dance halls. One fellow was thrown out of a saloon, pushed back his hat and entered the next one, and a minute passed before his next removal. This was a man with a thirst as he stood up and staggered into the third bar, but must have calmed down since he was not ejected.

Tradesmen, miners, well-dressed men and ladies pushed and shoved to obtain a view. Shouts were mixed with recommendations of cheap beer, fresh bread, and fine hotels. Administrative buildings, hotels, warehouses, and homes filled the valley. It took a while to get my luggage and once in my hotel I decided to see the sights and started on First Avenue. Walking along the street towards the Klondike River I encountered a nauseous smell that almost made me book a passage back to Whitehorse.

Garbage had been placed on two barges at the end of First Avenues with a temporary sewage drain that was blocked by ice and garbage, which was the cause of the horrid smell. Many frame buildings tilted like a two-day drunk since Dawson City was built on permafrost, and as the ground shifted, so did the buildings and it was common to see long boards that held up houses or shops.

Everywhere I walked it was, "Hello, good day, or, how are you?" as it was the custom to greet neighbors. Until the end of June, you wore rubber boots to overcome the constant mud. I needed to mine but how and where could I begin? I had not conducted any preliminary research other than articles in the *Globe* and it seemed that I had jumped before thinking. I had already spent three hundred dollars on supplies, trains, and boats.

The Royal Alexandria Hotel became my first home. It was a two-story building that had the most amazing bar. Attached to each end of the bar were gold emblems with scales to weigh gold. My first night at that bar began my research where miners answered my questions in return for drinks and by the end of the evening I was not sure what was true or their tall tales. A member of the North West Mounted Police told me Grant was out of town.

Mining required ample running water. When I arrived the spring freshet floods provided additional water for sluices, dredges, and hydraulic equipment. The gold fields never stopped, with perpetual noise day and night, and the scraping of metal on rock and from a distance the sound of sluices created a rhythm that never seemed to end. One miner permitted me to hold a long round cylinder attached to a hose with a handle that sent powerful streams of water to push away overburden.

Dredges were in constant use on Bonanza Creek, Bear Creek, and the Klondike River Flats. Another miner told me the Golden Crown Mining Company had a dredge of over one hundred tons and four stories in height. To float a dredge water is trapped in an excavated area. When the dredge moves forward, a series of bucket belts extend the front to remove vegetation, rocks, and gravels that are fed into sluice boxes. A dredge has two endless chains of buckets that occupy the front and rear of the structure. At the bow, there is a chain of buckets, which act both as an excavator and hoist. The rear holds the tailings stacker to process the pay dirt from which gold is extracted. The lips of the buckets were armed with strong prongs of nickel steel to aid in the process. The boilers fed with wood, powered the immense excavators and buckets.

My fascination was not just mining, but the people. I heard many languages and the different way English was spoken by Australians, Englishmen, Scots, Americans and Canadians. There were also Norwegians, Germans, Frenchmen, Russian and Japanese in the mix. Most miners were from south of the Canadian border, from all parts of the United States.

A week later, Grant and I had a reunion. Well not exactly, since he found me passed out in the Royal Alexandria Hotel bar attached to one of the gold emblems. He said that I had quite the spification as he deposited me in jail to sober up and I had to rely on his story since I had no recollection of the night's events. The next day Grant invited me for breakfast. I reminded him we were to have a drink but that thought made me ill. He looked at me and said he would tell me my escapades another time and to have our drink. When he returned to Nova Scotia he did not want to go back to farming and the North West Mounted Police was searching for recruits. A series of events resulted in his present position as an acting corporal. He told me the police in the Yukon Territory numbered about three hundred. Grant asked me where I was living and I told him at the Royal Alexandria Hotel.

"That hotel and your meals will bankrupt you and you will encounter men with bad habits which seem to be to your liking. You need to escape from downtown and I know of a boarding house on Sixth Avenue that is run by a wonderful lady named Mrs. Rivest. Her husband was Louis Rivest who mined on King Solomon's Dome, twenty miles southeast from Dawson City. He shared thirty claims with an Englishman named George Martin. Louis died in a mining accident when he tried to separate permafrost from the gold channel. He used explosives to blow the walls of a drift at the end of the tunnel, but the roof collapsed. I investigated the accident and met Mrs. Rivest.

After breakfast, we walked to the Rivest boarding house, which was a two-story log structure on Sixth Avenue that overlooked the City. Mrs. Rivest greeted us but would not let me into the house until she was satisfied that I was of good character. My French was fluent and told her I had independent means to cover the rent. Whether it was my French, my money, or Corporal Tupper, she finally invited us to the house. She looked to be about forty, with a red face, hair in a bun and brown eyes. She had a beautiful mouth and spoke with a deep accent. As I entered the kitchen the smell of peach pie overwhelmed me since I lived with restaurant food with cooks that knew more about drinking than cooking. She took me to a second story room that overlooked the city and rivers. I complimented her on the wonderful house, room and how beautiful she looked. That resulted in a long silence that transformed to laughter.

"Young man, when you tell me such stories you must try harder to make them believable, but I like your spirit. Come to the kitchen for pie." I now had a home and it was time to get a job. I came to the Yukon Territory to mine so I needed more reliable information. The next day I visited the Mining Recorder's office and met Henry Lloyd, one of the clerks, who was about thirty, short, bald, stout and always with an unlit pipe in his mouth.

"I will soon be the same size standing up, or lying down," he said. Later I heard him always telling that story and each time he smiled. He had a long face with wide set eyes. His mouth was crinkled from a perpetual grin and he supplied constant jokes, some of which were funny. I started to bring him snacks from the bakery on Second Avenue and from time to time he offered me one, although I always refused since he enjoyed them far too much.

Henry explained that in 1898 over thirty-four thousand free miner certificates were granted. Claim registration had now declined, but the earlier claims were still active. The amount of gold production had declined for individual miners but some mining claims still produced enormous amounts of gold. Hand mining was difficult and deadly with dangers that ranged from fires and death from explosives. Drift mining, where a miner excavated deep pits, created many untimely deaths, due to the collapse of unstable ground with the miner buried with his gold.

"Mining can create riches but can cause large numbers of deaths. From the Klondike River in the north to the Indian River in the south, there are thousands of mines, tunnels, and dams." Henry continued with his somber subject.

"Some of these claims contain the graves of unknown miners. It is a barren landscape, which sometimes makes me wonder if that is a vision of hell on earth." When he noticed my serious look, he became more positive.

"The biggest returns," he emphasized, "are from hydraulic mining and dredging which are with the big consortiums." He paused then continued, "Between 1899 to last year, over one hundred hydraulic concessions were granted, usually five miles in length, which is almost five hundred miles of waterways." When he described it, his hands stretched across his body. He stood and elaborated further.

"Imagine using water pressure to open up creek beds through the removal of vegetation and permafrost. Flumes and canals transport the water for dozens of miles. Steam thawers and heat boilers are used to pressurize water to melt the overburden." He explained that the biggest gold production came from the claims at Bonanza, Eldorado, Hunker and Dominion creeks. The gold claims at Bonanza Benches are exceedingly rich, but only a few control that wealth.

Talking to Henry and various miners, it was clear that for every thousand gold seekers that came north, only a few became rich. I had arrived in the Yukon Territory too late since all profitable claims had been staked. Hydraulic sluicing had started on Fox Gulch. Companies such as the Anglo–Klondike Company had created new wealth. This combined with the dredging on Bonanza Creek, meant big companies had overtaken small miners. These large consortiums made huge amounts of money and shipped large gold shipments south. Shipments of gold, if not properly protected, opened the door to theft.

One night I visited the Palace Grand Theatre. Arizona Charlie Meadows built it in 1899 from two abandoned sternwheelers. He was a showman who earlier had toured in western entertainment shows. Arizona Charlie came north to find gold and then sold his claims, to set up this three-story theatre.

A long bar was on the side with the theatre at the back. Filled tables offered roulette, faro, and poker. The night I was there, a waiter told me a continuous game of poker had stakes of over forty thousand dollars and several mining claims had changed hands during the evening. Miners in various stages of intoxication stood or leaned against the bar. Caution restricted me to coffee and I chose to sit at a table near the front where I noticed a little fellow alone at the next table. Suddenly the sounds of malamute howls and moose bellows resounded through the theatre and a waiter took bets for the best imitation.

The show began when Arizona Charlie rode his horse along the center aisle and onto the stage. I liked his flowing moustache and long hair. He slowed his horse at center stage where he stood and took out a six-shooter. On the other side of the theatre, a woman held a filled champagne glass in her hand. Once his horse stopped, Arizona Charlie aimed and destroyed the glass into tiny pieces.

His wife Mae was the one who had guts because she was the one who held the glass. I was tempted to check to see if she had all her fingers but this might tempt Arizona Charlie to have a new target. When he rode off the stage, the show began with wild yells, whistles, and howls. A few men danced on the top of the bar and then knocked over drinks on the men below who just moved away. One tried to jump on the bar but fell on to a miner who had passed out and ended up on the floor asleep next to the other miner.

The first act was knife throwers but no one dared heckle them. The next act was trained dogs that danced around wearing silly hats, which I enjoyed, notwithstanding various rude comments. Dancers followed to loud yells and whistles and the final act was an acrobatic couple, who interrupted their act to duck bottles thrown by drunken miners. One bottle was thrown at the little fellow at the next table. I did not know if he was drunk but he grabbed it and threw it back.

Two miners approached and he stood to face them. He was small, about five feet five inches and maybe one hundred and twenty pounds. They were much taller, wider and drunker. They staggered up to him, and I told them to leave him alone so they approached my table and I stood. My additional height of six inches and my broader size should have prompted their retreat, but they did not know me and were extremely drunk.

They stopped as I walked in front of them and asked if they heard me. One took a swing at me as I moved and hit him in the face. As he fell, I kicked his friend in the chest. I looked down and asked if they wanted more. They both struggled up and rushed me so this time I hit them harder. I picked up one, grabbed the other and dragged them down the center aisle to cheers with more husky howls. Everyone stepped aside or patted me on my back and I wondered were these two regular bullies or I was the new entertainment? At the entrance, I threw them out into the mud to hear Arizona Charlie Meadows exclaim.

"I was about to do the same," as he yelled they were barred for the week. He came over and shook my hand and hired me to be a part-time enforcer and instructed to come for lunch the next day at the theatre. As I returned to sit, the little fellow at the next table invited me to have a whisky and said his name was William Willard, and after a drink, invited me for dinner. I told him that the next time this happened he could do the same for me but I was not sure he knew that was a joke.

Lunch the next day with Arizona Charlie Meadows was overwhelming. A showman, and a talker, he never paused for me to speak. His wife sat across from him and knew his habits because she loved to cut him off. He ignored her efforts, blew her a kiss, winked and continued and I never knew if this was part of an act or not.

He told me about his tours with Buffalo Bill's Wild West Show and his own western show. He created *the Klondike News* and a fortune with just one edition. I heard him start to warn me about American's involved in some underhanded scheme when Mae cut in and said for him to tell me about the job. It seemed she did not want him to tell me that story so he moved on to discuss my work.

"Caldwell, you will be in the theatre every third night and your whisky is free, but no drunkenness. You will be with the girls for protection." I interrupted to ask how many miners caused problems? He laughed at that.

"You don't get it. The protection is for my paying customers since these girls are tough. They carry knives and razors in places I do not want to know and they do not take kindly to unwarranted attention as they all have rich miners." He started to turn red and looked to the ground and I felt he was embarrassed. He gave me a wink before he continued.

"The other problem is they love to fight amongst themselves. They are vicious so just fire a shot at the ceiling and that usually stops them, if they are not too drunk. Otherwise use your fist, but not on their face and I think you will figure it out. I like my customers to drink and spend money, so keep them happy. Only act if it threatens serious safety. Any question?" I didn't know what to say and kept silent. That was my introduction to the great man. I wanted to know about this American scheme but would have to ask someone else since he would have to anger his shooting partner and I knew he would remain silent unless he hid from Mae.

Mr. Willard took me for dinner the next night to a restaurant on First Avenue situated between a dance hall and a saloon. He told me he chose that place to be near his clients and asked me to call him William. He said he was from a small-town west of Toronto called Saint Mary's and had trained as a lawyer in Toronto until he heard of the gold rush.

"Everything was dropped so I could travel here. Recently I sold my claims and joined the recently created Yukon Law Society. I practice criminal law and legal disputes between miners. Business is outstanding since most miners never put anything in writing." He paused to take his beer.

"Miners are stuck in their cabins from October until May and emerge for the first cleanup, sell their gold and drink. Some use nuggets in the bars as money, they gamble, go to Lousetown to hire ladies of the night, fight with other miners or the police and end up in jail. The end result is Magistrate Court is busy and so am I."

Soon William joined me in Mrs. Rivest's boarding house on Sixth Avenue. He was twenty-nine and his glasses made him look like an owl. His long face had a small nose and deep brown eyes. He always looked serious with a perpetual scowl since he never seemed to have a proper prescription for his glasses. He was the kindest and politest friend and loved me telling about my time in South Africa. He was most proper except when he had a few glasses of whisky and then he would sing and try to tell jokes, but either told the punch line first or forgot them.

Another newcomer to the rooming house was Sven Laursen, captain of one of the mining dredges. He was taller and bigger than me and I am six foot five and two hundred and fifty pounds. He was forty, blond and with a scar on the lower part of his face with pale blue eyes and a pronounced chin.

Our talk around the dining room table could be politics, books, music, mining or current events. Sven did not join in as I think his command of English was limited. One day a piano arrived, brought by horse and cart and Mrs. Rivest had it placed in the living room. Sven arrived that night and before eating, looked at the piano and at Mrs. Rivest. She read his look and nodded and the most amazing music came out the piano, some of which I recognized, but many were Italian operas.

That night he talked. His father was Norwegian and his mother Italian. His father was a drunk and his mother escaped and took him to Italy when he was thirteen. They moved to Naples where he learned both piano, opera, Italian and French. It ended when his mother died of consumption when he was sixteen.

"My life got worse since I had no place to stay and dropped out of school. I lived on the streets and drifted into a rough crowd where we fought gangs of young men. One was stabbed and died when I was there, but I did not kill him. The police looked for me since they believed I was the culprit." He paused as if to consider speaking further.

"Some friends came up with money to buy me a ticket to Marseilles. He stopped and looked at us and went on with his story.

"A few days later I found a recruiting office and joined the French Foreign Legion. They did not care what I had done as they just wanted someone fit and perhaps stupid, to fight their wars. For me, it was an escape out of Europe. I told them I was eighteen and was sent to Algeria to serve as an escort to engineers." He looked at us with a sad expression.

"War changes you. I was with many men who escaped from Italy, Germany, and Poland to join the Legion. They were hard, tough and never surrendered. From time to time local tribesmen attacked us. I put in seven long years in Algeria until 1886, which was when I left." He looked at us deciding if he should continue.

"I returned to Marseilles where I started my journey with money from my time in Algeria. One night as I drank in a bar by the docks I saw one of my friends from Naples. When he sat with me I learned that another person was charged and convicted of the murder. The irony was that the police had never looked for me." He stopped when he said that and laughed.

"What a strange world this is, and if I had known this I never would have spent seven years in Africa, but perhaps those years have made me the person I am." Sven stopped as if to decide if he wanted to continue.

"My decision was to go to America and I ended up in San Francisco where I found another Norwegian, who trained me to become a mechanic. His name was Herald but everyone referred to him as the fist, because if you fought him, you found his large hands would knock you senseless. We never had a problem between us and I helped him out when he drank too much. I heard about the gold rush and came up in 1899. I failed at mining myself so now I work on the dredges, which is another type of gold extraction." I admired his perseverance because miners never stop since the sun is up before four o'clock in June and sets after midnight. Sven, like many other miners, worked a sixteen-hour shift and when he arrived back at the rooming house after midnight, he ate a cold dinner.

Mrs. Rivest complained that the new Carnegie library had many English books, but not French. She loved historical biographies and books of romance. My cousin Marigold lived in Montreal so I wrote to her and she sent French historical biographies and romance novels to me. One evening, I presented a package of books to Mrs. Rivest. She was so overcome she cried and kept saying poor boy, you should not have while the whole time she grasped the books. I wanted to help Mrs. Rivest and was fond of her but I also wanted to start something new and needed her cooperation. I asked her if I could have the members of the rooming house and my guests play cards on Friday nights. She was so overcome with enthusiasm that she agreed and that started my Friday night poker games.

CHAPTER 3

Those wonderful Friday evenings when the sun did not set until long after mid-night and you never needed sleep. We played poker, drank, smoked and any story we told was entrusted to a respectful audience. To laugh and let loose in the safety of friends was a great gift since we were far from our families and the letters took forever to arrive. Our comradeship was a bond that maintained, protected us and often made us laugh.

Henry Lloyd loved to play and was always the first to arrive while Grant was usually not there because of his evening shifts. A newcomer was Bob Innes, who I met while playing small stakes poker at the Palace Grand Theatre. He was from San Francisco and worked as a surveyor to draft plans for the Klondike Mines Railway, a narrow-gauge railway from the docks at Dawson to the gold fields. Bob was thin and tall with a huge moustache that overwhelmed his thin glasses. His laugh was loud and infectious, and even if the joke was not that humorous, after hearing his laugh you joined in.

James Riley, also from San Francisco, was a friend of Bob's and worked for a hydraulic mining company. He was down to earth, funny and made you feel welcome as soon as you met him. Thirty, with gray eyes and a blond beard, he had a habit of always talking, even when someone else started the conversation and finished your sentences before you had a chance. We drank whisky, beer, brandy, and rum, so long as Mrs. Rivest received an unlimited supply. During those Friday night games was when I learned the secrets and scandals of Dawson City. There was corruption in the mining recorder's office permitting registration of invalid claims or bumping a valid claim as invalid. In the gold fields, a miner moved registered claim markers, contrary to the law, while others stole gold from pay dirt when the owners were occupied. Shady people leased claims to new operators and then kicked them off the claims at the first cleanup of gold. Other crooks salted the creek with traces of gold that was never there, took the money and booked the next steamer south. The police were too busy with various administrative duties to investigate every criminal act.

Gossip and politics filled our discussions. Grant was a conservative and Henry a liberal while I disliked politicians of both parties, since I found the topic tedious and all governments in power corrupt. To work for the government, you had to be in the same political party as the one in power as evidence of the spoils of power. During our Friday nights, we shared stories of ourselves. I told my story about school, the war in South Africa, my experience in a bar in Toronto and at the Palace Grand but I did not talk about my family's wealth. They asked me about the dancers and I was tempted to tell them to ask them for a date but kept silent since these men were my friends, while the dancers were bloody dangerous. I expected William to fall in love with a viper, which would deplete his money and drop him, without a kiss or a goodbye.

At first, Henry's shyness prevented him telling his story but gradually it came out in small amounts. There were eight children and his parents died soon after he was born. His oldest brothers and sisters helped raise him on a farm in Aurora, north of Toronto. He went west to find work with winnings from a poker game that gave funds to travel north to join the gold rush. He learned there were better ways to make a living and found work for the liberal candidate until one the staff of the mining recorder's office drowned. Henry asked if he could apply for the job and was accepted.

Bob's family's business was in Boston but he decided to go to the United States Military Academy at West Point. That was not the family way but his Congressman wrote a letter on his behalf to West Point and he entered the class of 1886. He became an engineer and was assigned to work on improvements to bridges and canals. When the Maine cruiser was blown up near

Havana in 1898 he joined the expeditionary force in Cuba and fought with the guerrillas against the Spanish Army. He left the army in 1899 and worked for a mining company in Colorado before coming to the rivers of gold. Like most of us, gold escaped his grasp so he went back to engineering and explained to us how to float dredges and how to make estimates of gravel overburden. He assumed we were fascinated and the code of our friendship meant that all topics were assumed to be of interest.

Over time we learned about James Riley. His father worked in the Civil War for the Pinkerton's Detective Agency. After the war, his father joined the San Francisco Police Department and was a police lieutenant in the detective section and who spent time telling James about his work including various ways to catch a criminal.

"Father said unless the silly fool was drunk, and did the crime in front of him, he needed to rely on undercover agents, informant's tales and confessions and an investigator needed to keep records and newspaper clippings about his clients." For some reason, this was a topic that I never grew tired of hearing.

We decided to call ourselves the Dawson City Singing, Marching, and Shouting Society. That caused a lot of laughter since we could not sing, except for Sven, we could not march and Mrs. Rivest did not like shouting. William's story came from our fishing expeditions. Saint Mary's was a place of granite buildings and his was an old Ontario family. After graduating in law, he headed north. He explained that the Yukon Territory was established three years earlier after separating from the North-West Territories, because of a dispute over liquor revenues. There was limited self-government with the authority in the liberal appointed commissioner. There were two courts, the Territorial Court and the Justice of the Peace Court. A Justice of the Peace could include a commissioned officer of the Northwest Mounted Police.

"My clients are miners who allege theft or fraud against their partners or I have a property owner who has a dispute with the operator. Nothing is ever in writing and the court usually gives up on conflicts in the evidence and cannot convict so it no longer is a criminal matter but a civil one." He told me in criminal matters the courts used the recent Criminal Code that was enacted in 1892.

"I am retained on the criminal matter and then do similar arguments in the Territorial Court. I have different people prosecuting and different standards of proof, but more billable hours," he laughed. He related a recent case with a barge sinking on the Yukon River where he had to go to Admiralty Court in Ottawa and returned to present an enormous invoice. I knew in talking to William that he had spent many hours helping his poor clients and not sending any accounts. He acted for the local Han Indians to help recover unpaid wages refused by greedy miners.

He was a welcome visitor at the Indian reserve at Moosehide and it was in June he invited me to come with him to Moosehide. As we drifted downstream fish swam around our boat. William told me to wait until July when the salmon would appear and we could see fish camps along the river. He told me the Han Indians originally had a small settlement at the mouth of the Klondike and Yukon Rivers but the gold rush caused the government to set up a reserve further down the Yukon River.

Moosehide was smaller than I expected and had a few small timber cabins in a circle. I was introduced to Joseph and Mary who told me that about seventy people lived there, but many were out cutting wood and setting up fish camps. Miners thought nothing of the local Indians and depleted the supply of wood, fish, and moose. It was now difficult to find them near Moosehide so the families had to go further for wood or to hunt and fish. The elders did not speak English but spoke their traditional language. I was told that Han was short for Hankutchin, which meant people of the river. Returning and struggling against the current I thanked William for the invitation. Each time we returned, we brought flour and other supplies.

My first encounter as an enforcer with the dancers at the Palace Grand Theatre was a few days after I was hired. I was not sure where to watch and sat by the theatre stage to observe our customers when a scream rang from the dressing room. I rushed into the dressing room to see two dancers fighting on the floor. One dancer was squeezing the other dancer's neck while others bet on the result. I yelled to stop and was rewarded with a chair across my skull.

"Put down the chair or you will live to regret it," I growled while trying not to collapse. I thought I was going to throw up and sat down to assess these ladies who also scrutinized me and whispered to each other but I could not hear them. I took out my bayonet and asked the dancer if she wanted a tattoo, which prompted a new bet on whether I would do it and yells that I was too chicken. I explained I was new to this and asked if they would help me protect them. A tall and large one with reddish hair grumbled at me.

"From what? We take care of ourselves and do not want you. Get it." A dancer looked at her and said, "Soak it, Maude, I like him." Dancers commented on my looks, height and smile, and whether they wanted me around. The vote went in my favour and I was permitted to stay. I was an innocent in a room full of tough and experienced women, who I found more worrisome than the Boers I fought in South Africa.

"Arizona Charlie told me you all carry knives and are tough." That generated a new round of laughter, guffaws, and jeers.

"He likes to kid new enforcers," jeered Maude. "We are tough, but Arizona Charlie exaggerates." I was not sure whom to believe but the piano started a jangle and they flounced out for their next dance. Some became friends and a few distrusted me but they always entertained me since they lived a life so different from my upbringing I never knew what they would say or try. I knew they had fun with me and were always out to shock me and their knowledge of swear words exceeded most of the troops in my squadron. Later I learned they bet amongst themselves to see how much I could blush.

Most miners were lonely and showed up at the theatre to have a little fun and company. For the most part, they were pleasant, except when they had too much to drink, which was every night. I learned to joke and work with my problem customers and a victory was to persuade a problem drunk to leave without a fight. The Palace Grand Theatre was only part of my life and over time I developed a routine. As the sun entered my open window, I dressed and walked down to the river on Front Street. These expeditions became earlier every day since by late June the sun rose above the mountains as early as three-thirty in the morning. My walks took me from Sixth Avenue down to the waterfront.

At that time of morning Dawson City was quiet but in another two hours, it would be a hub of activity. Wagons would load, while at the docks, men would place freight onto steamers. One bakery on the waterfront opened at six where I often stopped to take a coffee and French bread. My walks brought me peace and during these weeks I decided that mining was not for me. Hand mining was risky and I was too conservative and cautious to invest with a partner.

As I walked I listed my qualities. I was a soldier and although I did not like war I had survived and learned to follow orders. I had experience fighting in the bar in Toronto and several times with troopers in South Africa. I handled my work at the Palace Grand, was an excellent rider, marksman and could read and write. Dawson City had grown on me and I loved to travel its rivers, enjoyed my walks and liked to observe the changes in mining methods and who benefited from the new wealth. William was swamped and had asked on several occasions if I could assist him and it was time to agree.

His law office was in a rental building on First Avenue. On the main floor, his clerk made appointments and accounting. Clarence was about twenty, with glasses and an inability to sit still. His pudgy face hid his narrow eyes that darted back and forth and from the beginning, his task was to be unpleasant to me. It did not take long for me to think of him as Uriah Heep since he reminded me of that awful character in *Dickens'* David Copperfield.

William was so busy it took time for me to be trained. To prepare me, William acted as a witness and made up rambling stories for my notes that became statements. Next, he provided me with sworn affidavits to review and explained the purpose for each. He asked me to read texts on evidence and cases that involved examination of a witness and cross-examination. William brought me to the Justice of the Peace and Territorial Courts where I spent a week observing lawyers in action with witnesses. His little library became my second home where I reviewed *Anson on Contracts, Best on Evidence, Broom on Common Law, Clement on Constitutional Law and Williams on Property Law.* Law became my companion from morning to night and I was surprised how well I understood it.

We invited lawyers to our boarding house for dinner and after a few drinks, they came into their element to recall stories of trials, judges, and juries. My job was to examine their exaggerations and nonsense to discover any truth in their stories. Soon I drafted witness statements and my size and experience in fighting meant I could travel with William to assist in taking evidence. I travelled to his client's mining claims and if the dispute was about staking locations then I took measurements. I brought James and watched as he used his equipment to measure the claims.

For each mining dispute, William told me what he wanted and emphasized that every witness needed to state what they knew, or what they believed to be true. Most times it was necessary to take statements on a claim while the owner actively sluiced gold. When they produce gold, miners never leave their property, since they are wedded to that gold, whether it was in the ground or on top. They never let me near their cleanup or nuggets while I visited and protected their gold like a first-born child. I learned the trails and paths in the goldfields and became friends with numbers of miners.

My idea for a second job came about from talking to these miners who suggested I act as an escort for their protection in transporting gold. Security to the small miner was essential and once I started to act as the bodyguard, Sven helped me, since he was bigger and tougher. The large corporations used the police but the smaller miners went unescorted until I arrived to offer my service.

It was about this time I learned that my grandfather had died from a telegram. He was a big part of me and I would miss our times together and mutual love. I withdrew from Dawson City and took a long river trip to nowhere to try to find peace and when I returned a letter from my mother awaited me with my grandfather's letter dated May 21, 1901.

"Dear John. My heart has been giving me problems over the past few years. I believe I have a few days left to live, and I wanted to send you a final letter. Of all my family, you are the most like me. To live a life filled with interests, to maintain love and kindness, is the life I have tried to live. And I see it in you. You have always filled me with pride and being together this past year has meant so much to me. You must live your life the way you wish and not what your father wanted. I cannot control nor influence what your father has done. I would have done it differently, or perhaps I would not. Your world is not coming home each day from a bank or factory. You are living the life you want and I believe in you and want you

to remember my love for you and always. I am doing something for you and not to annoy your father. I wish he had not assumed he owned the business as I have set aside one-quarter of the business in your name and left you one hundred thousand dollars. At the end of my life, I have many regrets and many accomplishments and I am tired of doing what others want. This gift is for you since you deserve it. Think of me with affection, a scotch in one hand, a book in the other and a smile on your face. William John Caldwell"

That evening I drank some scotch and enjoyed happy memories of a life well lived. My earlier trust fund continued and with one-quarter of the business it would work out to almost two thousand dollars a month, which left one hundred thousand dollars to invest. This was a fortune since I remembered a discussion with a male teacher in Toronto who earned under a thousand dollars a year. I was blessed and realized that I need to be careful with this legacy. It could be used to create my independence in Dawson City so I talked to William about becoming partners in a building.

Three thousand dollars purchased a vacant large two-story building on Second Avenue with an adjoining lot, caretaker quarters, a stable and a little house. William put in one-half while I put in the rest. It was large and on the main floor we set up rooms for a reception area, a library, a conference room and three offices. William had one office and I had the second with the third as a spare. William had a sign painted in black and gold hung prominently in front. William Willard, Barrister, Solicitor and Notary Public.

James registered as a Dominion Lands Surveyor and we agreed to let him take the third upstairs office. I told William that I wanted to use other upstairs for mining security and two more signs were hung out front, James Riley, Dominion Land Surveyor, and Caldwell's Security Agency. We decided to stay with Mrs. Rivest, as our cooking skills were dreadful. We furnished the separate house into three bedrooms with a sitting room and a kitchen and named the house "Bummers Roost."

CHAPTER 4

In late June, the theft of a large amount of gold from a riverboat captivated the citizens of this city and you could not walk down any street without this robbery being discussed. When I first heard of it but thought it was a distant event, but as time passed the theft became my major focus. The *Klondike Daily News* was the first newspaper to report on the gold theft from the *Casca* paddlewheel steamer. When it stopped for wood, five thousand ounces of gold was removed, of a value of about one hundred thousand dollars. I was surprised how easy it was to steal gold and a reminder for me to take extra care with my clients.

Two days later I agreed to handle protection for a miner named Big Pierre and to escort him from the Indian River to Dawson City. Big Pierre's name is a joke as he was about five feet and about one hundred and ten pounds. His real name was Pierre Cloutier but he always was known as Big Pierre. My job was to protect him but not his gold. He signed a small contract that confirmed this. I was not sure he could read English so I read it to him, gave him a copy, and brought in James to hear our conversation.

Not long after my contract with Big Pierre I was asked by another miner to stand guard, so I asked Sven to take the job for Big Pierre. I was satisfied that Sven, with his size and experience with the Foreign Legion, could handle, it since he knew how to fight. A few days later Sven came to my office so upset he barely could tell me the story. Ten miles from Dawson City they stopped for the night with Sven in charge to protect the gold. The problem was Sven's working day was between sixteen hours to eighteen hours and he should have remained standing but he was tired.

About nine o'clock, Big Pierre fell asleep by the fire since the July weather at night is cold and they had walked all day. A few hours later Sven fell asleep and when he awoke he discovered the luggage bag that contained the gold was gone. They searched the campsite and Big Pierre searched Sven but no gold was found. I asked Sven if he had searched Big Pierre but he shook his head. I said not to worry and brought in William and we went to the Police Detachment. Sven was not charged since no evidence existed he took the gold. The amount of gold was about one hundred ounces. Later that day in my office I had it out with Big Pierre at an unpleasant meeting.

"You stole my gold, and I want it back," he shouted and these exclamations and curses continued with his hands moving above his face. He was red, tired and excited and kept jumping around like a poodle on its legs. I did not say anything as I listened behind my desk and tried to remain calm since one of us had to act as the adult. Big Pierre approached me with his arm out which was a mistake since I am six foot five inches in height, with a broad chest and weigh two hundred and fifty pounds. Compared to me Big Pierre was a shrimp standing next to a shark but I remained silent and then slowly stood. Big Pierre took one look and sat. I took out the form that he signed and read it to him with his signature. I calmly told him that I agreed to protect him and not his gold. I asked if he was alive but he just looked at me and said nothing. I asked if he was hurt and he shook his head.

"Why on earth had you not taken shifts."

"After a long day of travelling, that was the only sensible way. No one could have stayed awake through the night." He started to protest, but I interrupted.

"If you agreed with me to insure your gold, I would have charged you a deductible of about one-third of the gold weight. I would weigh the gold, place it in locked postbags, and hired two armed guards." I stared at him.

"My fee would have been thirty dollars." I added, "But that was not what we agreed, was it?" Big Pierre sat silently with his mouth clenched, then he looked at me.

"What can I do?"

"I will refund your money and attempt to discover who stole the gold. Where did you camp the night when the gold was taken?" He showed me the location on my map.

"Did anyone at Indian River know the time you left," I asked? He said several miners worked near his claims including an American named Dalton Weigand and an Englishman, Edward Marston. He added he had not seen Marston this year and that Weigand was the only miner who was in his camp. He understood Weigand had mined different claims the year before and in late fall bought the adjoining claims. He heard Weigand had leased out his claims but had never seen the person. My next question was their description?

"Weigand has a moustache and talks fast." He added, "He has a long face, wide-set eyes and is always smiling with a cigar in his mouth but usually not lit. Weigand bragged he only smoked Cuban cigars." He described Weigand as six feet in height and his age to be about thirty.

"He always has one fellow with him who is called Victor who is about six foot five, clean-shaven with a short haircut. His face is dark with a large nose and when he speaks, he has an accent." I asked if anyone else was on those claims? Big Pierre said, just Weigand and Victor. I asked about Marston.

"Pocked marked, with a beard and balding, with large ears, a big nose, and is fat. He is a little taller than me."

"What is your claim registration number," I asked?

"Why do you need that?"

"I want to check something out." He pulled up a piece of paper and gave it to me.

"When you camped, had you seen or heard anyone?" He told me they were asleep. I asked was there anything else he could think of to tell me but he shook his head. Big Pierre got up to leave and told me to not refund the money.

"I survived," and added if I found his gold he would pay me a reward.

"The Police should be told and I will find out about the thefts," I answered.

"Sure, my gold was robbed ten miles from Dawson City by unknown persons. It looks like yellow nuggets and dust. I don't think so." I looked at him and said he should do it. He looked at me, shook his head, and walked out with a defeated air. My anger was gone and replaced by compassion and admiration since Big Pierre had lost three years of wages and returned to mine. The little guy gets knocked down but he's up, and ready to fight again. Good for him I thought. That night I talked to James and William. Both were interested but I noticed James made notes. I told them the next day I would spend time at the mining recorder's office and speak with gold buyers. I would visit the bars and the Palace Grand to hear local gossip and it was time to visit Corporal Tupper. I asked James to give me advice on investigations.

"You need witnesses, informants, gossip, and confessions, keep records and file clippings from newspapers." I thanked them and left.

The next day I found William in his office and asked if he had jobs for me that day? He said in two days I was to take a statement from a miner on Bonanza Creek but I could entertain myself so long as I took care. I told William I would try to find Big Pierre's stolen gold and asked if I could buy some of his legal pads. William replied for me to take them but keep him posted and told me to be careful. In my office, I wrote out the information I learned from Big Pierre and Sven. On a pad, I set out investigative procedures and decided to keep future copies of the *Klondike Daily News* for theft and police reports.

Big Pierre's robbery bothered me as I felt it was a stain on my reputation. I had the money and the time to investigate but the challenge was to find who did it since my witnesses were asleep. I needed information and lots of it and thought this might work with my security work. Today was a good day to start but I did not know where this path would take me.

I went to the North West Mounted Police Detachment. Grant asked if he could meet me after his shift so I told him I would treat him to dinner. My next stop was the mining recorder's office. Henry was there and I asked to look at the records for Big Pierre's claims and the adjoining ones.

Big Pierre was right. One adjoining claim owner was Edward Marston while the other adjoining claim was registered to Dalton Weigand. The registry showed a royalty agreement between Dalton Weigand and Frank

Thompson. Thompson was permitted to work the claims and pay royalties to Weigand. Big Pierre had told me the only persons on those claims were Weigand and Victor.

Where was Thompson and why did Weigand mine if he had assigned the right to operate the claims to someone else? Nothing was registered on the records that showed that the royalty agreement had expired or was canceled. I handed the files back to Henry and said I would treat him to lunch at the Royal Alexandria Hotel at noon.

"Pleasure or business?"

"Both." And I was off to my next stop The *Klondike Daily News*. When I spent time at the courts a few weeks earlier I had met a police reporter whose job was to attend court and report the proceedings. His name was Seamus O' Toole but he was not in the office. I went to the courthouse during an adjournment and found him in the corridor. I asked if I could buy him early dinner at six at the Royal Alexandria Hotel and he agreed, and realized this investigations would cost money.

I returned to the office to talk to William and noticed he was in the process of preparing notes for a cross-examination. He agreed he had time for questions on mining law so I read out my notes of the royalty agreement between Weigand and Thomson. Thompson was assigned the right to mine with an obligation to pay a twenty percent royalty to Weigand. I told William that Big Pierre had only seen Weigand and Victor on the claims and there were no records filed that showed the royalty agreement canceled.

"Who prepared the agreement," William asked?

"Weigand, since no lawyer's name was mentioned in the agreement. The agreement was simple and on one page." William said that was strange but his only thought was that Thompson was sick and appointed Weigand to mine on his behalf.

"There may be other explanations why Thompson was not there," I remarked. William gave me a strange look and I moved to another question.

"When a miner sluice's gold, what do they do with it?"

"It depends? If they do not need the money right away, they may put it in a safety deposit box, or hide it. Some miners do not like to pay the royalty tax on gold production." He added, "Although they take a chance," and looked at me to try and understand where I was going with my questions.

"Most miners sell the gold, and pay the tax." William went to his shelf and pulled out some books.

"The earliest requirement for taxation on gold was the *Dominion Mining Regulation of 1889*. It required a payment of four percent of gold production. This was increased to ten percent in 1897. The *Yukon Act* was again amended in 1901 to reduce the royalty to five per cent on gold and silver. The police have powers to investigate and seize any personal property of the miner if the tax is not paid." I asked if someone wanted to sell gold, would there be records of the amount of gold, where it came from, and the name of the seller? William said all that was required. I told him this information was important but I needed to go since it was almost noon and I quickly walked to my lunchtime meeting with Henry.

We had a table near the front and once we ordered, we caught up on recent activities. I told Henry about Big Pierre and his stolen gold then reviewed the details of the Weigand claim and the Thompson royalty agreement and emphasized that only Weigand and his friend were on the claims. Henry thought that odd, but said often miners do not comply with the requirements of the law and cautioned me to not assume anything until I had further information. I asked if he knew the process for gold sales.

"Miners must pay the royalty on gold to the gold commissioner. Often gold buyers act as agents and remit the royalty to the commissioner. The government has records of the claim number, the creek's name, the miner or agent, and the gold weight. The government charges royalty on the gross weight of the gold that is now five percent, which does not account that placer gold is not one hundred percent pure. It could be eighty-six percent purity, or less."

"Why do miners declare their gold, and not keep it hidden," I asked? Henry scowled at me since he was one of the few honest men in the office and then muttered.

"It is the law that all miners pay their share. When a miner has a clean-up from sluicing, other miners know of it. The most common reason is that the gold certificate, issued by the gold commissioner's office, allows the miner to show it to the bank, the police and anyone else as to how they obtained their money. To send money through a bank then you need that certificate."

I asked if I could have access to the records at the gold commissioner's office. Henry said he did not know but that all records in the mining recorder's office were open to the public. If the gold commissioner had a reason he probably would give me the information. We talked about the comings and goings of Dawson and politics and finished lunch around one.

Big Pierre was in his room at the Majestic Hotel packing supplies so I assumed he would return to mine at the Indian River. He looked refreshed but still unhappy and asked me if I had anything to tell him. I explained Weigand owned the adjoining claims with a royalty agreement for Frank Thompson to mine the claims. I asked if he had ever met Frank Thompson but Big Pierre said no.

"When was the last time Weigand sluiced?" Big Pierre said six weeks ago and added something I found interesting.

"I do not think Weigand had much of a find. On that day, I went over in the morning to see him, Victor stood next to him but did not talk. Weigand made coffee and we talked. He asked me how was my sluicing and I answered ok." He looked at me with a serious expression.

"You never tell your production to anyone," he added. "You know I had one hundred ounces from my cleanup and that that was not my first this year. I will be back soon to do a small one before freeze up."

"Did Weigand say anything on that day?"

"Weigand looked upset and exclaimed loudly he could not find the damn channel although he had dug in, under and around the creek. As he carried on I did not say anything, finished my coffee and left."

"Who watched your last cleanup?" Big Pierre said it took almost the whole day while Weigand watched. I asked if that other fellow was with him.

"Victor is always with him," and I wondered what the relationship was between those two? I thanked Big Pierre and told him I would spend time following up some ideas. Just before I left, I asked which route he would follow to the Indian River. He told me he would move southeast though King Solomon's Dome and then to his claim.

"Come see me if you have anything," Big Pierre said.

"I will be out to check on your claim within the week. Will you be there?"

"My friend, you can count on that." I wondered whether Weigand would make a declaration of gold at the gold commissioner's office and could this be something I should consider? Based on what Big Pierre told me, he believed the production from Weigand's claim would be non-existent. However, if I found a large declaration, how could Weigand account for it?

If Weigand, or whatever his name was, stole Big Pierre's gold he could state it came from his own claim and he could obtain a certificate. Once the smelter processed the gold then the balance would be sent to him or to his account in his bank. I knew the next step was to obtain records from the gold commissioner's office. Dawson City had a large population and the chance of meeting this official again was slight but I would have to use my own name.

This was a small deception but I would act as an agent for Frank Thompson. Up until now I had never lied in my life but I felt that if Frank Thompson was alive, he would want to know this information, and if dead, his family would want to know. A lie to uncover a fraud tilted my moral compass. It was a sin I could live with and if I was to act like a detective I would need to be resourceful.

In my suit, white shirt, and tie, I departed to the gold commissioner's office. I asked the clerk if I could see the records of payments made by Frank Thompson on the Weigand claims and provided the claim numbers. The clerk asked my interest and I said I was the agent for Mr. Thompson and gave my name. I provided the details of the royalty agreement and said I was to verify that the gold from the claims had been paid since Mr. Thompson had not been present to verify the payments.

The clerk checked the records and said there were recent payments representing royalties at five per cent and one hundred dollars was paid. I calculated that this represented one hundred ounces and then it struck me that I was catching a weasel asleep since this represented the same amount of gold that was stolen from Big Pierre. It might be a coincidence, but I would give it less than even odds that Weigand was behind this. I wrote that down and asked his name, which was Roland Caton. Before I left I asked who had paid the royalty?

"The man did not give his name," so I asked for a description.

"He had a moustache and seemed to be sharing a series of jokes because he always smiled." As I was almost out the door, he called out.

"Mr. Caldwell, do you want to know the other declarations this year?"

"Of course," I said and went back.

"The records show a payment of five thousand dollars was made for five thousand ounces. A further payment was made of one thousand dollars that represented one thousand ounces." I wrote that down and it was now clear that these claims were used to cover other gold thefts. I thought of the gold robbery from the *Casca* of five thousand ounces. Did Weigand have other legitimate operations or was he a master thief? Suddenly I realized I had blundered using my own name since the commissioner's office had it and my investigations on Weigand's claim. It was bad enough to be a target in South Africa and I might be one again but there I was one of the thousands while here there was just a large fellow on his own.

My final question to Mr. Caton was how long had he worked at the office? He replied about a year after he returned from South Africa, having served in the Second Mounted Rifles. I said I served with the Strathcona's and asked if I could treat him to coffee.

"I have worked through lunch so sure, why not?" We went to the Royal Alexandria Hotel since they knew me and always had my special table. Roland and I shared stories, including my friendship with William Willard, and Corporal Tupper. I told him I needed to trust him. It took a while to get around to my theory of stolen gold and Weigand. I told of the potential threat to me if my name was revealed. The sins of omission included not revealing that I was not Thompson's agent. My only request was could he remain silent on my inquiry. Roland paused and said that was highly irregular. I told him that I was meeting Corporal Tupper, who also had served in South Africa, and I would tell him everything.

"I will not say anything and you are not bribing me. I will simply forget to write a notation and anything I wrote accidently could be destroyed." At my office, I wrote more notes summarizing information from Big Pierre, William, Henry Lloyd and Roland Caton. Who was Dalton Weigand, and did he have other rich mining claims? Only the large hydraulic and dredge concessions employing dozens of workers could mine that much gold. No one doing hand mining could achieve those riches. I knew that at Indian River he did not have profitable ground. I had the gold commissioner's office record's that showed six thousand one hundred ounces paid but no apparent source for the gold. If I believed Big Pierre, those ounces of gold never came from Weigand's property. What motive would there be for Big Pierre to lie about Weigand's production on his property?

Big Pierre's gold was not insured and he did not report the loss to the police so there was no benefit to him to lie. The gold was lost and I believed he did not fake the robbery and he knew I did not guarantee the protection of the gold. I was satisfied that Big Pierre told me the truth and that Weigand had not sluiced any gold from his claims on Indian River but where did the gold come from, if not from his claims on Indian River?

Weigand could have other active mines, but if he did, why not use those claim grant numbers and pay the royalty? The snake used his claims as a front to pay royalties from gold including robberies from the *Casca*, Big Pierre, and other miners. I knew the North West Mounted Police were busy and perhaps Weigand and his gang relied on that.

To carry out my investigations I needed to travel to the robbery site and to Big Pierre's mining operation. I also wanted to meet Weigand, but to do that protection was required, so I needed to hire someone who was experienced and tough. My pocket watch showed it almost six o'clock as I headed to meet the reporter. Sean was late and when he arrived it was the first time I had a good look at him. He was tall, about twenty-five, lean, with slicked back hair and glasses. His coloured cheeks contrasted with his small moustache and his tie was at half-mast.

As he sat down, he told an amusing story about the Territorial Judge and a lawyer. I told Sean it was my treat and once he had his drink we ordered dinner. Over our meal, he continued with lawyer stories and I think he knew every trial lawyer in Dawson City. He explained his lateness was due to the copy editor, who nipped out for a drink and never returned, so he had to fill in to cover. His stories were entertaining as he could mimic judges and lawyers to raise his eyebrows and often laughed with his tales. It was a pleasure to be with him and I did not have to say much, just look, nod and laugh and from time to time, he would nod at the waiter for a refill. I was worried as his nods and whisky increased and since I was a regular at the Royal Alexandria Hotel restaurant the service was outstanding. Each time a new whisky was brought for Sean, he would stand and make a toast but I did not match his drinks since I had to keep sharp and remember.

After several more drinks, I asked him about his work. Sean liked to talk, so it was a matter of direction to respond to my questions. I had to resolve the story of the gold robbery before he became drunk. It was a challenge because if I did not soon get the story, there would be a repeat performance, and I was already into a small fortune for whisky. It turned out I did not have to ask Sean about the steamer robbery be he was the reporter assigned by his paper and found out it was an inside job. Two hydraulic companies, the Anglo-Klondike Company and the Bonanza Mining Company agreed to share security and transportation costs. The North West Mounted Police escorted the gold to the boat, where it was weighed, and the royalty was paid to the gold commissioner. The gold was placed on board in iron boxes in the hold of the *Casca*. Normally the police protected gold, but for some reason, the companies used private guards.

The *Casca* travelled against the flow of the Yukon River and required a stop to take on wood. It was around eleven o'clock at night as the crew began to bring on logs that four armed men with masks rushed up the plank and into the open hold to tie up the crew. No one noticed anything on the upper decks. A wheelbarrow was used to load the boxes out of the hold, down the ramp, and into a long wagon, and they were gone.

About twenty minutes later one of the crew untied his knots and reported the theft to the captain. There was no telegraph office at the logging stop so it was not until the next day that a theft of one hundred thousand dollars of gold was reported to the Detachment. It was several days before the crew was interviewed and it took longer before the North West Mounted Police investigated the river camp. The police found the abandoned wagon and evidence that the horses travelled north towards Dawson City. They followed the trail until it joined the main overland route.

One of the inspector's informed Sean that the gang was near Dawson City. The police could not obtain descriptions of the culprits, except their large size since they wore masks. The men were between five foot ten to six feet and the few words they spoke to the crew were in English. They did not have an accent and were thought to be American.

"They were smart and left no clues," was Sean's conclusion. My next question was whether he had heard of people spending money or selling gold? Sean said he tried to follow this inquiry, but found no other witnesses, or evidence. I decided not to inform him of my searches since the gold robbers were intelligent and could be dangerous and to entrust this information to a reporter who liked to drink was a needless risk. My last question was whether he had run into Frank Thompson or Dalton Weigand? He said he had never heard of Frank Thompson and then put his face close to mine and said in a soft voice.

"Watch out for Weigand and stay away from him if you want to live." That was not what I wanted to hear since I had spent time checking his claims and royalty payments. I told Sean that I needed to go and paid for the final whisky and the bill. I found that the liquor costs were ten times the cost of the meal and swore that if I needed to interview Sean again it would be at breakfast in the Salvation Army tent.

Outside I waited for Grant and hoped Sean would not appear. I had booked the Majestic Hotel for dinner number two and Grant's shift ended at eight. I noticed a man who had just left the hotel turned to look at me and gave me a long stare. I did not get a good description other than he was short and fat. I was tempted to follow him but decided to wait for Grant who approached and stopped.

"Change of plans, let's walk and talk while we go to the Majestic." Grant muttered that he did not want to talk about police work. He looked exhausted and as he walked he exclaimed.

"You and I will talk books, politics or the weather but I need a break after a twelve-hour shift." That was what we did on the way to the restaurant. I told Grant I would pay and he gave me a look, which implied, what do you need? I did not jump in with any explanations until Grant had a beer and dinner. I requested something small to eat.

"You are up to something and I hope it does not involve me," was his opening salvo from an old friend who knew my bad habits.

"This might involve you." He snorted, and asked, what was going on? I told of my agreement with Big Pierre and the robbery of one hundred ounces of gold. I moved to the results from the mining recorder's office and my searches of the title. I told him about the royalty agreement between Frank Thompson and Dalton Weigand.

"Be careful of that fellow." and I said I was hearing that warning. I told Grant about my discoveries in the gold commissioner's office and that Weigand had paid for over six thousand ounces from his claims, but Big Pierre stated that Weigand produced either no gold or a tiny amount on the Indian River. I finished by mentioning two matters that concerned me.

"Weigand uses his ground as a front for the payment of royalties. I also have no knowledge if Frank Thompson is alive or dead, and hate to say it but this may be a dangerous investigation." I stopped and looked at Grant who sat and sighed.

"You need to bring your story to Inspector McDonald tomorrow and he can decide the next step. You have landed in something that might be dangerous which will depend on the facts. I tend to agree with your theory but the Inspector may have a different view." He gave a long stare and then shook his head.

"The Inspector is at the Detachment and not the Town Station." I knew the Town Station was the building that handled matters for Dawson City while the Detachment handled policing for the Yukon Territory. We talked about other things until Grant said he was tired.

"Come by the detachment about nine and I will first have a chance to talk to the Inspector." I paid and we said goodnight.

On the way to the rooming house, I thought of what I learned that night. Before turning in I wrote down my conversations with Sean and Grant. I made a note of the description of the fellow who looked at me at the Royal Alexandria Hotel. The name Weigand I marked as dangerous. I needed a new employee, and fast and first thing in the morning I would clean my rifle and with these unpleasant thoughts, I fell asleep.

Chapter 5

During our breakfast, I told William what I discovered at the mining recorder's and the gold commissioner's offices. He was somewhat interested until he heard the name Weigand and moved from interested to alarmed. This was unfortunate since I needed to tell him what I had found and more to the point, whether these facts supported my theory. William remained silent with a scowl and grumbled at me to find a bodyguard and fast. I knew I overwhelmed him and returned to my room to clean my weapons. Dangerous times had arrived as I attached my bayonet and revolver and walked down to First Avenue.

At eight the Detachment was quiet and then the sudden sounds of policemen on the parade square and a scream of "Keep in step you bloody fustilugs," which took me back to some awful memories of sergeants I wished to forget and clumsy recruits. The constable on duty asked why I was there so I explained my appointment with Inspector McDonald. He said I was early and resumed his coffee. I did not know Inspector McDonald but many of the officers and men of the North West Mounted Police had served in the military. I sat and went over my story when at nine o'clock a different constable asked me to follow him into a large office. Behind a desk sat an officer and a sergeant while Grant sat next to the desk. I was about to explain why I was there when the inspector started.

"My name is Inspector McDonald, to my right is Sergeant Raven and I believe you know Corporal Tupper." Inspector McDonald was tall, about six feet with short gray hair. He had blue eyes, a deep scar on his cheek and an intimidating expression. Sergeant Raven was short, about five foot eight with short brown hair that matched his eyes and a moustache. As I spoke the sergeant wrote on a pad.

We sat with Grant to my right and the Inspector asked me to relate my story and leave nothing out. I explained I escorted miners to Dawson City and worked as an assistant to a lawyer. I was hired by Pierre Cloutier to take him from the Indian River to Dawson City but I was busy so I sent my associate to accompany him. I recounted what Big Pierre and Sven told me about the robbery and then set out the next part of my investigation, that Dalton Weigand had his claims next to Mr. Cloutier. Mr. Cloutier cleaned up and packed one hundred ounces of gold, which was the amount of gold that was robbed, and the two persons who watched were Dalton Weigand and his employee, Victor. Their expression changed as soon as I mentioned Weigand's name. I noticed the inspector and sergeant looked at each other but I continued with my story.

"Weigand did not produce much gold in his cleanups," and I summarized the results of my searches at the mining recorder's office. I handed them my notes of the royalty agreement between Weigand and Thompson. Weigand owned the claims under the royalty agreement, with the right for Thompson to mine, but Thompson never used his rights to mine and there was no cancellation of the royalty agreement. The inspector and sergeant looked interested.

"My real concern was the findings at the gold commissioner's office where I discovered that Weigand paid for six thousand and one hundred ounces of gold. The only source were royalties from his claims at the Indian River, but Pierre Cloutier was clear, that Weigand had a minimal return of gold. I was now excited and noticed I was not alone.

"These are significant royalties since these claims are not on Bonanza Creek, nor do they come from dredges or hydraulic mining. This is basic hand mining that has produced an incredible return in less than three months." I paused and looked at them.

"My only explanation is gold thefts that could be from the *Casca* or others and I believe more royalty payments will be paid to the gold commissioner's office unless Weigand becomes suspicious. These are my thoughts but I need to find out more information." For a while no one spoke. At last Inspector McDonald asked me to wait in the entrance so I returned to the front. Twenty minutes later I was asked to return and sit. Sergeant Raven spoke to explain he had been a police officer in the Dominion Police in Ottawa, assigned to protect members of parliament and the federal buildings. The creation of the Dominion Police was after the murder of Darcy McGee, a member of parliament.

"I perform investigations which usually requires witness statements and informants. Four months ago, I was assigned to the North West Mounted Police and my job is the same since I perform detective work but in a different part of the country. Now, you, on your own, have given us the first links to the *Casca* robbery." He stopped and looked to the inspector who asked me to set out my background.

"After leaving school in Toronto, I went to the North-West Territories, in the District of Alberta, to work on a horse ranch where I learned to ride and shoot. I joined the Strathcona's Horse, fought in South Africa and came here to mine but gave up on that and now I am an assistant to a lawyer, William Willard where I help with witness statements and affidavits. I sometimes visit mining claims to take measurements and conduct interviews and you know about my escort of miners to town." I did not mention my work for Arizona Charlie and did not expect what Inspector McDonald would say next.

"How are the dancers at the Palace Grand Theatre since I hear you like to stop their fights?" He laughed and continued, "Some of the best informers are hidden in the most unlikely places. He looked at me and said he had grown up in Toronto. He asked which school did I attend and I answered Upper Canada College. He asked what sports did I play? I replied rugby, boxing, and hockey.

"My predecessor Inspector Steele left Dawson in 1900 to command the Strathcona's Horse." I knew the name of my commanding officer but had no idea he had been in Dawson City. His next question was if I would like to do investigations under Sergeant Raven.

"We think you have the capacity and intelligence to do this." I did not expect this and it flattered me but I liked my freedom and I did not want to return to morning inspections, picket duty, and other unpleasant tasks. I remembered my time in the army and hated the discipline and the North West Mounted Police was based on military lines. I hated the drill and the thought of these men outside under the command of a corporal were not an incentive for this job.

"I appreciate this and I know this is an important position. However, my time in the army taught me what I do not like and I enjoy my freedom too much to take up your offer. Besides I enjoy my work with Mr. Willard and my new business, so the answer is no." While I spoke, the inspector studied me and I felt he expected my answer.

"There is a compromise offer since we have eighty officers, non-commissioned officers, and constables and that leaves some discretion in how we run the Detachment. We employ special constables who work part time and as a special constable you would be free to do your other work and perform detective work with Sergeant Raven." Now he was in the game since I wanted to be a detective and I think he knew that with this offer.

"Let me talk with Sergeant Raven as I think I am interested," I replied. I followed Sergeant Raven to his office and after we sat I told him I would like to be special constable for six months to see if it suited me. He replied it normally was a two-year commitment but he would see if that was possible but before he took the next step for my enrolment, we returned to Inspector McDonald's office.

"He has agreed to be a special constable." The inspector gave me an unsmiling long look that was totally different from his earlier expression. What had I agreed with this look?

"Caldwell, if your application is approved your life will be at risk. I know you faced danger in South Africa but I need to tell you that this might be more dangerous. You can refuse, and leave."

"How risky?" I asked.

"Extremely risky", the inspector replied." I surprised myself by saying I was still prepared to join. He looked at Sergeant Raven and nodded. Were these the evil twins to bring me into a perilous adventure and was I ready for it?

"One more thing, you will be working out of uniform and you must not tell a soul."

"I need to have a confidential discussion with William Willard and if I continued working with him, I could not be involved in criminal cases."

"Fine, but tell him to keep this information secret, or your life may end sooner than you like." Great, I thought, what have I agreed to? I suddenly thought of *Kipling*, "We have forty million reasons for failure, but not a single excuse." I had no idea why that came into my mind but it was what I thought might happen if I failed.

We left his office and returned to Sergeant Raven's office. He came back with the application for engagement in the force. The form asked three questions which were my work over the past five years, experience with horses and military experience. It required age, height and a physical description and I had to be checked out by the police surgeon.

That was how my fourth job in Dawson City happened. My enrolment required the approval of Superintendent Zachary Taylor Wood and I was enrolled a few days later as a special constable and provided a regimental number. I met William in his office and told him I would work undercover for the North West Mounted Police and no one else must know. I added that I could no longer work on criminal files. William shook his head and gave me a long stare.

"Are you crazy? Just when you are settling down as my assistant and I keep you busy, so why do you have to do this? I do not understand you." I knew he was both frustrated and worried.

"William, I survived the war and I can deal with this." That remark did not help since he was giving me an evil stare and I expected him to lecture me about my foolish nature and be fired.

"I am very busy with civil cases and new corporate file and it is not a problem to give up my criminal work, although I will miss their stories. I do not know whether to provide my blessings or to curse you. Take care, I need you as a friend and a partner." We spent some time on our schedule and as we finished I reminded him not to say a word to anyone. He just looked at me and sadly nodded. I was glad we still would work together since I enjoyed my work with William.

King Solomon's Dome had been mentioned and I would be heading there but I did not know why it had that name. I asked James Riley why the small mountain east from Dawson City was called King Solomon's Dome. He explained the richest gold creeks flowed from there and it was perceived that the Dome was the mother lode of gold. I told him I would be away for a week and would see him when I returned.

Maps were my next requirement and after I bought them, I spoke to a couple of miners to ask for directions to King Solomon's Dome and the Indian River. One map was the Grand Trunk Railway System and its connection to the Klondike Gold Fields. A more detailed map was George Dawson's map from the Geological Survey of Canada. At lunch, the Palace Grand Theatre was quiet and so different from the sounds at night of shouts, howls, yells, brawls, and laughter. Arizona Charlie was occupied with his liquor order when I asked to speak with him.

"I am heading to the gold fields and will be back in a week." For some reason my statement made him look uncomfortable.

"John, this place is special and you help with that. You have an ability to handle my customers so they return and not end up in a hospital or in jail. My clients like to drink and talk and my job is to maintain confidentiality like a priest at confession." Mae's expression was like ice as she shook her head back and forth. Arizona Charlie turned away from her and whispered.

"I have to tell you a piece of information but I can't tell you the whole of it. Someone wants you dead and that is all I can say so be careful and watch yourself. Make an acquaintance with Mr. Winchester or Mr. Smith and Wesson and come back alive." I thought Mae would jump on him, although he was a head taller. I told him I would take care and as I left, I heard Mae dressing him down.

My lessons with Sergeant Raven included principles of investigation and the first subject was sources of information, witnesses, and photos. The next topic was how to interrogate a suspect or a witness. In his time with the Dominion Police he had heard about fingerprints and had requested a book on this topic, but it had yet to arrive. I moved from lessons to practice at the firearm range outside of town. There were three of us that day and I was anxious to finish to get started on my investigation. The range corporal introduced himself as Corporal Meighan and at first, I had difficulty understanding his Scottish accent but he explained the details of the weapon. I did not tell him about my service in the Strathcona's Rifles, or my experience with the Lee–Enfield cavalry carbine. That carbine fired a .303 bullet and you had to firmly grip it and if you lay prone with the rifle next to your face, you needed a strong grasp, otherwise the kick from the discharge gave a bruise. The range corporal handed us the North West Mounted Police rifle, which was also a Lee-Enfield but slightly longer than the cavalry one. After a few shots in the center of the target and in the absence of a bruised cheek, Corporal Meighan smiled.

"Lad, you have used this before. Let me guess, South Africa?" I nodded. He said Sergeant Raven wants you to train on the revolver as well since you passed the rifle test. He produced an Enfield revolver.

"The problem is weight. It is a reliable weapon if it is new but as they age, problems arise. To start, use one hand to steady the hand holding the weapon." I knew revolvers but I needed the practice, so I spent the day standing and moving which resulted in an aching arm. As we rode back to Dawson, Corporal Meighan suggested I buy a Smith and Wesson handgun. The next day was the riding range but after a few hours, I was told to leave. The physical examination and photographs were next.

After the photo shoot, I met with Sergeant Raven who asked what private weapons I owned? I told him an old Martini-Henry cavalry carbine from my uncle, who served in India, and my Lee-Enfield cavalry rifle. He said to take the Lee-Enfield as it would be better than the police rifle. He told me to look for a Smith and Wesson revolver. The final interesting meeting was with Inspector McDonald who called me to his office. He had telegraphed an old friend with the Toronto police.

"You have a prominent family and I am surprised you are up here." He smiled and asked, "How was the horse?" There was a long pause and then laughter as he escorted me to the door. I worked for a couple of days with William before I met again with Sergeant Raven and asked if I could travel out to check up on Big Pierre and Weigand.

"Not alone," and he told me he would also come, but not in uniform. We sat in his office to discuss investigation techniques when the sergeant said there was a chance we could encounter nasty strangers on the trail and he was a terrible shooter. This was an incentive to practice with my firearms so that day I bought a Smith and Wesson. It felt light in my hand compared with the police revolver and I needed to try it out, so we went back to the range where I spent many hours with my own Lee-Enfield rifle and my new Smith and Wesson handgun. Watching the sergeant, he was correct, he was a terrible marksman to the point of a danger to anyone near him.

Once we finished we were tired and did not speak on our journey back to Dawson City. I knew how to ride and shoot and anything else would be a learning experience. That night we packed and checked our weapons, which meant me, since Sgt. Raven was without a doubt hopeless. In my room that night, I sharpened my bayonet and practiced holding my revolver. As I lay on my bed I heard the long mournful howl of wolves and wondered if that was a good or a bad sign. I knew I was as prepared as I could be, but I did not know what awaited me. It was like South Africa when I awoke and never knew if it was my last day but each day I survived and had to trust my luck would continue.

CHAPTER 6

There was no light when I awoke at five o'clock. It was the end of August, which meant I was almost three months in the Yukon Territory. I checked my gear and weapons and placed my carbine in a leather holder and my revolver in a holster on my belt. I took my agreement with Big Pierre, some maps and the *Criminal Code* to study. I dressed and went downstairs to discover breakfast.

"You need a good meal before you travel," Mrs. Rivest exclaimed. I forgot to tell her about my trip and her knowledge of my habits and plans amazed me. She fed me coffee, eggs, toast and ham and I told her that I would be away for a few days into mining country.

"If you go past King Solomon's Dome, see if you can find George Martin. He mined with my husband and I have not heard from him in two months. He paid me my share of the profits but I have not had any messages from him. It was as if he disappeared, which is not like him since he is a good man." She looked worried.

"Why did you not mention this before?" She looked down at the floor.

"I kept thinking he would arrive but it is too long." I looked at her and said I would try to find him. I asked her how much she received from her share of the profits.

"After George takes a wage, I receive fifty ounces from every cleanup since it is a good mine." I asked if she had a map of the mine location. She went into her room and came out with a map and the partnership agreement and I asked if I could take it with me.

"You now have a son named Jean Rivest." She looked confused so I explained.

"If someone, other than George Martin was at the mine, I would show the partnership agreement, which gives me the authority to ask questions." She agreed with my plan. The map set out the location and under the partnership agreement, Martin and Rivest jointly owned thirty bench claims on Hunker Creek, near the Dome. I showed her the agreement and she said the claims were around the Dome but not past it, so I wrote this information on my map. My final question was George Martin's description.

"He is about forty-five, short maybe five feet, four inches in height. He is a bit fat and bald and has a moustache and during the summer, he wears a peaked flat cap. If he asks about me, he calls me my little flower," she whispered as she blushed. Rivest looked at me and said for God to protect me.

It was six thirty when I arrived at the Detachment with my bedroll and pack and the guard let me in. At the stables, Sergeant Raven waited with the horses saddled and I added my packs and told him I had the route mapped out. As we left, the sun started to cover the City. It was a cold morning and we rode in silence southeast over rough ground and soon we were out of the city.

"While on this trip, call me Bert."

"Your mother must like the Royal Family so I presume Bert is short for Albert, Queen Victoria's husband." That remark went unnoticed but I persevered.

"Please call me John." He nodded and I thought this is going to be a long trip since this fellow is not much of a talker. About an hour into our trip I needed to confirm my theory.

"You are not a morning person, are you?"

"Nope," he curtly replied and that ended our conversation. We continued our ride in silence and a few minutes later I asked about his family. He did not respond for about a minute.

"Do you a wife, and daughter," I asked. But there was no answer. As we rode, I could see the snow in the mountains. We travelled around dams, creeks, and constant mining activity because everyone wanted the last push on the creeks before freeze up. You need constant water to mine but once it turns to ice, you can do excavation, but not to sluice. We rode for another hour when he at last spoke.

"Let us stop for a smoke," and after we dismounted Bert lit his pipe. I was tired of not knowing what he was investigating and decided to ask.

"Why are you here?" That caught his attention and he looked at me carefully, without immediately responding.

"I am here to help organize some investigations," but there had to be more. I told him that I had asked members of the police about detective work and they told me that they were too busy with maintaining the peace, customs, escorting gold and different duties. One told me that fifteen years ago Inspector Constantine considered establishing a detective section but decided against it since there did not seem to be much here in the way of detective work. Bert looked at me with a smile.

"Nothing escapes you but this will take some time to explain. We remounted our horses when he started.

"I was from a small town near Ottawa. When I was twenty and looking for work, one of my father's cousins was a clerk in the department of finance who told me that the Dominion Police were on the lookout for recruits. I applied and was accepted which was in 1877." He explained the Dominion Police were established in 1868 after Darcy McGee was murdered. To assassinate a sitting member of Parliament was a national disgrace.

"When I joined, the Dominion Police was small but it has expanded to protect naval ports, canals as well as government buildings in Ottawa." He looked over to study me.

"The Dominion Police protect important people like members of Parliament but we also deal with counterfeiting and trafficking. We are like a secret service and this is common knowledge. What I am now telling you is not and it is highly confidential. You keep your mouth shut with what I am about to tell you." He paused and I thought he decided to not tell me anything more, but he continued.

"You know about the Fenian raids in the 1860's that were launched from the United States into Canada. The United States government was not happy about England during their civil war so this was a bit of payback, permitting a blind eye for these raids." He looked at me and continued.

"America likes to flex its muscle. Look at Texas and Cuba. There is a chance the Yukon Territory is on their list for interference or worse," which caught my attention.

"Why is the Yukon Territory on their list?"

"This becomes more interesting so let's look closer to home with a history lesson. In the 1820's the Russian Czar and King George juggled trade rights in this part of the world with an agreement that the Russian fur traders could trade up to a certain point in the present-day Alaskan Territory and the Yukon Territory. This was in a signed treaty between the Russian and British Empire almost eighty years ago." Bert continued seeing my interested look.

"Then Seward arranged in 1867 for the United States to buy Alaska from the Russian Empire, which includes the treaty from the 1820's that set out the rights of Russian traders to enter British Territory and the geographical limit of Russian interest. Now you have the Americans replacing the Russians, but it no longer is trading rights, it is now the ownership of land." He paused to check his horse and then discussed the next part of the story.

"The exact boundary was not defined and left quite vague, which was not a huge problem until 1898 when United States infantry was shipped to Haines in the Alaskan Territory, south-west of Whitehorse. Then in 1899 American infantry were sent to Skagway with more forts established in various parts of the Alaskan Territory. Fort Egbert was established on the Yukon River at Eagle, next to the Canadian border, and has a company of the Seventh Infantry Regiment." I looked at my map.

"That is not far from the Klondike gold fields. Why did they need infantry so close? He studied me and I felt he was deciding whether to continue with his story.

"Canada needs an outlet from the Klondike gold fields but the nearest port is around Skagway, in the Alaskan Territory. So why establish a fort near the gold fields? Were these soldiers placed there to put pressure on negotiations that will take place? Or is there something else, since most of the miners in the Klondike are American. I do not put it past the American government to remain behind the scenes to help create a new conquest? If they achieved that, the infantry that is stationed near the gold fields could move in to establish law and order. I just do not know the answer but I my suspicious nature makes me very distrustful." He looked distressed as he told me this story.

"I was sent by the Dominion Police to the North West Mounted Police to conduct a very secret investigation. My work is to discover if a secret society plans to take control of the Yukon and the mining areas near Dawson City. The name of this organization is the Order of the Midnight Sun and some members include Fenian and Boer sympathizers. We know they have members and supporters in Seattle, San Francisco, and Skagway. My, or should I say, our investigation, is to find out if they are active here. I am so glad you practiced on the range since I cannot shoot worth a damn." That was not what I wanted to hear but I knew he was truthful about that.

"During the Gold Rush, almost forty thousand Americans came to look for gold. Many left, but they still form most of the population. We have constables out of uniform from the Dominion Police in Seattle, San Francisco, and Skagway to investigate this organization. My superiors in Ottawa do not believe there is any serious threat by the United States government, but they are asking questions."

"What evidence have you discovered?"

"Unfortunately, the facts support the possibility of a conspiracy since we have a copy of a manifesto written in March. It states the Midnight Sun Order wishes a new republic for various reasons including corruption in the mining recorder's office, taxation, timber permits, and excessive royalty payments. Miners hate these costs and just want to leave alone to search and produce gold." This reflected some stories I had heard in my visits with some miners. The sergeant looked at me to estimate my reaction.

"If this group takes over the gold fields, they will run it without our government. We lack adequate police to properly cover this large area. Outside of Dawson City there are more than thirty police outposts with just a few men, so we are very thin on the ground. This clandestine group believes it will be simple to seize the Yukon Territory." We were interrupted, when a horse made a sound. We checked around for wolves but did not see any.

"Our agents identified two men, Clark and Grehl whose purpose is to obtain the sympathy of unhappy miners. In the manifesto, they wrote of the greed of the present government." Bert sighed and shook his head.

"In June, a letter was sent to citizens in Skagway which asked them for financial support. We know money was provided and unfortunately they have the support of important people including some Senators in Washington." His face looked miserable as he continued with the story.

"Ottawa's concern is the local American miners declaring the Klondike gold area as part of the Alaskan Territory, but these miners do not want the rest of the Yukon Territory, just those gold fields. Some argue this area was always part of the Russian Empire under this loose treaty that will be finalized in London." I did not believe it, but he seemed more upset the longer he spent in telling this tale.

"It is even worse since we learned that Grehl was in Dawson City to search for financial contributions. Grehl was so concerned the police might search him that he left his plans at a trading post. The owner gave those papers to the North West Mounted Police and they were forwarded to the Detachment. Those plans included donations of money for the purchase of weapons, but they left out the robberies of steamships. I do not know his description, but we have his name and are searching for him. We have another suspect named Cedric Barton, and again we do not know what he looks like but we heard he might be part of this group." He looked over with another unhappy expression. These constant expressions of pain made me consider a quick exit but I felt sorry for him.

"More bad news has come to our attention including a gold robbery from a smelter in Seattle, where the robbers stole over two hundred thousand dollars. That did not concern me until I learned that money was sent to St. Michaels in the Alaskan Territory to be used for weapons and the recruitment of men. He looked at me.

"Have I answered your questions?"

"You have opened a box that leads to more questions. Have you been able to find evidence of attempts to overthrow the authorities here?" Before he answered I jumped in with another question.

"Was the *Casca* gold theft used to finance the Order of the Midnight Sun and were these American's the gold thieves?" Bert looked at me with a frown.

"Those are two questions and I will attempt to answer both. This is an enigma and I am not sure of anything at this point but if I were a betting man, I would put my money on a link between the robberies you have talked about and the plot to create trouble here." He looked ahead and paused before he continued. He seemed to exhibit a reluctance to tell this story but also felt it was required for me to know this information.

"We have yet to find conclusive evidence and that is why you and I are taking this little trip." The sergeant remained serious but determined to re-gurgitate an unpleasant tale.

"I pushed the Inspector to hire you. I was impressed with your inves-tigations at the mining recorders and gold commissioner's office and your conclusions. You have potential as a detective and your main value is your war experience. I spoke with Corporal Tupper who told me you could handle yourself when shots are fired but you do not like army rules. I do not believe in too much discipline but you will need to obey a few orders when you work with me, but I am more of an administrative type. I am forty-five years of age and a little soft and never was a great marksman, but you are. Maybe I lured you in but you have a chance to back out. Whatever might happen, I think the danger level is high."

What was I riding into? It was one thing to sit in my office and wan-der the government offices in Dawson City. Now I ride to something, or somewhere that may kill us and was there a link between Big Pierre's theft, the steamship robbery, and a potential conspiracy? Another question was whether this had anything to do with a missing miner? He asked if I wanted to hear more so I told him I did.

"You may not like the next part." So far, I did not like anything he had told me.

"We hired an undercover agent to work with American miners named Alfred James who is also a miner. Every Saturday night at eight we had an ap-pointment. During the last meeting, Alfred told me of a miner named Cedric

Barton, who was assembling supplies of guns, and among the weapons were four Maxim machine guns and four hundred rifles. I warned Albert to be careful since I would rather have him alive without information, then dead." He looked at me to see if I was scared and I tried not to show it.

"That was the last time I saw him. We searched all of Dawson City and outside of the city but soon found it was next to impossible with thousands of miles of diggings, two rivers, and the wilderness. We never found him and I presume he is dead." I was sure I did not want to hear more.

"I have several scenarios. Either he decided to leave the Yukon Territory or he was killed in a robbery. The third possibility is one that keeps me awake at night that he was killed by the Order of the Midnight Sun, and if that is the case it leads credence to the plan to take over the Yukon Territory. Why else would anyone want to kill him except to maintain secrecy? If this rumour were correct, why would they want that much weaponry except to cause trouble or worse? The North West Mounted Police are supposed to have matters under control since this is not the Alaskan Territory. My only conclusion is that these guns are to bring about an uprising." He looked at me to see my reaction.

"Do you still want to travel with me? I should have mentioned this before and you can turn back and resign as a Special Constable and nothing will arise from that." I did not say anything but thought of the chance to learn from an experienced detective and to discover what happened with Big Pierre's robbery. I still had the same trait that took me to South Africa with a desire for adventure. I knew the war was not what I expected. Here, I could make choices. I am a good shot, a good horseman, and I would attempt patience and someday I might achieve it. I wanted to learn investigative skills and if I left Bert now, he would be alone, and that bothered me since he was useless with a weapon.

"I will stay," and added, "Because I enjoy your morning conversations." His annoyance turned to a grin, since he was relieved I would remain with him. Whether my future turned bad, or worse, I was not going back to Dawson City.

"What is the connection between Weigand and Barton?"

"Weigand is an American and my reports indicate illegal gambling, assaults and extortion. Your evidence about royalty payments at the gold commissioner's office was the first link to the gold robberies. If you are correct, that money might be used to buy guns and pay recruits. We are not sure if Weigand is part of Barton's gang but my guess is he is." Bert paused and looked ahead.

"I believe Barton, or his gang, killed Alfred James but I cannot prove it but if we squeeze Weigand enough, his confession might connect us to Barton. We just need to find him alive." Based on the maps we had arrived at the area the robbery took place. Due to the passage of time, it would be difficult to find evidence, since it had rained, and other miners may have camped here. After dismounting, we tied our horses near a stream and found wood to make a fire for coffee and stew. No one else was there so I used our privacy to describe Weigand, which included his habit of smoking Cuban cigars. Bert told me they only had rumours about him but never obtained sufficient evidence to charge him, since he scared anyone who might approach the police.

It was time for our search as Bert walked to the south and east, while I walked to the north and west. After about ten minutes I returned to check the fire and found that the coffee and stew were ready. As I stirred the stew I heard a shout but I could not see Bert and I walked south on a slight elevation and as I moved over a hill I heard his voice for me to come. Over an incline there was a miner's tunnel and I found a long rough path and walked three feet to an old campfire. Bert explained he had picked up a few objects and showed me his small silk bags. We walked back to our campfire and reheated the coffee and stew and while we ate I asked about his small silk bags.

"It is for evidence. I never know what I will find so I always keep them with me and I found two things of interest." He removed some items and showed me the small end of a cigar and some partially burnt pieces of paper. I asked if he could determine the cigar's manufacturer but Bert could not see any label on it.

"Often I cannot find a piece of conclusive evidence. Remember John that a piece of evidence forms part of a chain, and it is the connections from these separate objects that is important. What are we trying to prove with these items? For us to decide what is relevant we must ask, does the cigar stub help us prove or disprove the facts involved with Big Pierre's theft?" He paused and looked at me before proceeding.

"Weigand smokes cigars but so do many miners, so to connect a list of suspects to the evidence, I look to motive and opportunity. Big Pierre had gold and from what you told me, Weigand did not, which is the classic motive of greed." He asked me to take notes since it could be months before this went to trial.

"Opportunity is the next issue. Weigand had the ability to follow Big Pierre and evidence that may or may not link Weigand to this site. If he followed Big Pierre it would make sense that he waited until they fell asleep" He scrutinized me to see if I understood.

"The standard for relevance is fairly low and only requires some movement towards proving, or disproving a fact in question and I am satisfied the cigar is relevant to the gold theft." I felt as if he was testing me.

"John, do you think the cigar stub can be used in a court of law? The point of the case is to show Weigand followed them, hid in the miner's shaft, and when they slept, took the gold bag." He sighed and said this why his job gave him a headache.

"With just the cigar stub and burnt papers to show Weigand was here, the Justice of the Peace would throw this case out, and demand why it was brought. We cannot prove that without a witness or a confession and it never would get to Territorial Court. But we have something to work with which is a theory." He moved to another topic.

"The other piece of evidence is more interesting. In the light, I can see it is a map of some claims but I cannot figure where they are located. Have a look," and handed the burnt documents with the map to me and I took out my own maps and compared them. As I looked at the burnt map I thought it set out the location of certain mining claims near Indian River but I needed more information.

"The burnt map might be the Rivest and Martin claims or some other claims," I said.

"The mining recorder's office can confirm this and I am a friend with one of the staff so I can ask, on the basis I was interested in buying those claims."

"John, if you believe the cigar to be relevant to the gold theft, can you explain why the map was burnt and for what purpose?"

"Whoever was here tried to destroy this map but failed, which meant they suddenly had to leave, and never looked back to check. The map may be related to other mining claims used to finance this operation, such as the payment of bribes or to hire men, and maybe the burnt map will show the location of guns." He did not say anything for a minute but studied me.

"You have the beginnings of a detective and I agree with your analysis but check out the mining recorder's office when we are back." We finished lunch and organized the horses. We did not travel fast due to the necessity to avoid creeks and trails. I asked if we could check out George Martin at King Solomon's Dome as I said we were headed that way. I repeated what Mrs. Rivest told me this morning.

"Do mysteries follow you? First Big Pierre and now Martin. Is there anything else you need to confess as I can look the other way?" I said that was it for now.

"I am going to change the topic to talk about our boss Superintendent Zachary Taylor Wood, who is the head of the North West Mounted Police." He asked me about my American history.

"Was there not an American president named Zachary Taylor?" Bert grinned at my response.

"He was the twelfth president of the United States. Zachary Taylor Wood is the great grandson of Zachary Taylor, a graduate of the Royal Military College and has military experience. You have cavalry experience and are a horseman and I think that is why he approved your joining the North West Mounted Police. I am not sure my recommendation about hiring you made any difference." He looked around to give me a secret.

"Do you know many of the constables named their dogs Zachary? Four of which I am aware, but there may be more. Can you imagine that?" He raised his voice and pretended to be a constable calling his dog.

"Zachary heel, Zachary, sit. Zachary, good dog." He laughed but then turned serious.

"Wood is a strict, but fair commanding officer. He likes that his men have military experience, which does not include me. He is not pleased to have Ottawa involved here. He told me on more than one occasion, that by the time a decision is made by the federal government in Ottawa, the world here changed. Obtaining instructions requires a letter, which can take a month to arrive in Ottawa, two to three months for their decision to be made, and another month for a reply and on something urgent, it is always too late." He stopped and resumed.

"Perhaps I should not be explaining so much detail to you but I sense you will not repeat what I tell you. The big problem for Superintendent Wood and Inspector McDonald is the possibility of the overthrow of the gold fields by the Order of the Midnight Sun. If the rumour is true we must act on it and perhaps request military assistance, since there are less than one hundred police in and around Dawson City. We know we may call on Canadians and members of the Empire that served in South Africa, but they are less than one hundred men, which is problem number one." I remained silent.

"Problem two is if this rumour is false and it gets to the press, then relations with America will become unpleasant. Great Britain handles the boundary negotiations but we have some influence. If the plot is no more than gossip and is published in either the *New York Times* or the *London Times*, we will look like an immature Dominion with no ability to conduct foreign affairs and London will send our delegation home." My new boss looked unhappy at me as he spoke.

"The government has warned us this is a very secret investigation. Until today when I spoke to you, only Superintendent Wood, Inspector McDonald and myself were briefed. Extreme discretion and confidentiality are to be maintained. We do not record any material unless it is locked, which creates problems for communication with Ottawa and we use a code." Now I heard an actual sigh.

"I think that is why I have problems sleeping so mornings are not my best time of the day. This is a devil of a problem, which is how to perform an investigation while pretending not to do one? I am damned if I do something and damned if I don't. Welcome to my world." We go into danger no matter what we do and I was a good thing I was the constable and not in the person in charge. Suddenly I felt sick, what would happen on this trip if my sergeant dies? I suddenly had an awful vision of Bert, dead on the back of his horse, while I fought off a bunch of screaming Yankees with pistols and swords. I shook my head to clear that nightmare and knew it was on me to protect him. We rode in silence for a while before Bert asked me to tell my story. I was glad to move to something normal so I told him everything including my upbringing, my departure from school, the South African War, my family and my trip to the Yukon Territory. I left out the incident with the horse and my money. I asked about his background. He told me about his youth and the Dominion Police and a description of his wife and daughter. The Married quarters in the Detachment were recently built and his wife and daughter were on their way to join him. Bert said his daughter had finished her education and was on her way to teach elementary school.

It was late but the sun was still over the mountains. We had one more hour before it was dusk so it was time to stop for the night. We began to search for a place to stay and found an abandoned cabin. Inside it had a stove and while he looked for wood I fed and watered the horse and discovered a spot for them to graze. We cooked and cleaned up, and whether we were tired or had spoken enough we remained silent. I suggested he sleep first and I would wake him up at one o'clock to replace me as a sentry. I sat alert with my worries when the cabin erupted with the most earsplitting snores and I was glad we took turns on watch since there was no way I could sleep with those kettledrums of sound.

Chapter 7

The moon in the clouds and the stars a faint glow in the endless sky I felt transported to an alien but wondrous land. Every fifteen minutes I walked around the cabin and checked the horses. My experience was to carry weapons I could reach and use, with a bayonet on my belt, a knife tied to my leg, a pistol, and my rifle. I listened for the sound of horses or voices but heard only wind in the trees and shivered, both with the cold and fear.

It was my first night in this wilderness and I tried to stay alert. I started to relax and enjoy the moon when the sound of wolves interrupted my peace. I stood up and placed my rifle on my chest but decided the wolves were at least a mile away. It was midnight when I heard bushes rustle and spied a man carefully approaching the cabin, then the clouds shifted to cover most of the moon, but there was enough light to see smoke from the chimney, so he knew someone occupied the cabin. I slowly raised my rifle and looked around to discover a second person creeping towards our horses.

My problem was two men at different locations, which meant I had to apprehend one before the second one entered the cabin. If I shouted or made a sound, they would escape or shoot me, and I wanted to capture both alive. I gently put my rifle down, took out my bayonet and slowly crept towards the stranger near the horses. I had spent many hours sharpening and practicing with it and knew I had one chance to surprise him. His rifle was pointed at the ground as I approached him from behind, reached around his neck, and gently pushed my knife to touch his back. He tensed as I softly spoke.

"One word and you are dead," but he was a good little lamb and kept quiet. The darkness made it difficult to obtain his description. I told him not to turn around because my friend had a pistol pointed at his back. I stepped back picked up a rock, and clobbered his head. As he fell, I reached to catch him before he collapsed. In the dark, I had a glimpse of a beard and a big nose. I removed his small haversack and put it on my back since I needed to find out his identity.

I grabbed my rifle and lay on the ground with the barrel aimed at the second man. He was at the door when I shouted.

"Don't move, or I will shoot," but he turned and ran into the trees. I jumped up and tried to follow him, but he was gone, and I worried about an ambush, so I headed to the cabin as Bert stepped outside with his rifle.

"Bert, we need to find him. He may be armed, have your weapon at the ready and come with me." The darkness and an unknown enemy created a tense situation as we headed to where I last saw him. We searched but found nothing.

"Well, at least we have one, come to the horses" I explained I had knocked out the other one out, but when we arrived at the spot, he was gone. I started to shake and felt sick and leaned down to think what was I doing here. Bert came over and helped me to the cabin. I told him about the two strangers and what I did to the man near the horses. When I finished my story, he looked at me.

"You sneaked up and disabled him without being shot?"

"Maybe he was careless and perhaps I was lucky, but I have no idea how I did that. I did not want to kill him, just stun him, but I did not wallop him hard enough." Suddenly my excitement had turned to exhaustion. We entered the cabin and lit a lantern.

"Were these two just trying to steal from us, or did they follow us here," I asked? Bert did not answer and looked concerned before he responded.

"I prefer them to be robbers because if they pursued us, we are in trouble since they may have information from Alfred James. If they trailed us from the Detachment, it is the end of our undercover role."

"We have nothing to suggest this was anything other than an attempted theft. I did not get a good look at the fellow I hit, other than he was an inch or two shorter than me and with a beard and a large nose. Why would they try and stop us since we have not discovered any evidence and our investigation has not even begun?" I thought there might be more to this.

"If they followed us we should set a trap," but Bert said nothing and started to pace before he spoke.

"John, if you are a victim what do you prefer robbery or murder? Dead is dead." And then he laughed and stopped pacing which made me nervous, but I had to give him the benefit of the doubt.

"Tell me how you would set a trap," Bert asked.

"First we have to find them. Many miners have beards and ride together, but if they are travelling in our same direction, we could plan an ambush. They may or may not fall into it, but it is the best thought I have this late at night and tomorrow might bring a better idea." Bert said he could not sleep so I told him to keep watch and have his rifle ready.

At first light, I went to the stove to heat the kettle and Bert told me nothing else had happened during the night. After our breakfast, I opened the haversack to discover a canteen filled with whisky, biscuits and an envelope with a paper that had my picture and some writing. The sketch was my face, and the unsigned note said to find and kill him and I read it out to Bert

"I know why they were here, but I do not understand why you are the intended victim."

"Probably my investigations have stirred up trouble, and I would give anything to know who ordered my death?" I examined the haversack and found that someone marked the initials E.S. on the back. We went outside and placed our bags on the horses and headed towards King Solomon's Dome. A cloudy morning greeted us with a bit of wind, and it had snowed during the night.

"We needed to be extra cautious," which prompted Bert to glare at me for stating the obvious as he shook his head. We followed the tracks of the two men but lost them at a river. I told Bert that we needed to check on George Martin since he has disappeared and relayed the history and ownership of the mine.

"If I find people on the claims operating the mine, I will introduce myself as Mrs. Rivest's son, and ask why my mother no longer received her gold." Bert snorted and shook his head as I heard him mutter. Mining activity increased as we approached the Dome and no one looked at us as we rode. We stopped to ask a miner for directions to the Rivest and Martin Bench Claims, and he explained we were close to them. I had my map that pointed to a slightly elevated spot that overlooked what I believed to be their claims

After lunch, I did a reconnaissance with my Chevalier field glasses. I crawled to a small hill covered by bushes. With my field glasses adjusted, I observed two men at work sluicing gold through a wooden rocker. They focused on their work and did not look in my direction. One was tall, with a beard and bushy black hair while the other miner was shorter, with blond hair but no moustache. They had two rifles about ten feet behind them.

There was no short, fat man with a peaked cap and a moustache, so George Martin was not on his claim. I let the bushes fall back and crawled out of sight. Bert would hide in the bushes and cover me with his rifle while I went onto the claims.

"Are you a good shot with the Lee-Enfield?"

"It depends on whether I have my glasses and he checked his pockets.

"Hell, I left them at the Detachment." I was about to end my investigation when he laughed and said he did not use spectacles.

"How accurate are you at three hundred yards?" Bert replied that he probably was not.

"Shoot in the air if you see they are trying to kill me and use the field glasses," and Bert asked if I should rethink my plan, but I said I had the element of surprise.

I gave Bert my rifle, but took my revolver and bayonet and hid them under my jacket. It was a nervous and long walk to the claims. Approaching any miner who sluices gold is dangerous at the best of times, and this walk was worse, since these two could be part of Barton's gang. When I arrived, and introduced myself, what would be their response? They could order me off the claims but if I spoke in a quiet voice, would they approach me, away from their rifles? One of them could pretend to be George Martin, or they could say they worked for Martin, or that he sold the claims to them.

When I was about two hundred yards from their activity, one of them looked up. I said something, but they could not hear me. I tried not to shake and trusted that they would not reach for their weapons. They stood and watched as I held my hands in front and stopped ten feet in front of their cleanup. Both men were thin and much shorter than me.

"My name is Jean Rivest" but I did not tell them of my relationship with Mrs. Rivest, or Louis Rivest, but they did not recognize the name and remained silent. I was tempted to ask, why the hell they were on George's claim but kept quiet.

"Where is George?" I asked.

"Never heard of him," the blond one answered. My next question could require my pistol and my coat was now partly open with the hidden revolver.

"George Martin is one of the owners of these claims. My father owned the other half, and it is a mystery why you are here." They looked at each other and then the bearded one spoke.

"Listen, kid; we have no idea what this is about but we are finished with you, and you have thirty seconds to turn around and get out, or you will regret trespassing."

As we spoke, I inched closer. My view is strike first and hard which is something I learned in the bar in Toronto. I punched the blond fellow in the mouth hard enough for him to fall backward. I expected the bearded one to hit me, or run for the guns but he swung, and I ducked and connected my fist into his stomach. He fell, and Blondie tried to get up to run to the weapons. I kicked his head, and he dropped. Mr. Beard started to get up again, so his stomach connected with my foot. My foot was fine, but it affected the bearded one as he lay and moaned. I backed up, took out my revolver and barked at them.

"Sit down, and don't move or I might try a leg shot. That should not kill you, but it will hurt like hell." They sat and did not move then I heard Bert who sounded concerned.

"Are you on top of this?" and I said I was.

"We need to tie them up," I said, and Bert did it while I covered them with my revolver. I asked Bert to get their weapons and bring them, so he grabbed them and gave me one while he kept the other. They had slings, so we put the extra pair of rifles on our backs as spares.

That feeling came again as I sat down and shook. My stomach churned, and my heart pounded, and I thought if this does not end I would change jobs. It had taken several minutes before I stopped my shakes and my heart level returned to normal. Bert watched but kept silent and then told me to follow him out of earshot of the prisoners. Before he spoke, I whispered that I needed to say what bothered me.

"I have a bad feeling about this. Are these two alone, or are there others? We need to search the cabin and the miner's drift and to confirm if there are any more of them. Those two must come with us, so we will put them in front, have a quick look at the cabin and then go to the drift." Bert looked surprised but never questioned me as he checked the cabin while I guarded the prisoners. When he left the cabin, he raised his hand and moved towards me, and we helped the men up.

"You two walk in front of us while we inspect the miner's drift." They looked at each other but did not move. It was control time, and I was ready.

"Listen, you two mugs, I do not want you to do a scoot so move, or you get a leg shot. Do you understand?" I was worried that their friends were around the corner. Bert gave me a severe look, but I did not think he understood my game of bull and bluff. Either he would learn my way or fire me, and at that point, I did not care, since I had been on high alert for some time and wanted someone else to come to the rescue. Uncharted waters lay ahead, and all I wanted to do was to stay on shore and watch. The two men at last moved and I could not think of a better shield.

We found two lanterns at the entrance, lit them, and started into the tunnel. The descent continued with flickers of light on the walls and ceiling. The limited light made our progress difficult and soon bent forward, we started to trip over loose rocks and areas where the roof and sides had crumbled.

The descent continued and never seemed to end, and I stopped when I discovered that I could no longer fill my lungs with air. I thought we had gone far enough when we turned a corner, and I saw something on the ground. In the shadows from the flickering light, I could see a body that I assumed was George, and we were too late. Blondie stopped, and I went around him to see a man tied to a post. I knelt to touch him, and he suddenly sat up.

"Who are you," he croaked?

"George?" I asked.

"How do you know my name?" I whispered, "I will tell you later, but Mrs. Rivest sent me." He looked at me and sighed.

"Thank God," he exclaimed as I cut him from the ropes, I could see we were at the end of the tunnel. As I looked at the rocks, George told me that was where the cave-in killed Louis Rivest. George stood up, and I told him to follow us. At the entrance, I checked for any threats and once satisfied, we took them out. We walked towards the cabin where I tied them to trees about one hundred feet apart. Once I finished this, I waived to Bert, who took George into the cabin.

After they had entered the cabin, I blindfolded both prisoners. I went to the blond one and growled, "You want to be a tough guy, so here's my thinking. I came across some fresh bear scat this morning, and I am not sure if it came from a grizzly or brown bear. It is unusual to see bears this close to a cabin, but maybe that is your destiny. Later, I am going to take my bayonet and give a little cut on your arm, and I may or may not stick around because I am tired and the cabin calls me." His high-pitched scream brought Bert to the window, and I realized I should have gagged them.

"Shut up. You almost killed George since you knew that part of the tunnel was unsafe and I am surprised he survived. I have no compassion for you and if I had my way your life would end tonight. Let me tell you it is dark, and I am nervous in these mountains, so I need the protection of the cabin." I started to walk away he cried out to me.

"Don't leave."

"Why not? A silent fellow like you will not talk, so why waste my time. Besides, I am tired and hungry." His crying started, but I had to be tough and not let him know I would stay to protect him. I used the same threat to the bearded man who reacted the same way as Blondie. I tried to remain quiet as I entered the cabin.

"Our two prisoners seem to be in a cooperative mood and wish to confess." Bert gave me an irritated look that confirmed I was now learning his expression. I asked if George had told his story.

"Give me another ten minutes with him and then bring in the first one." I snuck out of the cabin to stand behind them. If they were new to the wilderness among wolves and bears, they would be petrified, and any animal sound would frighten them. At that moment wolves howled over the next ridge and both men yelled and made as much noise as possible. Ten minutes later the bearded one was untied and brought to the cabin.

After I had closed the door, I crept softly to stand about twenty feet from the blond one who was now silent. It was time for a new scare, so I cracked some twigs, and his screams started again. Enough light at the window showed an irate sergeant shaking his hand. After half an hour, Bert opened the door, and I took Blondie inside and the bearded one out. The basic rules of investigation are never to interview both suspects together.

"You will be tied but if you tell me your name I will not put on the blindfold." He said his last name was Peters, whether it was his real name or not and I explained I would stay.

"If you help me then I will help you. What is the other fellow's name?" I asked, and he said it was McMillan. I told him shortly we would eat and get warm. He remained quiet but looked more relaxed. Bert stood at the window and motioned me to bring him in. The cabin heat felt wonderful, and I was tired and hungry, and no one spoke as the two prisoners ate in the corner. We had our revolvers on the table ready for problems, and neither Peters nor McMillan looked my way. If we need to get out of here fast, it would be easier to have compliant prisoners. When we finished, Bert gave one of the rifles to George and told him if they moved to shoot them.

"I need to talk to my partner," he angrily muttered and I was sure he meant his soon to be former partner. Outside he angrily exclaimed I threatened the prisoners.

"How could you do that? I thought I knew you."

"Calm down and let me explain. I understand that police in Canada beat up prisoners to get them to talk, but we can't do that. Remember when you were a boy, the effect of ghost stories told around a fire at night? What I did was to prey on their minds. I was always there to protect them, notwithstanding what I told them, and I would never have cut them. We have limited time for a confession because their associates could be here tonight. We may need to leave in a hurry, so all I did was provide them with a slight prod.

"That was a prod? I am surprised you didn't give them heart failure, and exactly how am I to explain this to the Inspector?

"Just tell him that you had no idea what I was going to do." He grumbled he did not need this.

"Peters and McMillan would not have talked until my mention of bears while they were tied. One they were sufficiently stimulated they talked, and we needed the information. When the Inspector reports to his boss Wood, who was in the army, he would probably not have a problem. What did George tell you?"

It took a while for Bert to tell me George's story. Two months earlier Peters and McMillan showed up. When he looked out at his sluice box, they suddenly grabbed him and took him to the cabin. After he was captured they mined, but during gold cleanup, they tied George at the end of the tunnel. Before the first cleanup, George was forced to sign a written contract that appointed Robert McGill as his representative to deal with the gold commissioner and gold buyers. The document stated that the gold production had been one thousand ounces.

George felt the actual production was no more than one hundred ounces. He explained the mining custom was that once a gold buyer paid royalties and received the gold, the buyer paid an advance. Once they smelted the gold, the balance was paid to the owner. The signed document authorized all payments to Robert McGill.

The next month he was forced to sign a written agreement that sold his interest in the thirty claims to McGill, for one thousand gold ounces, which he never received. George saw someone else had signed on behalf of Louis Rivest. When I heard that I knew they had made a huge error and they were now in an all-round muddle, once that was discovered. The police knew Rivest was dead while these robbers assumed he was still alive. I wondered if they intended to keep George here until they left the Yukon Territory or was he living on borrowed time? During cleanups and when he was in the tunnel, he had heard different voices, which meant others had come to pick up the gold. Peters and McMillan never left the camp. George said they were in the third cleanup and someone might be here at any time to take the gold.

I asked what was the name of the boss but Bert said he did not receive much information from McMillan, but Peters said his name was McGill, who was about six feet in height, had a moustache and smoked. Peters said McGill scared him and was always worried that he would die each time McGill came to the camp. He warned them if he thought they held back the gold, or told anyone about this camp, that he would slowly kill them and enjoy each hour that it took. Peters said McGill was never alone as there were always three others with him. Each time McGill came with his men, there was a search of the camp.

"Weigand might be McGill," he whispered which was what I thought.

"Bert, we need to leave at first light or shall we stay here to set up an ambush?"

"Give me strength John; there are four of them, and we have prisoners. I have no idea about George, but I am the worst shot, so you could not rely on me. You are beyond belief to suggest this foolishness, and I now doubt my wisdom to bring you on this investigation, so prove me right, or I will cancel this trip." I said nothing, which seemed to mollify him. If we did not have prisoners and if I had another soldier I could do it, but Bert was correct, I sometimes speak first before examining the consequences.

During the night, we all took turns on watch. At first light, Bert told me the nearest North West Mounted Police outpost was at Grand Forks, and we agreed that was our next destination. While he cooked breakfast, I scouted the area and checked on the horses. It was time to get ready, so I gave them food and water while George organized his gold and equipment. As I took the prisoners out of the cabin, I had one question.

"Do you know two men that were hunting me? They are in this area, and one has the initials E.S." They looked at each but kept quiet, and we had no time to wait or to push them for an answer. Peters was tied to my horse while Bert had the same arrangement with McMillan. McGill or Weigand would not want information about a murder to be broadcast since this required secrecy. Would the two men, ordered to kill me, report back and say they failed? Or would they quietly take the next steamer? I did not know but hoped their choice was a quick exit, but I needed to make inquiries about them. Men assigned to eliminate me made my skin crawl since it was too soon to organize my funeral.

Our rifles were in our hands as we rode since I assumed McGill and his gang were in pursuit. I sighed since this was not like the war in South Africa and I was a vulnerable target. I was scared and desired a simple life and not one with a mastermind plotting my murder. My senses were confused, with anger and fear in a struggle for supremacy, both of which made my stomach churn. We stopped for Bert to smoke and to make a fire for coffee while I started to read parts of the *Criminal Code* out loud enough for Peters and McMillan to hear. I listed potential charges against them.

"Bert, let's see what crimes these boys did? They fit the offence of extortion, theft over two hundred dollars, assault, and kidnapping. If they knew what McGill did, perjury, false pretenses, and fraud are the crimes that fit their actions. Peters and McMillan looked ill and sat there with a glum expression.

"That is enough, I do not want to get to the penalty part which could be the lash or prison, but that is for the police and judges to decide. It is not for me to sit in judgment since that will come soon enough." Bert sliced a hand across his throat.

"Thank you for the law lesson constable, but it is time to keep going", which I took to mean for me to shut up. We rode without incident, and after a few hours, we stopped for lunch with turns on watch. At two we arrived at the Grand Forks outpost where two constables came outside to gawk at the two tied prisoners.

"Could someone explain this," one constable demanded. I thought either Peters or McMillan was going to open their mouths, so I gave my look, and they kept quiet. I asked if Corporal Tupper was there, but he was on patrol. Bert dismounted and went with the constables inside the police cabin. We had waited for about half an hour before they returned. Peters and McMillan ran into the cabin and Peters yelled something about a man off his chump outside. It was a relief to be free of them, so we could now continue our trip to the Indian River, but I felt a slight remorse for my treatment of these scallywags but knew it was required.

George was politely asked to check on our horses so I could hear Bert's story. It took a while for the constables to accept he was a sergeant. I was dressed more like a policeman than Bert, as I had on my Stetson hat and Strathcona boots, issued to me in South Africa. We had not taken documents with our identification as police officers since there was a remote chance of our capture. The outpost had three constables and a corporal and any escort for prisoners could take a week. Bert outlined George's story to the constables including potential charges against the prisoners and warned them about McGill's gang. George returned and said he needed to talk with us.

"That gang put me through hell, robbed me and treated me like a dog. You have protected me, and I trust you and I do not care about danger, but I am not going anywhere without you." We explained we were going to the Indian River and it could put our lives at risk. He said he was coming and that was that. I was about to mount my horse when one of the constables gestured and asked if we could take a little walk.

"I am not sure who you are, but the prisoners have filled my ears with complaints about you. I like your style and have a safe journey." He turned, but before he walked to the cabin, I needed to warn him.

"Be careful, those two are part of a dangerous gang." We rode for a few hours and found shelter under some trees. The next day we left to search for Big Pierre's mining claims. I kept checking my maps, and it was some hours before we stopped and looked down to the Indian River. With my field glasses, I could see a person mining below on the Indian River. We rode close to the camp and as we approached George said that was old Scotty. He waved and shouted, and Scotty bowed.

Scotty invited us to his cabin and gave us coffee and biscuits but the biscuits were so hard they required softening in my coffee. When Scotty saw this, he laughed and said that was the correct way to deal with hardtack. He was blue eyed, which contrasted with his red face, and nose. His ears stood out through a mass of gray hair, and he had not shaved for a week. He was short, and a bit stout, but he made up for it by endless talking. My guess was that he had not had visitors for some time and was glad for our company. I asked if he knew the location of two mining claims owned by Dalton Weigand and Pierre Cloutier.

"They are located three miles to the east. Thompson has an agreement to mine on Weigand's property, but I do not know if there is anyone there." He paused and continued.

"Perhaps I should not say this, but at the end of last year's season, I met Thompson in town. He took me for a drink, and after a few, we got to discuss our favorite topic of mining. He leaned over and told me Weigand scared him because they had a disagreement about the mining contract. Weigand's complaint was the shortfall in gold and demanded that Thompson pay him another one hundred ounces. Thompson told him that he paid every ounce of gold under the agreement, but Weigand shook his head and warned him to take care." Scotty stopped to see if we paid attention then resumed.

"I have not seen Thompson since last year." He looked worried and added, he should have checked on Thompson, but mining kept him busy. I told Scotty we would look for him. As we rode, we discussed this new information. As I started to speak, I tried to ensure that George would not hear me but then suggested to Bert that we reveal part of our investigations to him. As soon as Bert explained that we were the police he was cut off.

"I knew you were police and I won't say a word to anyone," George exclaimed. I thought, so much for our undercover operation. Did we have signs on our horses that advertised police at work? We stopped three hundred yards from Big Pierre's camp, and I told them I would go alone to Big Pierre's cabin. I knew Bert was useless with a rifle and asked George if he could shoot. He laughed and told me he learned when he was a boy and for me not to worry. I asked George to take my field glasses and to shoot if necessary.

I was on my own and tried not to show my terror as I started my slow walk to the camp. If someone waited for me in an ambush where would they hide? I stopped every few feet with my rifle cocked and listened but only heard the croaking of ravens. Was this a welcoming committee, or a message of danger but it did not matter, I was committed and would leave it to fate as I crept forward.

CHAPTER 8

To walk into this danger was something I forced myself to do but every sound made me jump, and I had to overcome gruesome images of pain and death. It was unfortunate that *King Richard the Second* popped into my mind, "The worst is death and death shall have his day." I needed to shake this melancholy and look for the men who had tried to kill me. There were two cabins, one without chimney smoke, so I decided to investigate that one first. I knew that this was the perfect spot for someone to lie in wait, but I forced myself to confirm it was empty. I kicked open the door and jumped in to find it empty. When I was about ten yards from the second cabin I shouted.

"Big Pierre, it is John Caldwell, and we need to talk," but I never expected what next happened. The door opened and out stepped an attractive lady with a rifle pointed at me, and I could not decide whether to check the weapon or her. I lowered my Lee-Enfield and looked to see a tall woman, five feet eight inches tall with short brown hair, brown eyes, and full lips. She wore a necklace, with a small pearl and had tall black leather boots, brown pants, and a brown jacket. Her rifle was a Winchester.

"Who are you?"

"John Caldwell, a friend of Mr. Cloutier, and why are you in Mr. Cloutier's cabin?"

"Suzanne Cloutier, Pierre Cloutier's daughter." She studied me, and then told me to come in. Both her smile and her name gave me an assurance.

"There are two friends with me, but I guess you know that." She told me that I was the only one who could come in. I told her I needed to speak to my friends and to explain not to enter the cabin. When I approached Bert and George, I gave Miss Cloutier's description and instructions and Bert gave me a funny look.

"Good lookers can make you careless." I laughed at him not to worry about me and that I could protect myself. They agreed to scout around while I was in the cabin.

I removed my hat and gloves and put them under my arm and was prepared to shake her hand but that never happened. The charming smile disappeared, replaced by a hostile glare. I examined her rifle pointed at my chest and thought of *Macbeth*, "There's daggers in men's smiles." In her case, that should be a woman's smile as I carefully dropped my rifle, hat, and gloves and cursed my gallant upbringing. I had a horrible thought that she was to be my executioner and I was next in line for the eternity box. What a colossal fool I was, wishing to impress a beautiful lady, and I had walked right into this mess. I needed to concentrate on an escape or a capture, and she had all the cards.

"Mr. Caldwell, I have questions." She ordered me to open my coat, so I dropped my revolver and bayonet and only had my hidden knife strapped to my leg. She smiled as she studied me, like a wolf about to dine, and I was the meal.

"Lift up the bottom of your pants." I smiled sheepishly as I carefully dropped my last weapon while the whole time the Winchester pointed at my chest.

"You seemed prepared with that collection?"

"Doesn't everyone have those?"

"Not often," and laughed as she kicked away my weapons. She told me to sit, and I grabbed the nearest chair as she sat in a chair across the room.

"Relax, you are just upset because a lady beat you."

"Drop your rifle and see how long you would last, at the most maybe ten seconds." She gave me a smile.

"You wouldn't hurt a lady, would you?" Out came my stupid response.

"Miss Cloutier, I am not sure if you are a lady and I have reached the stage where I might take a swing." She surprised me by laughing.

"You are a troublemaker, and I like that." She explained she wanted answers since three men who arrived uninvited at her father's place made her nervous. I told her about my agreement with her father to transport gold, his robbery and my concerns about Weigand. I explained Weigand might be involved in other robberies and had a bad feeling his tentacles had reached Big Pierre. It was bad, her father was missing and I was now worried that something sinister had descended on this part of the gold fields but I needed to focus on my problems. I knew Big Pierre was shorter than his daughter, and plum ugly, but Miss Cloutier was beautiful. Between her father's height, looks and her skill at disarming me, I wondered if she was his daughter.

"I never heard him called Big Pierre, he was always just Pierre, and I am his daughter. My mother was taller and beautiful, so I take after her. My brother taught me to handle weapons and to take care of myself." I was not sure if I believed her since she was an expert in disarming me and how could someone as homely as Big Pierre be married to a beauty.

"Have you found out anything?" She looked at me and told me to call her Suzanne.

"Two days ago, I tracked down my father's mining claims, but after a search of this camp I found nothing and plan to leave early tomorrow and travel to the next North West Mounted Police outpost." That was of some use, but I remained nervous about the gun pointed at my chest.

"Would you please put down that Winchester? An accidental discharge comes to mind, and I prefer my body intact and without holes." She analyzed me and then pointed her rifle at the floor.

"I will call you John, but do not mistake politeness for friendship and you are a potential enemy, so if you try to stand it will not end well."

"There is a copy of my agreement with your father in my pocket and could I slowly remove it and throw it to you?" She nodded but after she had read the agreement, she studied me.

"Why was my father robbed, if you agreed to protect him?" Here we go again and thought that she must be Big Pierre's daughter. I had to repeat what I told Big Pierre, so she reread the agreement, and became more relaxed. She stood and asked what I intended to do now.

"Our next step is a visit to the police outpost at Indian River; then we will search the mining area at King Solomon's Dome." I asked if I could talk to my friends, and she agreed but said for me to leave my weapons. I remained in the chair and shook my head.

"Nasty encounters seem to follow me. Recently we stayed in a cabin when armed robbers tried to kill me. They escaped but I am still their target," and I told her of the rescue of George and the capture of two armed men.

"These two kidnapped, extorted and robbed a miner, and like your father, he did nothing wrong. McGill is the leader of a gang that includes these men and they could be here at any time." I looked at her and attempted a smile.

"That smile is terrible so give it up. Really, if that is the best you can do consider becoming a clerk if you can't stand danger."

"Your suggestion is for me to go outside without weapons? I am not leaving, and you get to protect me." I grinned and put my arms behind my head. She studied me then sighed and said for me to equip myself. I strapped on my ankle knife, bayonet, revolver, and grabbed my Lee-Enfield and told her I would be back soon. Just around the side of the cabin, I found Bert who stated he had checked out Weigand and Marston's mining claims and saw no signs of a struggle. It was hard to tell Bert about Miss Cloutier and the loss of my weapons. Once I began, Bert could not stop his laughter.

"Let me understand this. We have a six-foot, five-inch soldier, with experience in the South African war. You managed to overcome robbers at the cabin, rescued George from armed men and yet you allowed a five foot eight lady to capture you?" More laughter erupted, and I muttered my concern.

"I hope you do not repeat this?"

"Repeat this? John, you have no idea. This will be a legend in the North West Mounted Police for years to come. We will sing of the legends of Nelson, Napoleon, Hercules, and the big fellow bested by a little lady. John, you have no idea how this story will be passed on, generation to generation. You will be famous." As Bert laughed some more, I was not pleased with myself, or Bert. He noticed my expression and told me to take it in stride.

"By next year, you will think back that this was a funny story," but Bert spoiled that by his guffaw. I was annoyed but tried to not show it and told him we should travel to the police outpost at Indian River.

"I expect that Big Pierre's daughter may come with us." I also asked him if we were to be treated in a serious fashion, not to mention at the outpost, my loss of weapons to Miss Cloutier. Bert struggled not to laugh and agreed, but his smile drove me crazy. We motioned for George to join us then I returned to the cabin to explain our plans. Suzanne asked to come, and I warned her about possible dangers. She said she would be safer with us than alone in these hills. I thought if this lady was alone what had changed? I should walk to the next hill to see if she had someone with her, but decided to leave it since we needed to move. Her lovely smile did not mean I trusted her.

She walked over to a hill and returned with a horse loaded with equipment. When I first arrived, I had not heard horses and reminded myself in the future I needed to conduct a better reconnaissance. As we rode, Bert talked to Suzanne, which was just as well because my annoyance had not left me. We stopped for coffee and for Bert to smoke.

Suzanne was attractive, experienced and with an odd sense of humour and the same description could apply to me. I survived the war, and I liked to laugh and enjoy practical jokes. I did not know what I could believe about her but knew I could not rely on her. She applied her charms to the old sergeant, which created problems. If we were to remain undercover, we needed to talk to the police without her around. If we met the policemen without her, she would be more suspicious but I did not want her to know our business.

My trustworthy sergeant was entranced and oblivious to my attempts to catch his attention. The gospel of Bert that fancy lookers can make you careless applied to him but he was under her spell, and her good looks masked her dangers. Suddenly I had the same feeling I experienced in my scouting missions in South Africa, that someone was behind us and I needed to stop and check it out.

As we rode, the sky clouded over with an increase in the wind, while rain and snow lashed our faces. The bright autumn weather had left us with no indication of a return. We stopped to put on our coats and gloves, and I went over to Bert and asked if we could move away and talk. I explained at the police outpost I needed him to go in alone and I wanted to check if were being followed.

The change in weather gave me time to climb a slight hill. I took out my field glasses and looked, but whatever was behind us was gone. I returned to shake my head at Bert, which did not go unnoticed by Suzanne. As we rode, I noticed she often looked my way and had watched my private discussion with Bert. Since we left the cabin, she had not said a word to me, but that did not stop her from studying me.

I wondered if she thought I was with the police since I wore my issued Stetson hat from South Africa, which was tan felt with a flat brim. I used the hat when I arrived in the Yukon Territory, and I refused to surrender it since it offered protection against the accumulating snow. I had the tall brown leather boots provided by the Strathcona 's Regiment, and the laces on my bottom shoes had a high gusset that covered my lower legs. Some of the officers and men of the North West Mounted Police also used these, but I was not going to change my hat or my boots. They served me well, and I never could find replacements in Dawson City.

At four in the afternoon, we saw a Union Jack flag flying on top of a building and knew we had arrived at the Indian River outpost. As we approached, a policeman came out to meet us. We dismounted and entered the North West Mounted Police main cabin. I needed to warm up and was thankful for the fire in the stove. George took our horses to be fed and watered in the corral. The constable's name was Jerome Scott who offered us coffee and fresh biscuits, which we gratefully accepted. We made our introductions with Suzanne providing the biggest smile to a new conquest, who seemed overwhelmed. The constable observed my hat and boots, looked at my face but kept quiet. He looked at Suzanne and asked what she was doing alone in mining country?

"I am looking for my father Pierre Cloutier who has disappeared. Do you know where he is?" Constable Scott said two constables were on patrol to find him, which left him alone since the other member was in Dawson City. We helped with dinner, and George fell asleep on a chair near the stove, as I moved next to him. He woke and I said not to say anything in front of Miss Cloutier. When we were alone, Constable Scott told me to call him Jerome. He was about five foot ten, lean with a moustache and square face.

He seemed friendly, about my age and I told him to call me John. He told me we could stay the night and the lady could sleep in the main cabin, while we shared the adjoining sleeping cabin.

After dinner, we left Suzanne and went to the other cabin. The snowfall had ended and in the still night was a full moon and countless stars. Bert and I agreed to keep watch, but Jerome said not to worry since he was a light sleeper and would take care of us. As soon as I put my head on my blanket, I was asleep since I had spent too many nights on watch but sometime during the evening Jerome shook me.

"Wake up; I heard something," whispered Jerome. Outside the moon gave enough light to see that a horse was gone from the corral and I ran to the main cabin to discover Suzanne Cloutier had left. We followed her trail, and by the moon's glow, we saw several sets of horse tracks. She had made sure of a silent departure and had joined up with others. She was in this country with others and what was their purpose and more importantly, were they with us or against us?

CHAPTER 9

We walked back to the main cabin in silence. I was angry for being played such a fool and mistakes like that could kill us. I needed to be smart, not stupid and there was a lot to learn in this business, including vigilance, caution and to ignore beautiful women and the last one would be the hardest to overcome. Jerome noticed my frown.

"Let's have coffee." He lit the stove and some lamps as he studied me.

"Did you serve in the Strathcona's," he asked?

"I served with them, but I now work undercover as a special constable with Sergeant Raven." He laughed and said he thought he recognized me and I learned he was in another squadron in the regiment.

"Why did you not want her to know that you were with the police?"

"To be honest, I did not trust her, so the less said about what we were doing might keep us alive." I reviewed the robberies and fraud and my theory about Weigand. I watched his reaction, but he nodded for me to continue.

"We were on our way in our search for Big Pierre when it turned into a trip from hell with encounters outside a cabin with potential killers and the rescue of George from kidnappers. Then I met Suzanne Cloutier, who is capable and dangerous." I described how she disarmed me and found it suspicious that she left at night.

"What bothers me is either McGill is her boss or she is in a team to investigate him. Two detectives and a constable let her waltz out of here without us stopping her and that is what drives me to distraction." Jerome whistled and then laughed.

"For a detective, you seem to be a little slow to pick up clues, but I am sure you will figure it out, perhaps by Christmas. You need to watch out for these fancy popsies, they will get you in trouble." His giggle did not help but then I smiled. He was right I had much to learn, including never to trust a looker. Jerome looked at me and said to take out my notebook for some evidence.

"A miner showed up three days ago concerned that Big Pierre was not at his camp and he had not finished his season. Two constables went to investigate and returned yesterday. They reported they searched all cabins, but in Weigand's cabin, under a board, they found maps and papers with claim numbers, which they left in this office. Another request from a miner sent them out to investigate and they should return in the morning. The maps and papers with the claim numbers are in a file marked evidence in the desk."

"Jerome, don't bet on it. Miss Cloutier has skills you do not want to discover." Jerome ran to the desk and shuffled files.

"I don't believe it; she took them. What kind of policemen would let evidence disappear?" He looked so shaken and sad I did not know what to say, and it was not the time to kid him. To explain the truth about this lady was difficult but we were the victims, and I wanted to comfort him since he looked like he might break down.

"This is a highly skilled person who knows what to do and how to do it and around her, we are the country cousins in the city. There was no indication that she would take the evidence and leave in the night," but I was not sure that helped. Jerome looked at the floor and remained quiet and it was clear I failed to make headway with him.

"When I get back to the Detachment, I will make inquiries about Suzanne Cloutier. I had no idea that she had others with her and I failed to check the area, so I also made mistakes." As we drank our coffee, I tried to get Jerome's mind away from the loss of the documents, but it did not help. I moved to discuss our time in London, but that did not shake his desperation. It was like being at a wake, where Jerome had lost his best friend

Dawn brought the return of two tired constables. Before Jerome could speak, I introduced myself. I explained that for decorum, we had to leave a lady in the main cabin and it was a surprise that she took the maps and papers with her. One of the constables, about my size and weight, looked me up and down.

"Be quiet. We need coffee and food. My name is Jonathon Davies, and that one is Samuel Taylor. You soldier's stuck together and always protect each other. We wrote out the details in our notebooks, which we have in our jackets, so nothing is lost." He looked at Jerome.

"Except the original evidence. Scott will face charges, but we have enough to investigate. Now excuse us while we eat and drink." They took packages of meat and biscuits and silently ate. Jerome said nothing and I thought if I could help him, I would try but I just did not have a solution.

Bert and George entered and gave their names. Davies had heard of Sergeant Raven, so they made small talk as they ate while we prepared breakfast. As we ate, Bert gave a summary of what had transpired over the past few days and asked for their investigation results. Bert added they could trust George. Davies began to read from his notebook and provided details of the list of claims found in Weigand's cabin. I took out my maps and the burnt documents that showed the claims we found at Big Pierre's robbery site. I provided a comparison and made notes, and I cross-referenced the claims at King Solomon's Dome.

After breakfast, we thanked them, checked our horses and rode north towards King Solomon's Dome. The weather had changed, but with the sun the snow had melted the tracks, and we lost the trail. We stopped for a meal, coffee, and to smoke. There was a stream so I tied the horses near it and went a distance to practice with my rifle and pistol since I was concerned about what we might meet that day.

As we resumed riding, I discussed Suzanne Cloutier with Bert and concluded that she was looking for something in Big Pierre's cabin but was not part of McGill's gang. The question was whether it was that miner or others, and for what purpose? I thought around her I needed to have extreme caution, but I did want to see her again. I was now on the search for Big Pierre, Frank Thompson, my assassins, McGill, Weigand and Suzanne Cloutier.

Lunch gave me time to check my maps, and I suggested we stop to seek directions at the next mining camp. About four o'clock we entered claims to see three men at work. As we approached, all three grabbed their rifles and waited until we stopped about fifty feet from the sluice box. George dismounted and raised his hands and approached them, since he was the least threatening.

He was there for about ten minutes before he returned and asked for my maps then he went back. Another twenty minutes passed before he returned and remounted. He told us we had another two hours to travel north into higher country. The clouds covered the sun, but it did not look like snow for that night. Around six, we approached the peak of a hill and checked our maps and my notes for a camp with mining claims.

We found the camp we looked for, and I knew twilight would be in an hour. I raised my rifle, and we rode to about fifty feet to a cabin. No smoke escaped from the chimney, and I could not see any lights from a window. I told them to cover me as I got off my horse to hold my rifle and to listen but heard nothing suspicious. The wind swirled leaves as I walked to the porch. The sun cast a reflection in the window, but only darkness showed inside. I knocked on the door, waited, turned the handle and pushed open the door.

A shot splintered the wall next to me, and a piece of wood hit my nose as I jumped into the cabin to the floor. To escape death by inches brought such intense fear it was incredible my trousers remained dry. More shots followed, and I had to concentrate to determine if there was more than one shooter. Bert and George now returned fire and I needed to stop these shakes and do something. I crawled to the back door and kicked it open but the sun's reflection did not provide cover. If I went out, the shooter or shooters in the woods to the side of the cabin might see me. There were some bushes and rocks about three feet from the back door that provided cover.

After my count of three, I jumped and rolled, but no one fired in my direction. I took out my field glasses and was worried that they might see me but I could not see anything. If I crawled into the woods and fired, Bert and George might shoot me. Bert was a bad shot, but George had hunted since he was a boy. If I had cover from the side and front of the cabin, I could try it. I crawled along a path and moved closer to the area from where someone had fired. The shooting had stopped, and I listened but heard only the movement of trees.

I crawled and stood when the sound of a crack against a tree brought me down into some brambles. My curse probably gave away my location, but I was furious with these shooters. I dropped and shouted for them to stop shooting. I was directing that order to Bert and George but then heard horses moving in the trees. I had to assume that this could be a trap and these shooters might leave others to make more mischief.

As I stood, I listened then carefully walked towards the area where I heard the rifles. I fired off my Lee-Enfield, but there was no return fire. I stood behind a tree, reloaded and then took out my field glasses, but I could see only trees and bushes. I turned to see Bert and George holding their rifles.

"Go the cabin and set up while I stand guard," I shouted. About twenty minutes later, I took the horses to a stream, tied them and gave them food. My shaking started, and I almost had to sit and felt ill. Why did I take these risks and was there a reason I was again a target? I wanted this to go away, and as I walked to the cabin, I looked but heard only silence. Inside the cabin, lanterns gave a pleasant glow complemented by the heat from the stove. George went outside to stand guard, and I was thankful for the fire and moved close to it. The shaking started again even though I was warm. Bert came over and said for me to sit there while he made dinner. I was exhausted. As we ate, it was time for my question.

"Who fired on us?"

"There was no us in those shots since you were the target." I knew Bert was right and this led to a discussion of suspects and their motive. I knew the two men at the first cabin had their orders to kill me. I felt they might be the shooters since they were directed to kill me and I did not think Suzanne was out to murder me. It also could be a new player for my assassination, but I was too tired to work on theories. After dinner, we set our bedrolls and determined who would stand guard. I said I would take the first shift, so I went to the door and called for George.

I went outside, but the darkness gave me limited protection since the moon was full and stars filled the endless sky. The moon's light cast a glow on the hills and trees, and I could hear a stream gurgling over rocks. If I wasn't involved in a dangerous journey, I could find this to be a place of peace. In the distance coyotes howled but I kept my movement around the cabin, and at one o'clock Bert approached and told me to get some sleep.

In the morning, we a discussed our next steps. We needed to search this camp, but before we did that, we needed to explore the area for unpleasant strangers. I went to the woods where someone had used me for target practice. Horse tracks and expired rounds were the only clues that I found, and no one had the courtesy to leave me a calling card. Bert walked up and used a handkerchief to place the expired rounds in his silk bag. I estimated there were two horse tracks and Bert told me to make notes. We returned to the cabin, and George agreed to act as the sentry while we investigated. We walked over a hill and discovered a mineshaft. Bert went back for lanterns while I stood outside the entrance and wondered if last night was to deter us from finding this tunnel.

When Bert returned, I went in first with my pistol. I carried a lantern; but that did not give enough light to show any detail. We descended the mining shaft, which narrowed, and as we turned a corner, a foul stench hit us. The last time I experienced that smell was abandoned corpses in the war. The darkened lamp revealed a man on the ground. I stood over the body to give increased light, while Bert turned him over.

"Now I know what happened to Alfred James so we can stop that search." The cold had kept him preserved, but he was stiff as we touched him. We took off his jacket and shirt and lifted him to see a large wound in the upper part of his back that looked to be three inches in width. Bert put his face closer and said it was a puncture wound. I put the jacket back on the body. I knew he was dead, but it seemed the proper thing to do.

"John, when we get outside I again need you take notes. With what has happened on this trip, including missing suspects and evidence, it would be my luck to lose this body but we will leave it here. Our officers have the powers of a coroner, and we need to return to report this murder and to send a patrol and an officer." I asked if there was something we missed?

"We should see if there is any identification or notes in the pockets." Bert searched but found nothing but I decided to check the jacket and took my bayonet to open a seam. I found a letter and with the lantern up close, I read, but it had nothing to do with a report on the Order of the Midnight Sun. A lady had written a love note and the signature was signed Louise, but we could not make out the last name. What a terrible end and why did he hide the letter in such a fashion? Was he worried that someone might find it if it was not hidden?

At the surface, George had pointed his rifle at persons riding towards us. They were too far away to determine their identity, but I was jumpy and did not want unwelcome visitors. I took out my field glasses and saw four men in Serge with Stetson hats. It was a patrol of the North West Mounted Police and suggested to George that he put down his weapon before they fired at him.

They arrived five minutes later and dismounted. The corporal recognized Sergeant Raven and approached to speak to us and after our introductions, the corporal explained they were in search of criminals that had freed two prisoners at the Grand Forks outpost. A miner showed up at that outpost and requested assistance for a gold theft. That night there was only one constable on the watch to guard the prisoners while the corporal slept in the other cabin. Several men overcame the constable, freed the prisoners, and when the corporal ran out of his cabin, they shot him. Five patrols were out on the search with a command post not far from this camp.

"How is the corporal?"

"Just a graze to his arm and we think he will recover," said the corporal. As soon as I returned to Dawson City, I would see Grant, but I could not leave now. Bert said that we needed to report to the commander of the post, so one of the constables waited until we mounted our horses and he took us to there. We left George outside and entered to see Inspector MacDonald talking with a sergeant and a corporal. When he noticed us, he raised his voice.

"At last, where have you been? I am waiting for your report." Then he laughed as it turns out he was surprised to see us. Hot coffee, biscuits, and warmth were a pleasure after so many days in the damp and wretched cold. The stove sizzled with wet wood as we sat at the table. It was time for us to tell our story and the service regulations required that the person in charge do this, so Bert spoke.

"We have discovered a murder victim near here. Do you want our report and can you act as a coroner?"

"The deceased won't go anywhere so give me your report," the inspector replied.

"Sir, I wouldn't count on that," I said. "Lately our evidence has been either stolen or rescued." Inspector MacDonald was not bothered by my comment. Bert knew the sergeant and corporal so he made my introduction and then set out our maps, the claim papers and our notebooks on a table. The story included what we found at Big Pierre's robbery location, including the cigar end and the burnt evidence. Bert described the late-night incident at the cabin and emphasized how I had overcome one man and scared away the other. I told them about my death threat and the two shots directed at me last night.

That had their interest. As Bert described how I captured Peters and McMillan, they kept looking at me. I reviewed my rescue of George Martin from the tunnel and the information from Peters and McMillan, including the evidence of fraud, forgery and McGill's gang. Bert added that I liked to push suspects to obtain information, but Inspector MacDonald said that sometimes that is required. Bert continued with the report.

"We delivered Peters and McMillan to the Grand Forks outpost and they are the escaped prisoners." The last topic to be discussed was Suzanne Cloutier, and Bert continued with his story.

"During the night, she removed evidence from a desk at the North West Mounted Police outpost and departed with some others. We do not believe she was part of McGill's gang, but had carried out her own investigations." When he heard that the Inspector scowled and made a note. The next part was what we learned from the two Constables at the Indian River outpost. Bert linked the claim numbers and maps to what we found at the site of Big Pierre's robbery and how we followed this evidence to the nearby claims to discover a corpse.

"Did I miss anything," he asked me, not expecting me to answer, but it was my chance to help Jerome. I was relieved he omitted how Miss Cloutier disarmed me.

"No, but Constable Scott could not have expected Suzanne Cloutier to take evidence and escape in the night." The Inspector gave me an inquiring look.

"Why would you try to protect that constable? Is Scott from your regiment?" I nodded to see his smile.

"We shall see about this constable and what he has to say another time. I need to write a report, and at the same time I need to be a coroner."

"Constable Caldwell, you have the privilege to write my report for my signature." I stood and said thank you, sir. That was the last thing I wanted to do, but I realized I could write the way I wanted and make my own conclusions. Everyone else left to visit the miner's tunnel and the body when George came in for coffee, food, and heat. I looked at him and said I needed to write. I think my work preparing affidavits helped as I wrote rapidly and without errors. A corporal entered for a coffee and introduced himself as Kerry Loughlin. He was of medium build, blue eyed, about five foot eleven with dark hair. I finished writing and began to read it to him and when I mentioned something new, his eyebrows would rise and then fall. He sometimes grimaced at other parts of the report, but he never spoke and his facial expressions were a riot. When I finished, Loughlin gave me an evil stare.

"It was my turn off shift, and I came in to get warm and sleep. I am now warm but that was enough to scare anyone half to death." He gave me, a mournful stare, then laughed. A few minutes later the stove's heat made me sleepy. The sound of the door woke me and I had no idea of the time. The inspector looked at me.

"I have no idea if you have had a decent night's sleep since you left Dawson City. I will write out my instructions and tomorrow you head back. I have some further inquiries and work I need done. My coroner's report confirms that Alfred James died of unnatural causes, which appears to be the result of a bayonet or thin knife that created a puncture wound, which touched his heart. That impact and the loss of blood resulted in his death.

Now, you two tell me your thoughts on what you next should do in your detective work." Bert said he wanted to hear from me first. I stood up, stretched and poured another mug of coffee. My first thought was a need to empty my bladder and I thought about our next steps, but had not yet spoken to Bert.

"The first thing is a search at the mining recorder's building, since that office is open to the public and I can find out who is the owner of the nearby claims where we found the body. We need to review any documents registered on the Martin and Rivest claims to see when they were filed. I looked to see his reaction and once satisfied I continued.

"There will be a link between deliveries to the gold commissioner's office and the source of that gold. George Martin can come with me for his claims and I believe I can access the information for the Marston claims." The inspector and Bert made notes then the Inspector nodded.

"We need to put together affidavits and to apply to court for an order to determine if Weigand and McGill have accounts at the British North America Bank or the Commerce Bank. If they have them, we need the dates and amounts of the deposits. The rules require service on the account holders, and this will become public information. If Weigand and McGill are linked to these accounts, we may find out what they look like, but they will also find our descriptions. They may try to retaliate, so this phase is dangerous." They were still writing, so I waited until a facial expression from the inspector told me to continue.

"Finally, we need to investigate Suzanne Cloutier and to find out why is she here." I stopped and looked at Bert who said he had nothing to add. After a long pause, Inspector Macdonald spoke.

"Be patient, I need to read your written report." He finished reading and looked at me.

"I have nothing to add except to have Corporal Loughlin write your report as an order and I will include what you have just said. Have dinner then sleep. You two have gone far beyond my expectations, which were high when I sent you out of Dawson City and you have done well." There was another cabin, and after dinner, we went to it. We did not need to take turns on watch, so I lay awake asking what was I doing here apart from risking my life. We had not found out any evidence to determine if the Order of the Midnight Sun existed. I was pleased to have rescued George and captured the culprits, who stole his gold, but they escaped and Grant was shot. All we have now is one witness for this case. The thoughts of Suzanne took me to a happy state, which were replaced by kettledrums of noise, with George rivaling Bert for the loudest earth splitting snore.

I went outside and back to the command post for a chair. Corporal Loughlin's look implied I was the cause of his work but he let me sleep until he started to whistle a lively Irish jig. I opened one eye and growled.

"Any more of that and you will discover something you will live to regret and after I will whistle a funeral dirge just for you." I knew he was a corporal but I was beyond caring and did not care about a discipline charge, but the sudden silence in the cabin was a blessed relief.

CHAPTER 10

The awful weather delayed our arrival to Dawson City, which required a stop in a mining camp, where at cards George won while I lost. I told George he could stay at Mrs. Rivest's boarding house, and after I had left my horse and equipment at the Detachment, I went to the hospital to see Grant. As I entered his first words was an apology.

"It was my fault since you told us to be careful." I ignored that and we talked about his injury and my searches in the gold fields. I asked permission if I could be a detective to find out what he remembered. Grant grunted and began.

"I awoke when I heard a door crash. I grabbed my revolver and ran out in my long johns only to be shot. I had the misfortune to be wounded in my union suit, but the press kept that out of the papers. I was on the ground with terrible pain in my arm to see a man with a beard, a large nose and missing some teeth. The second one was about thirty, bald and had a scar over his right eye. That one was thin, with a small nose, a narrow jaw and it was strange; they knew I watched them but they never killed me, and I still wonder why they spared me? They took the two prisoners with them and they rode into the night. I passed out and was still on the ground when the constable found me. He managed to untie my ropes, but I was too weak to follow them. The one thing I do not know is which one was the shooter."

I thought if I find them I would take them into the country, blindfold and tie them, and hope to hear wolves. I promised I would return soon and went to the Detachment to find George. I told him to come with me and because it was a cold night and we moved quickly to the boarding house. Mrs. Rivest cried, ran and gave us each a hug. I left George in the kitchen and went upstairs, and after a bath and a shave, I descended to the kitchen. William sat with George and Mrs. Rivest and shared a bottle of whisky. She stood and saluted me.

"We have much to celebrate as George told of how you rescued him and told your other adventures. I did not know we had a hero with us." William shook my hand and exclaimed welcome home. The boarding house was another world to me. My search was dangerous, cold and exhausted me, but I had survived and realized I was a risk-taker and needed to be more cautious, or I would die. George had his rifle next to him on the floor, and I went upstairs to get mine but then sat on my bed and looked out to the lights of the city. Perhaps I should move to Bummers Roost and find help. Sven might stay with me, and I could pay him since he was capable and experienced as a former member of the French Foreign Legion.

I heard my name called for pot roast. I would drink a small amount since I needed to remain alert. I almost fell asleep, but George kept the party going drinking and talking while William asked questions. Before I left, I told George and Mrs. Rivest to come to the Mining Recorder's Office at ten the next morning. If someone filed the mining registrations for her husband and George, there would documents we could use for the police. At six I was up and put on my suit, shirt and tie. At breakfast, I told William I would meet him at five o'clock that afternoon, and he said he was still worried about my safety.

"So am I," I said, as I left the residence. My first stop was for a haircut and shave as I knew my undercover days were over. If I was to meet with the Crown Attorney, I needed to look presentable and at nine I was in Bert's office.

"Where have you been? The superintendent is waiting for you." I was led to a large building and once inside, I had my first look at the boss of the Yukon police. Of middle height with a hardened face, a prominent nose, and a long chin, he reminded me of my former colonel. He had a large moustache, thick eyebrows, and gray hair. I walked up to him, stood to attention and announced my name. He looked me up and down and told me to sit while he sat behind an oak desk.

"Before I start," he said, "I have examined an official report of a Canadian ship, the *Islander*. It sank on the fifteenth of August carrying gold from the gold fields. It hit an iceberg off Douglas Island and quickly went down with the loss of forty-two passengers and crew and over three million dollars in gold." He stopped to look at us and commented on such a massive loss of life. It was a tragedy, but as a detective what interested me was that ship carried a significant amount of gold. The mining fields still produced enough riches to attract confidence men, fraud artists and thieves. The lure of gold brings out the best and worst of men and my job was to weed out the swindlers that followed the money.

"I have read Caldwell's reports. The first one is your work at the mining recorder's and the gold commissioner's office. The second report is of your activities with Sergeant Raven. I must say I not often impressed, but I am and congratulate you both. I like it when my men handle problems in the field, but your investigations will be public and potentially dangerous." He stopped.

"Any questions?"

"Yes," I said, "Someone murdered the undercover agent and we now know of several mining claims that have a link to gold robberies. We do not know if McGill and Weigand are the same crooks, but if we can access these bank accounts and serve them with our subpoenas, then they should be discovered. The problem is this may bring our names and identities to these criminals. We are on the offensive and need to pursue all potential evidence including finding out the real name of Suzanne Cloutier. We also need to find why she was interested in our investigations and she may appear once we find McGill or Weigand." The Superintendent nodded at Sergeant Raven and asked any other questions?

"Could you meet the Crown Attorney to discuss this, which would be very helpful," Bert asked? Wood agreed and finished to remind us that the Order of the Midnight Sun remained confidential. The superintendent appeared to dismiss us but I had not finished my theory.

"Sir is it possible Suzanne Cloutier works for the Pinkerton's Detective Agency, on behalf of the United States Government? The affairs of the Order of the Midnight Sun are known in Seattle, San Francisco, and the Alaskan Territory and is it a real plan to take over the Yukon Territory, or a rumor? I am sure the United States Government does not want to create a potential war with England." I was amazed I threw this out and I wondered what would be their reaction. I made sure to avoid eye contact with the inspector and Bert but discovered the superintendent looked interested and did not stop me, so I continued.

"She left the Indian River outpost with two others. I do not know if the Pinkerton Detective Agency works in Canada, but the American government may wish to have some distance from this inquiry." I noticed Bert's distressed look but Superintendent Wood sat silently, and finally spoke.

"Caldwell, that would be a monumental breach of our neutrality, and I would dismiss your thoughts as far-fetched, except our government has used the same agency in the United States for tracking down fugitives who fled Canada. When that happened, I am not sure if we notified the United States Government. Your idea is a long shot, but then again you may be right. I will contact my Commissioner by mail, to advise him to make confidential inquiries and will do the same with the head of the Dominion Police in Ottawa but I will not discuss this with Mr. Sifton. Not now as we need more evidence before I contact him." He stood and started a slow walk to the door.

"You two have things to do," as we stood and followed him." He shook our hands, and we went to Bert's office. Since he slammed the door, I knew his mood.

"I don't know whether to discipline you or commend you and how do you make these leaps of logic? The inspector is threatening to notify the Minister of the Interior who will speak to Prime Minister Laurier. How far up the ladder do you wish this to go, to the Queen or God?" He glared at me and then stopped.

"But it makes sense the more I think about it." He examined me, which it seemed an eternity before I replied.

"We have facts that support this theory. Remember how quickly Miss Cloutier managed to disarm me? She pretended to be alone, yet she travelled with others and stole police evidence. It took research to be able to impersonate Big Pierre's daughter. I think she knew our identities, our investigations and hooked both of us in. We might as well put a story to the papers, police at work, come and watch. We no longer are anonymous in Dawson City, and this worries me." Bert studied my face and then grinned.

"You are on to something so get at it and let me know when you have something else?" I was late for my meeting at the mining recorder's office, so I told him it was time for my appointment with George and Mrs. Rivest, but would see him by four o'clock.

"This old detective was taken for a fool by a smarter and younger detective. I have tried to train you, but I believe this lady can do even better. If you find her again, spend time with her, if you find she is on our side, but take care as she is dangerous." The clock in the Mining Recorder's office showed ten o'clock and George and Mrs. Rivest stood at the counter waiting for me. Henry was standing with them.

"Are you here to visit, or do searches?" I replied it was for searches and introduced George and Mrs. Rivest. Henry pulled out the files and announced that new transfers were entered on the Rivest and Martin claims which included one to Robert McGill. I showed it to George who explained he had to sign it or they would kill him. Mrs. Rivest looked at the sale and said her husband's signature was a forgery.

"Only a ghost could sign that document since he died last year." Henry heard this, became upset and requested they meet with the police to state these transfers were false. I suggested they visit Sergeant Raven while I continued my searches. After they had left, I looked at the Weigand claim file to see if McGill or his cronies filed a lease termination for the agreement with Frank Thompson, but none was registered. I showed Henry the map and claim numbers where we found the corpse, and he cross-referenced the map to the owner.

"Those claims are owned by Robert McGill, with the right to mine for Dalton Weigand." Bingo, I had them and told Henry we needed to get together soon and left for the gold commissioner's office. I was excited with my discovery and the first connection between McGill and Weigand. They could be in the same gang, and the pieces of the puzzle had started to come together. It was strange that these claims were near King Solomon's Dome. Roland Caton was in the Gold Commissioner's office, and I told him I needed to update my last search for Frank Thompson. He pulled out his record book.

"There was another two hundred ounces for royalties." I thanked him, and asked about payments for the McGill claims on King Solomon's Dome and gave him the specific numbers. He returned with a large ledger and checked it.

"These claims are owned by Robert McGill with the rights for Dalton Weigand to mine them, and this season there were royalty payments of four hundred ounces." I showed my North West Mounted Police identification and said this was part of an investigation.

"I thought you were police the last time you were here since so many soldiers are now members of the North West Mounted Police." I asked about royalty payments for the claims owned by George Martin and Louis Rivest and provided the registration numbers for the thirty bench mining claims. Mr. Caton consulted the records and looked excited.

"Royalty payments for two hundred ounces were made this season for the McGill claims, which is a lot of gold." He had a questioning look, but I remained silent. I mentioned that George Martin would come to find out about royalty payments on his claims and Roland looked surprised.

"The written assignment was transferred to Robert McGill last month."

"Do you recall the description of the person who registered those claims to him?" I asked.

"No Mr. Caldwell, it was done by another clerk who is on vacation for a week. Perhaps you can return then." I made notes of my searches and said I appreciated his help. I walked to the Detachment to see if George and Mrs. Rivest were still there, but they were gone, and Bert was not in his office. I decided against lunch at the mess and headed out for the Royal Alexandria Hotel. After placing my order, I made notes and listed the next steps. We need Superintendent Wood to meet with the Crown Attorney while our job was to put together sufficient notes to form the basis for affidavits. I realized it would be many affidavits and I could list most of the required evidence.

George's and Mrs. Rivest testimony would be easy, and we required certified copies from the mining recorder and the gold commissioner. Added to the list were the constable's notes from the Indian River outpost and the partially burnt documents that showed maps and claim locations. Another document was the coroner's report. The body was in a tunnel on claims owned by Robert McGill and on the same claims Dalton Weigand had the right to mine. We had to link McGill and Weigand and have them explain why their mining tunnel contained a dead body. Hopefully, they would turn on each other, since murder is hanging offence.

They would also be required to explain where they obtained large amounts of declared gold. Whatever story they embellished would not prevent a court imagining some very long noses. They could not spin such a creative falsehood since they would have to swear those facts to be true or add a charge of perjury. Judges hate perjury, and this charge alone could result in a very long sentence. Weigand and McGill would head back south rather than contest the evidence. We had nothing on Barton at this point, but that could change. I thought this could take a week or more and finished the summary of what was required. It was almost four and time to see Bert in his office. He had a broad smile when I noticed a document on his desk, which was a telegraph faced upwards.

"Close the door. My wife and daughter are arriving soon in Whitehorse, and I am going to surprise them by taking the *Casca* tomorrow at eight. Sorry for the short notice and I expect you will have a busy week." He smiled and watched my reaction.

"The superintendent is not well so when you have enough information; you will meet with Wade, the Crown Attorney. Now tell me what you learned?" I told him about my searches at the mining recorder's and the gold commissioner's offices. Bert asked if I had made notes. Once he saw my nod, he told me to prepare subpoenas for those records.

"Once you finish, I require the signature of Inspector MacDonald as a Justice of the Peace."

"How do I do that?" Bert told me to look at the back of my *Criminal Code* for the *Evidence Act* and see examples of subpoenas. He looked to see if I followed him.

"A book I ordered arrived, and I want you to review it. It called *Ames on Forgery.*" He told me it was important to prepare affidavit evidence for Rivest and Martin and I must have that done within seven days.

"How could I do all of this within the week?" He smiled and said he would take *Ames on Forgery* with him. Bert explained that to assemble evidence would take from two to three weeks and it was important that I got it right. Bert told me Inspector MacDonald had returned and there would be a discipline hearing for Constable Scott tomorrow. Under the *Code of Discipline*, he was charged with the loss of police evidence. He looked at me when I told him I wanted to provide testimony at the hearing. Bert asked, was that wise but I felt strongly on the matter, and I was not in the police for advancement. I told him a suitable punishment for Constable Scott was to be my bodyguard. Bert laughed and said he doubted that would happen. I wished him well and said he deserved a break. Bert said he had not taken a day off since he arrived and had worked many weekends. He came over to shake my hand.

"John, you have been a good partner and detective, notwithstanding some occasional problems. Take care, and I will see you soon, and it is because of you I can take a vacation since I persuaded the inspector that you can do this." The walk out of the Detachment and to our building was slow, due to the deep snow. When I arrived, I went to William's office. His stove gave off enough heat for me to take off my coat and I was given coffee and told to sit. William looked at me and told me to close the door.

"Can you explain what you have been doing?" My story would soon be made public, so I sat and gave him a serious look.

"William, in confidence, I will tell you because it will eventually be public and I trust you to keep this information confidential," and I related the events of the last week, including my recent searches. When I finished, he looked at me but remained quiet and then told me to be careful. I told him of my plan to move to our house and to obtain bodyguards. I asked him to tell me about Wade the Crown Attorney who was the prosecutor for criminal matters. William laughed.

"You will need a drink for this story." He pulled out some whisky, and filled a tall glass.

"Politics is what drives this government and the appointments of civil servants. Patronage falls like manna from heaven to staff at the mining recorder's office, clerks, judges, and Crown Prosecutors. The Liberals were elected five years ago under the leadership of Wilfrid Laurier from Quebec. How is it that Judge Dugas, a police magistrate from Quebec, is the new Territorial Judge? You think he is conservative? He is a Liberal, and the same rule applies to lawyers here. George Black is a conservative so he cannot be a Crown Attorney, which is for loyal Liberals, such as Frederick Coate Wade and James Burleigh Pattulo. At present, it is Wade who prosecutes for the government." I interrupted to ask about Wade. William's eyes twinkled as he smiled.

"He is a character, smart, and quite opinionated, particularly in the defence of his party. He is in practice with James Aikman and Frederick Congdon and has quite the ability to find trouble. Two years ago, as a Crown Prosecutor, he also acted as a defence counsel for mining companies on the same matter, but he never thought there was a conflict. Recently, he assaulted a reporter on the docks in Dawson City. He is pugnacious and good in court but has his view of the truth. Have I said enough?"

"Wade is the key to this case," I said, "I need to work with him to get an order to subpoena accounts at the banks." William stared at me, laughed and said good luck on that.

"He will eat you alive if you try that. He will not take anything to court unless he thinks it is a winner as he has his reputation to maintain." I outlined the chain of evidence that linked Weigand and McGill. I mentioned we found a dead man on McGill's claims and summarized the declarations of enormous amounts of gold with no supporting evidence of actual mining. I reviewed George's testimony and documents of maps and mining locations.

"I do not care if we succeed in accessing the accounts, but we need to serve these men and obtain their descriptions." William shook his head and sighed.

"You have the enviable task to demonstrate these links in evidence to Mr. Wade, so good luck John, you will need it."

Some things are best left unsaid, including my earlier death threat and attacks. He was such a gentle and good friend I did not want to worry him. I told him I would not be home for dinner since I needed to visit the Detachment. The weight of what I was required to do overwhelmed me, and I wondered if I should leave a note for Bert and take the next steamer to Whitehorse since I felt like a fireman with long periods of quiet and then frantic and explosive action. I wanted normality to return and had quite enough of adventures.

CHAPTER 11

Once I left our office, I checked out the house, back buildings, and fence to look for entry points and went around the property to search for areas where a shooter could find a target. Danger was coming and I had an earlier entree, but now I would have the main serving of deranged and treacherous men. I did not know when, or where but thought of *Henry the Fifth*, "But when the blasts of war begin in our ears, then imitate the actions of the tiger." I was tired of waking and asking myself, was this my final day? I had been lucky, but there was no guarantee of invincibility. I loved this place, my work as a detective, good friends and the life the way I wanted, and no two-bit thug would take that away without a fight.

I was angry and tired of looking over my shoulder. They ruined George's life, shot my friend and attempted my murder, but who was the man behind his gang? Was it Barton? There seemed to be a connection between Weigand and McGill but were they working with Barton as part of the Order of the Midnight Sun? It did not matter since acting defensively was at an end, and I would seek them out and destroy the creature behind this, but I needed a plan, names, and locations. As I thought of potential suspects my thoughts turned to James Riley. He shared a small house on Third Avenue near the Klondike and Yukon Rivers and told of men who travelled the bridge to Lousetown to visit the bars and brothels. But had never invited me to his place.

As I walked to his street, I made sure my coat was open for easy access to my revolver. I found his darkened house with no smoke from the chimney.

I took out my gun and knocked on the door, with no response. At the back of the house, I looked through the glass window but saw nothing. I did not know where Bob Innes lived, but I could visit his work tomorrow, so I put my revolver in its holster and walked downtown. Was it a coincidence that my two American friends were both out of town when Suzanne was at the Indian River? My suspicious mind turned to the possibility that there was a connection and I should add them to my list of suspects.

The streetlights were lit when I arrived at the Royal Alexandria Hotel, and after my order, I went to the front desk and asked for stationary. Over dinner I made notes. I believed Suzanne Cloutier was an American who could escape by steamer to Whitehorse and take the train to Skagway. From there she could continue her voyage to Seattle or she could also travel downstream to St. Michaels and then to Seattle or San Francisco.

The Dominion Police in Seattle and San Francisco were occupied to investigate the Order of the Midnight Sun. If I worked for the American Government or Pinkerton's Detective Agency, I might take a steamer to report my findings, and I could not trust letters or the telegram. I decided to call this lady Josephine, as in Napoleon. She was a secret agent, which surprised me that a woman could do this but it was brilliant, and who would suspect her. I had tasks to do, and would recommend undercover work along the dock, but did not know if we had money to pay informers.

It was after nine when I left the hotel and as I left First Avenue, I took out my gun and walked to the river. No lights shone on me as I walked by the wharves and sheds. I stopped and watched two men as they smoked and talked while staring at a barge tied to the front of a steamer. They did not seem to notice me as I slowly slid into an alcove. One of the men said they would soon leave for St. Michaels. The other man asked if he had heard anything more but the other man said he was not safe to discuss this in the open. They walked ahead and crossed on a ladder to the barge and then pulled it onboard. I could not see their faces but thought I recognized a voice.

When I arrived at First Avenue, I put my gun away and questioned my wisdom to do that alone. I checked for the name of the steamer, the flag was American, and it was the *Sarah* owned by the Northern Navigation Company.

The boat would travel the Yukon River to Circle, in the Alaskan Territory and then down to St. Michaels on the Bering Sea. As I turned a corner onto Second Avenue, I saw a man trip over a sleeping dog. The dog was a cross between a husky and a shepherd and then I noticed a second man with him. The first man started to kick the dog when I was about ten feet away I yelled.

"Leave the dog alone." I ran near to the dog when one of the men told me to walk away.

"No," and repeated, "Leave him alone." I was close enough to grab the man who kicked the dog. He swung at me, and I backed up and hit him so hard in the face that I might have broken his nose. He fell, and I turned and expected the other man to attack. Instead, I watched him run as I helped the first man up, who immediately took off.

The dog stood and growled as I watched but did not touch him. The dog was dirty and his bones showed but beneath the dirt were a handsome creature. I had desert in my pocket, so I held it out in my open palm. The dog sniffed, came over and gently took it. His tail wagged, and I told him to go home. I started to walk uphill towards Sixth Avenue when I heard the tapping of feet behind me. I turned and pointed with my hand for him to leave. The dog sat and waited and as I started to walk, so did the dog. I was probably the only person who had shown the dog any kindness for a long time, and I gave up, and he followed me all the way to the boarding house.

Mrs. Rivest's place was silent with all the lights out. I put the dog in the shed and went into the kitchen to fill up a bowl with water and some bones and took them out to the dog. The dog sat in front of me as I put down the water and placed the bones on the ground. The dog sat and waited, and after I had said go, the dog drank the water and grabbed the bones. As he ate, he looked at me with his tail wagging. I said goodnight and went inside the house. I thought what on earth, talking to a dog, but it made me feel better

One more job was to find the owner of the dog. I sat and looked out the window at the stars. I was exhausted and still had not a chance to talk to Sven. He was always up before me, and by the time I arrived home, he was asleep.

The question if I had a dog woke me. It was my landlady, and I said he was a stray that followed me and I would try and find his owner today. She left, and I put on my red serge and my Queen's Medal for South Africa. When I entered the kitchen, Mrs. Rivest and William stood up and applauded. Mrs. Rivest told me she fed the dog and would buy more food from the butcher. William thought that my getting a guard dog was a fine idea. I told them about last night and that I would look for the owner. I could not take the dog with me, so I tied him to a tree. As I left, I heard the most mournful howl that continued until I was downtown. The clock at the Detachment showed eight when I entered the orderly room and asked to see Inspector MacDonald. The corporal took one look at my uniform and took me to the office and knocked.

"Come in," boomed Inspector MacDonald and inside two other inspectors stared at me. Their names were Routledge and McDonnell, and I assumed they were the discipline panel. I stood to attention, but Inspector MacDonald resumed his discussion with the other officers. After a few minutes, he looked at me.

"Speak your business."

"I can report on what I had discovered at the mining recorder's office and the gold commissioner's office." He seemed distracted but nodded.

"Secondly I wish to be a witness for Constable Scott." Inspector MacDonald asked me to wait outside, and he closed the door. After a short time, he opened the door and told me that they would allow my testimony if I limited myself to what I had heard and saw and I was permitted to remain in the room. At eight-thirty MacDonald said it was time and the three inspectors moved to sit behind a desk. I stood at the back as two constables with shoulder arms escorted Constable Scott into the room and left. Inspector MacDonald read out the charge.

"While on duty on September 23, 1901, at the Indian River outpost, Constable Scott lost possession of criminal evidence of the North West Mounted Police." I knew he was going to plead guilty, so I spoke.

"Sir he never lost possession of the evidence. They were removed without his knowledge when he permitted a miner's daughter to have privacy in that office." One of the inspectors turned red and exclaimed,

"Constable, be quiet." Inspector MacDonald ignored that outburst and almost smiled.

"If those are the facts the charge will be amended." He checked the Instructions to Members of the North West Mounted Police and wrote something down.

"While on duty on September 21, 1901, at the Indian River outpost, Constable Scott acted in a negligent fashion by permitting the removal of criminal evidence." I knew that was a distinction without a difference, but I trusted the inspector to do the right thing. Constable Scott said he was guilty to that charge. He told his story, and Inspector MacDonald asked if I had anything to add.

"Sirs, we knew that Suzanne Cloutier had searched for her missing father but she was a lady, and for decorum, Constable Scott permitted her to be in a separate cabin for the night. She could not share our cabin. It was unforeseen that she would leave during the evening and it was even more remarkable that she removed evidence.

"You mean stole the evidence," Inspector Routledge muttered and then gave a slight smile and I knew that this panel was not composed of hanging judges. I was told to leave at the same the same two constables returned and took Constable Scott away. I stood outside the closed door for about half an hour before Inspector MacDonald invited me in. He told me to sit and that he had provided the other inspectors with the information from our searches.

I walked them through everything, starting with the robberies, my first visit to the mining recorder's office and the gold commissioner's office. I reviewed our trip to Indian River and King Solomon's Dome, the evidence we recovered, the corpse and my near-death experience. I finished with what I recently found at the mining recorder and gold commissioner's office. That was new information for Inspector Macdonald, so it took some time, and no one said a word. Once I had finished, both officers shook my hand and left. Inspector MacDonald asked if I wanted coffee and had some brought in.

"Listen, Caldwell, I have spoken to Sergeant Raven and visited the superintendent. I do not know if you are the proper type for the North West Mounted Police, as we never know what you will do next. But you are on to something, which I think is important, and you are on the right trail. I will support you because you will need it. By the way, the change in the charge against Constable Scott reduced the penalty to fourteen day's imprisonment, rather than two months. We all felt that was the right thing to do."

He listened as I explained that my job had turned dangerous and could Constable Scott be assigned to protect me. I added he could also be of assistance in the investigations. Inspector MacDonald looked at me and said he would think about it as he escorted me to the door.

At two veterinary clinics, I asked if anyone had reported a missing dog but they had no information, so I bought a collar and leash. At the boarding house, Mrs. Rivest was outside in discussion with the dog, and I had a strange feeling that they were communicating, so I left them to their stories. I went upstairs to change into my work clothes and realized I would be staying the winter, so I needed to telegraph for equipment, winter clothes, and food. It was mid-September and the last steamer for this year would leave Dawson City in six weeks when the rivers freeze.

It was time to review my finances. The North West Mounted Police paid constables one dollar each day, and I was paid seventy-five cents a day as a special constable. In the south, that was great money, but here, costs were higher due to the freight. I pulled out my ledger. My trust fund paid one thousand dollars a month, and it had increased. Court probate for my Grandfather's estate had finished which left me one hundred thousand dollars and a quarter of the family business. My banking cousin, Egbert Lindsey's last letter stated that five thousand dollars was in bonds, at three percent return. That would increase by further contributions and each month I received five hundred dollars in my bank in Dawson City. I spent one hundred dollars per month, so I had over sixteen hundred dollars available. I was in a very fortunate position and did not need to work, but loved my work as a detective.

In the yard, the dog ran up to me, sat and stared, so I went upstairs to get the collar and leash, and we headed down to the docks. I did not put on the leash since the dog walked next to me. I needed a name. My grandfather had a favorite horse called Ben, so Ben it would be. My first stop was to the veterinarian Dr. Beach to have the dog checked out. He said that apart from malnutrition, Ben was in good shape and I told him I was in search for his owner, but Dr. Beach shook his head and said good luck on that.

"Each fall is a bad time in Dawson for dogs. Miners leave for the winter and abandon their animals. I have a husky puppy that was dropped off, and I need to find him a home otherwise, I must destroy him. Food costs are expensive, and I already have ten dogs."

"I can't take another dog; one is enough." Dr. Beach went to the back room and brought out a small husky that was white and gray with brown eyes. I tried to look away but gave up. I bought another collar and leash and swore to avoid veterinarian clinics in the future. Once I took the dogs back to the fenced in area of the house and I entered the office. Clarence sat in the reception area and tried to ignore me, which was hard due to my size and my constant greetings.

"Did anyone ask for my services?" He did not look up, but he knew I would pester him until he responded.

"There were a few who inquired, and I told them I did not know where you were and they left." That did it. I entered William's office; he looked up and saw I was upset.

"Clarence goes, or I will hire my staff to handle my business, and I do not care which it is." William looked down, hesitated and answered that Clarence was efficient and that he was not sure if he could find an adequate replacement. I told William I would be dividing the reception area to have two desks so I could have my own receptionist, or I would have to abandon my security business. William quickly agreed and asked if there was anything else he could do to help me. I asked William if could I borrow the law book *Best, On Evidence* and William nodded. He said he had work for me, but this could wait for a few days. I said I would be working upstairs on subpoenas and affidavits. The rest of the morning was the organization of my office. Before noon I went to where Bob Innes worked near the docks. As I entered, he put down his pencil and said his newest project was for a route for the narrow-gauge railway. I asked if he had been away and he told me for a few days on surveys.

"Do you know where is James Riley?" He seemed surprised by my question and raised his eyes.

"James was outside of Dawson City on land surveys. He returned several days ago and learned that his father was sick, so he left on the steamer the

Columbian." I told him I hoped he would recover, and after a few minutes of gossip, I said we should try poker Friday night, and Bob agreed.

Walking to the post office I wondered why both Bob Innes and James Riley left Dawson City at the same time we conducted our investigations. I knew they did work which would take them out of Dawson City and this might be just a coincidence. James father was in San Francisco, and he would travel there if his father was unwell, but my misgivings remained. James had Pinkerton's agency connections, and we had reports of the Order of the Midnight Sun operating in San Francisco. After obtaining my mail, I went to the Detachment to see Jerome Scott. I was told to return after seven at night since he was cutting wood.

Lunch at the Royal Alexandria Hotel was a treat, and I asked the waiter to provide me with a menu and stationary. I listed points to discuss with Inspector MacDonald, including payments for informants at the dock. After lunch, I returned to my office and started on the subpoenas. When finished, I asked William to review them. He apologized for Clarence and said it would solve my problems when I hired my receptionist.

William reviewed my work without changes. I told him we needed to hire a caretaker for the house and property and William said he would pay half. He mentioned that during his last trip to Moosehide, his friends Joseph and Mary had asked if he knew of any work for their son Frank, and asked if we might hire him. I agreed.

At seven, I went to the Detachment and Jerome thanked me for my help. At the Boarding House and time with the dogs and dinner I went to my room. The moon cast a glow over the city, and I made some more notes. I thought of Suzanne and wondered if she thought of me but realizing how foolish that was, I checked my weapons and lay to watch the stars. I realized that this was the one chance I had to relax and hoped the next part of this journey would keep me safe.

Chapter 12

It was Monday, October 1st and I was occupied in preparation for court while Frank fixed our buildings, acted as a guard, and trained Lucky. When I worked at my office, Ben and Lucky slept on my foot. If I had adequate information, these American robbers might lead me in pursuit out of the country, so I went to my bank and bought American gold coins, paper money, and Canadian money. I took out a wallet that fit around my lower leg and put in it four hundred American gold coins and dollars and the remaining hundred dollars I put in my pocket. The week never seemed to end and by Friday I needed a break, so it was time for fun.

The poker game included my reporter friend, Seamus O'Toole and as we played and drank, I mentioned I needed to hire a receptionist who also could help bring in work. Seamus laughed and said he had someone for me and said it was quite the story. A few reporters had visited the bars in Lousetown across the Klondike River. Scattered among the liquor establishments were houses used by ladies of the night. One of his friends knew of a clerk, Mathew Talbot who had recently arrived in Dawson City as a graduate from the University of Toronto. He came north to mine for gold and was not robust enough to help in the gold fields and ended up as a clerk in a general store. He fell in love with a lady in Lousetown, who worked in a restaurant. She was one of a few respectable women in living in Lousetown. He had the misfortune to discover, too late, that she had an admirer who was mean, jealous and about twice his size. A fight ensued, and poor Talbot ended up in the city jail. He was fired from his job and had no money to pay the fine.

In a card game, someone wins and this time it was not I, but Seamus. He was so drunk we carried him home to his lodging while he serenaded us to the filthiest songs I had ever heard. He would need to do at least five thousand Hail Mary's and his confession would drive the priest to drink or on the next boat to Whitehorse. I put my hat low over my face and hoped no one recognized me and tried to push our procession as fast as intoxicated men could stagger. As I returned to my room I thought that this might be the last time I would be in the boarding house. It had been a good start to Dawson City, but I could not take the chance that Mrs. Rivest, William or George might be hurt.

The next day I wandered down to the jail to conduct an interview with Mathew Talbot. He stood as I entered the cell and my first impression was of a morose and bedraggled fellow with a prominent shiner and who stank of sweat and whisky. He was about five foot six and thin with a prominent nose, small lips, and slight size that did not impress me, but I looked for a clerk and not a lady's man. My impression changed as I found him to be astute and he asked intelligent questions and kept apologizing for his condition. He had a sense of humour and charm and as I told him about the job and what it required and he immediately became excited and agreed to do it. I arranged to pay the penalty and hired him with the agreement that his first pay was my reimbursement to cover his fine for disturbing the peace. I could not understand why the constable arrested the victim but not the offender, but realized an overworked constable found it easier to end the fracas by removing the timid fellow and not the enraged bully.

I bought new office equipment and law books from a lawyer who left Dawson City. I placed a mahogany desk and chair in the reception area and the second desk was for my office. I now had a secure filing cabinet and added a lock to my office door. I had a large table, to spread out papers and texts. Notes and lists covered the table and floor as I listed points of evidence and their connections. Matthew had made friends in his short time here and brought in new customers. His referrals came from Lousetown that required security for trips to the bank from brothel owners. Bar owners also asked for help in safety, and off-duty police were happy to do these jobs. I paid them each two dollars, which was twice their daily wage, for a short walk from Lousetown to the banks.

Once Bert returned we met with Mr. Wade, who kept us waiting twenty minutes. He was well dressed, of medium height and slightly fat. He had a square face, gray eyes and cheeks that hid behind a large moustache. His voice was deep, and he looked about forty years of age. He told us to sit in the two wooden chairs in front of his desk. Bert introduced us and handed a letter from Inspector MacDonald. Wade read the letter and asked what we needed, so I set out an outline of our case. I thought we should start with something that created interest like the discovery of a murder. When I mentioned finding the murder victim, Wade interrupted.

"That is a question for me to determine and if the facts meet the definition of the offence of murder under the Criminal Code." I thought, what an idiot, but remained calm.

"The finding of the body and the open wound suggested he was murdered."

"I must make that determination," Wade grumbled and gave me a look to put me in my place.

"Someone, as young as yourself could not be the judge of what constitutes murder. Perhaps it was an accident?"

"An accident precludes running backward into a sharp instrument and impaling yourself," I replied. Wade scowled and was about to say something when I jumped in.

"The Coroner's report made a finding of death by unlawful means. I believe we have the evidence to show the method." His eyes bore into me.

"Well young man, perhaps I misjudged you. What is your name again?" I answered John Caldwell. He asked where I was from so I told him Toronto. He said he knew Ontario and that he knew of a major manufacturing company owned by the Caldwell's.

"Are you part of that family?" I acknowledged I was, but did not mention they were major donors to the Liberal party. My guess was that he knew it, but his manner suddenly became more respectful. I hated to admit my family connection but much rode on this lawyer's help.

I set out the story of the *Casca's* gold robbery. The theft totaled five thousand ounces, almost one hundred thousand dollars, while the second one from Big Pierre was smaller. That was around one hundred ounces or about two thousand dollars.

"Dalton Weigand owned a series of mining claims on the Indian River and signed a lease agreement with Frank Thompson. Thompson was to mine and provide royalty payments to Weigand. No agreement was registered canceling that lease agreement and this year only Weigand worked the claims. We also have evidence that Thompson is scared, but that is hearsay since no one has seen Thompson this year." Wade sat and looked out the window, so I waited and turned suddenly.

"Continue, since you now have my interest, but I think a judge will find this not relevant. It will be my job to entice him with promises that there is more to come." I was not sure what he wanted from me, but he smiled so I continued. He had the court experience and knew what judges wanted.

"The records from the gold commissioner's office are essential since they prove this season that Weigand declared sixty-one hundred ounces. The adjoining mine owner, Pierre Cloutier, told me that Weigand had minimal production. Cloutier went back to mine at Indian River but disappeared, and unless we find him, you cannot use this evidence." Wade grumped at me with an impatient expression, but I carried on with my story.

"George Martin and Louis Rivest own claims on King Solomon's Dome. A few months ago, Martin went missing, and I was asked by Mrs. Rivest to find him." I paused to add a new element.

"The gold robbers needed active mines as a front for royalties on the stolen gold and to receive money from gold buyers. They captured George Martin, and those claims were used as a front to create royalty payments for the stolen gold. The declarations filed stated that it came from those claims, but that was a false statement, and we believe this gold is from robberies. We captured the two kidnappers, Peters and McMillan, and Peter's confessed this. Their boss is Robert McGill, but unfortunately, they were freed from jail and are missing." Wade looked exasperated, threw his pen on the table scowling and muttering I wasted his time

"However, we have George Martin available as a witness. He can verify the actual gold produced and can swear he was forced to sign the papers granting the authority to Robert McGill to sell the gold. He also was forced at gunpoint to sell his share of the mine to McGill." I heard a chuckle and Wade exclaimed that it was clear sailing.

"It gets better since Mrs. Rivest can confirm her husband never signed any documents because he is dead, so the signature on the assignment is false. Martin can state he produced about one hundred ounces on the claims while the value stated in the Gold Commissioner's Office was two thousand ounces. I think any judge can figure that out." I waited for his look and continued.

"Another set of claims of a false gold declaration was near King Solomon's Dome. The owner is Robert McGill, but Dalton Weigand has the right to mine those claims. That links those two, and it was in a mining tunnel on McGill's property that we found the murder victim. Those two will need to convince a judge that they knew nothing about the dead man. We have maps and claim numbers that were found by the police at Weigand's cabin on the Indian River and the constable's notes that summarizes the evidence and partially burnt documents that show McGill's claims. We checked the location where Pierre Cloutier was robbed and found these burnt documents." Wade's motioned me to continue.

"I believe you can apply to the court for Dalton Weigand and Robert McGill's bank accounts since we have this evidence," I announced. He scowled at me and grunted.

"Maybe I can, but it will take a lot of work, and I am quite busy."

"Mr. Wade, I have copies of the mining recorder and gold commissioner records and draft affidavits." I took them from my briefcase and handed them to him. He looked at me.

"Who prepared the affidavits?" I told him I had using *Best on Evidence*, the *Criminal Code*, and my work as a legal assistant to William Willard. After half an hour, he looked at me.

"If you want to work with me, just let me know. These will do the trick and Mr. Caldwell you amaze me. I can review them in more detail this afternoon, and I may want to make changes, but I think we have the basis for an application to the court. I will have my clerk finalize them by tomorrow and file them." Mr. Wade escorted us to the door and told me to return at four this afternoon. As Bert and I walked back to the detachment, he congratulated me.

"John I had no idea that you came from a wealthy family."

"Bert, please keep that quiet. I am not going back to Toronto as I like Dawson City and my job as a detective." He said he would like to have me for dinner once his wife was more organized in the house. At four I returned to Mr. Wade's office. He had made changes to the affidavits, and I realized that the changes reflected his style but the content remained. He told me he would have them redone and would file them tomorrow morning. The return date for the court was for eight days, and Wade explained he needed to advertise notices for McGill and Weigand. He then asked if I was free for dinner. Although surprised, I accepted.

Dinner was at his house as he explained his wife would return in two days. He introduced Mrs. Stevenson, his cook and after he had poured us a glass of decent wine, he started to tell me stories. We discussed the law, politics and the problems with corruption in government. I discussed South Africa and why I came north. What surprised me was Mr. Wade's passion. His hero was Major General James Wolfe, who defeated the French at Quebec.

When I took my leave at nine o'clock, I felt I had misjudged Mr. Wade. He was opinionated, full of himself and looked like a bulldog, but he was intelligent and carried on a good conversation. He loved to tell stories of other lawyers, judges, and politicians. He divulged scandalous tales of the leading citizens of Dawson and often broke out in laughter before he finished his story. He looked at me in a stern fashion then smiled and said, "Don't repeat that John." I liked him and wanted to be in court for his application. I envisaged his leading a judge with promises of more tidbits of gossip and the revealing of hidden secrets. At his front door, he said if the weather turned clear, he would like to take me out on the *Spirit*. Mr. Wade grinned as he described his boat.

"It can hold twelve passengers, and alcohol vapors power the engine. I can take her out for up to twelve hours and can refill it with extra cans I keep on board." I thanked him for his hospitality and left.

As I returned home I checked each street and kept my hand at my revolver since I could not shake the memory of the death threat and my attempted murder and my mind went over who wanted me dead. There were clues including the note in the haversack and whom did Arizona Charlie overhear that he refused to tell? How did they know of my investigations at the mining recorder and gold commissioner offices? I trusted Henry Lloyd, but I was not sure of Roland Caton and other staff might have overheard my discussions. In any event, once they printed the notices of the court application to obtain the bank records, people could check the affidavits filed in the courthouse and find my name and once that happened I was out there as a target.

I moved to my training and knew I was improving. I had learned that one piece of evidence can link to another, which Bert called internal consistency. He talked about connecting a fact related to an issue in the case. The example he used was finding the burnt maps and cigar stubs at the robbery site. The burnt documents were maps and claim descriptions for the McGill claims on King Solomon's Dome. On their own they were not helpful but linked to other evidence they formed part of a chain and could relate to other pieces of evidence.

The next day I was early to work but Bert was already reading. He looked at me and said for me to sit.

"This is the second book I ordered. I have read the first book on forgery, which you need to learn, while this is book deals with identification from fingerprints." We spent the rest of the time in discussion about our investigations. Bert sighed and looked at me.

"I am not sure if I told you, but I have further reports on the Order of the Midnight Sun. They state they bought four Maxim machine guns along with over four hundred Lee- Enfield rifles. Ottawa has secretly sent two Maxim Machine guns to the Yukon Territory. One is coming here, the other to Whitehorse and they also sent Lee-Enfield Rifles." That was not what I wanted to hear.

"Bert, as soon as the ship docks at Skagway, the American customs agents will check the freight and discover these weapons. There is no other way into the Yukon Territory except by horse trail, and so much for the secret

shipment, since the Order of the Midnight Sun will know this before we do."
I thought if only the government had a port under Canadian control.

"How many additional police or soldiers are they sending?"

"None at present." Bert added, "The feeling in Ottawa is they do not wish to alarm the Americans."

"Yet the American's continue to increase the size of the infantry regiment in Haines. Our politicians have no idea of the potential threat here or is the Yukon Territory not worth protecting?" Bert stared at me.

"I do not know, but as soon as word reaches Washington of two Maxim Machine guns heading north, they will react." He gave me the book on forgery and said with a wicked smile, for me to read it in my spare time. I opened it and saw an inscription, Sergeant Albert Raven, N.W.M.P

Seamus O'Toole was next on my list. He was in courtroom one, and I sat and watched the end of a robbery trial. As the lawyers, and visitors stood for the judge to leave, I asked when we could meet. He said now, so we went to the Dawson Hotel in the adjoining bar. We each had a beer, and I told him about Suzanne Cloutier. I provided him with a description of her and asked him to pass this around to his acquaintances. There was a ten-dollar reward if I learned something about her and he said he would do this.

My next stop was the *Klondike Daily News* to obtain today's newspaper. In the official notice page was printed that an application would be made in the Territorial Court for an order to examine the bank accounts of Robert McGill and Dalton Weigand. It showed the dates and times. The opening salvo of this battle had begun. After some other chores, I returned to make dinner. As I ate, someone knocked on the entrance to the gate. I walked out to see Seamus who looked excited.

"John, my friend knows in which hotel your lady friend stays. You described her as pretty with brown hair and brown eyes and there are less than ten girls that good looking in Dawson City. Herbert saw her at the North Star Hotel and tried to invite her to go for a walk. She told him her name was Pauline as she politely declined his invitation."

The North Star Hotel was on Front Street, across from the docks. I gave Seamus ten dollars for his friend and five dollars for him. I thanked him as

I put on my coat, checked my revolver, slid it into my holster and attached my bayonet. Seamus stood, and I thought his mouth would drop as he asked where was I going. I said the hotel as we left the house.

It snowed as I walked to Front Street. The North Star Hotel was built at the beginning of the gold rush in 1897 and it was not the best hotel but was still acceptable for a lady. The advantage of the hotel was the location next to the docks. Entering the lobby, I stamped my boots to shake the snow and asked the man at the front desk to tell Pauline she had a visitor. The clerk asked my name, but I explained it was a surprise and gave him a quarter. Suzanne would not expect me, but I did not underestimate her. The lady who descended the stairs in a dark green dress was beautiful. She looked like Suzanne, and when she reached the lobby, she spoke to the clerk at the front desk.

"My name is Pauline Humphries, what is the message?" The clerk pointed at me and said,

"He wants to see you." I told Miss Humphries it was a mistake since I thought she was someone else. She stared at me and asked, "Describe her to me?"

"As beautiful as you, with short brown hair and brown eyes. This lady wore a necklace with a small pearl, tall black boots, brown pants and a brown jacket." She asked, what was the name of this lady.

"Miss Humphries, how about desert with coffee in the restaurant and I will tell you a story." She looked at me, smiled and said she would be delighted. After we had ordered coffee and port, I told her some of my stories and that my name was John Caldwell. I knew that some of this information was filed with the courts and would soon be common knowledge and I told her about my visit to Pierre Cloutier's mining camp where I met his daughter Suzanne. I finished by telling of her departure from the police outpost in the night and her removal of police documents. Miss Humphries sat silent and sipped her coffee before she spoke.

"Incredible how you can spin together such patent nonsense. I know this lady, and she is a respectable person who I am sure would never be out in the wilderness, impersonating someone else and stealing documents." She pushed her chair and stood up to leave. It was time to move from gentlemanly behavior to official business.

"I am a Special Constable with the North West Mounted Police involved in investigating major gold robberies and here is my identification. I am sorry to interrupt a wonderful discussion but Miss Humphries, this case involves murder, kidnapping, and fraud. This lady is not a suspect, but we need her to return the police documents and to answer questions. Would you like to follow me to the Detachment where they can verify my identity?" She seemed overwhelmed before she spoke.

"Mr. Caldwell, I am a writer for the *New York Times*, and I have been in Dawson City since July, and I leave in two days. I visited with Alice Freeman who writes under the name Faith Fenton for the Toronto *Globe*. She is married to the medical health officer, and she can confirm this."

"Miss Humphries, you are not under investigation, and I just need to know the name and location of this lady." It was time to find out Suzanne's real name. Miss Humphries had now sat down and stared at me before she spoke.

"I met her on the *Sybil* travelling from St. Michaels in the Alaskan Territory. She introduced herself as Mary Bertram from San Francisco and told me the reason she headed to the Klondike was to find gold properties. Miss Bertram said she would be here to visit mines but intended to leave before the end of October. Both of us dined often and shared intimacies. Since my arrival in Dawson City, we have seen each other occasionally." She stopped to ascertain my reaction, and I nodded for her to continue.

"She promised to meet me here tomorrow for dinner, since it will be my last night in the Yukon Territory. I will take the Northern Navigation Company steamer the *Susie*, to St. Michaels at eleven that night. I cannot tell you more than that, I am sorry." I asked where Miss Bertram was staying and Miss Humphries said she was at the Westminster Hotel on Third Avenue.

"Miss Humphries, you have been of great help to me. Thank you." She asked me about my background and what brought me to the Yukon. I told her I did not want to have my story in the press, but if she used another name for me, I would tell her. She promised to do that so I sat and the rest of the evening passed quickly, and I was sorry when it ended. We shook hands, and I said I was sorry that she was leaving. She smiled and said that she also would have liked the continuation of our talk. On my walk home, I thought my luck was never going to improve with the ladies, and I knew I needed to follow up with Miss Bertram. She knew me, so I needed someone who did not look like a policeman. I thought of my thin and tall clerk Mathew and I knew the Westminster Hotel, and it made sense that Miss Bertram would stay there since it was close to businesses and the docks.

Matthew's job would be to sit in the lobby until Mary appeared and then follow her. I would pay his registration. Frank's job was to dress warmly and stay outside, and if he saw Matthew move, he would run and get me. When I arrived home, I briefed them on Miss Bertram's description. I prepared my weapons and woke up with first light. After my breakfast, I went to the docks.

It was early Saturday morning when I arrived on Front Street. The steamer the *Susie* glided, and nosed up to the dock, reserved for ships of the Alaskan Northern Navigation Company. It was huge with three decks, a pilothouse and pushed a barge. I walked over the ship's office and asked the clerk for the departure time.

"Tonight, at eleven o'clock traveling back to St. Michaels on the Bering Sea. The ship will unload after clearing customs; it will be cleaned and take on new supplies. Passengers can board tonight starting at seven, and it will leave on time," and I thanked him and left.

I returned home to plan and considered whether I should meet Bert to inform him of my search for Miss Cloutier and the information I learned from Pauline Humphries. I rejected that idea since it was Saturday, his family had just arrived, and this might amount to another false lead. Monday would give me time to provide a proper report. I started to read the book Bert gave me, *"Ames, on Forgery."* At five the sun had disappeared over the mountains and I decided to eat at a restaurant across from the Westminster Hotel. I told Frank where I would be and once inside ordered dinner and coffee. I placed Matthew at the Westminster Hotel as a backup plan in case Miss Bertram cancelled her dinner with Pauline Humphries. After my supper, I took Bert's book from my haversack and as I read I made notes. I became so interested in the book I lost track of time until the waiter told me they were about to close. I put the book in the haversack, paid and walked into the cold. Near the Westminster Hotel, Frank motioned me across the street and told me Matthew had not left the hotel.

The clock in the lobby showed eight. Matthew was seated in the corner and ignored me. At the reception desk, I asked if I could leave a message for Miss Mary Bertram and gave the clerk a dollar. He said she had not gone out and I noticed he had glanced at room eight when he spoke. I did not know if he was aware of what he had done or he reciprocated my generous tip. I went to Mathew and tried to be discrete.

"Bring me to your room." We walked up a flight of stairs, and I told him to stand outside room eight while I accidently opened the lock. My small knife was not needed as I turned the doorknob. The closet doors were open with clothes and papers on the floor, and the bed was untouched. I grabbed the papers before I closed the door.

"Mathew move fast. Check out, go to the Police Detachment and find Sergeant Raven. Tell him to meet me at the docks, go home and have something to eat and take these papers with you." I left the hotel and told Frank to go to the house, warm up and have something to eat. Front Street was dark with a few lights with snow that obscured my view. Should I wait for Bert, or start my search? I had my leg knife, bayonet and revolver so I felt I could handle myself. I knew the steamer the *Susie* would leave at eleven and the whistle was continuously sounding to remind passengers to get aboard. I felt an urgent need to search, aided by the thought of helping Suzanne.

No one watched as I started my reconnaissance. Although the snow and clouds obscured the moon, Front Street and the *Susie* provided adequate light to show prints in the snow near a barge and one set were those a female. As I slowly moved forward, I heard someone's shout from the barge, but then it suddenly ended. I grabbed a ladder next to a shed and placed it across to the barge. Once on the deck, I looked in the cabin window, but it was too dark. The door was locked so I took out my small knife and worked on it until it moved. With my revolver, I slowly opened the door and descended the ladder into total darkness. When I reached the lower deck, I went to open a curtain and felt something cold and solid against my neck.

"Drop the gun." It fell with a thud on the deck and fortunately the safety was still on, so no accidental discharge occurred. The object against my neck remained, the curtain opened, and another voice spoke.

"Look who we have? Turn around slowly," and I looked to see the man who I knocked out at the cabin when Bert was asleep. It was one thing to go on the offensive, but to stupidly walk into this trap proved I needed to think before I acted. A chant of stupid, stupid, stupid danced through my mind. It was still dark as I gently removed my haversack and pushed it under a table. I was told to walk slowly to the center of the cabin and watched a man with a pistol pointed at my chest was the second man who escaped. The first man lit a lamp and told me to open my jacket.

When he saw the bayonet, he ordered me to take it out slowly and drop it. He checked my pockets, and I felt him gently slide my hundred dollars into his hand. He looked to see if his friend noticed when he put the money in his pocket. I thought no honour amongst thieves when he told me to sit. I still had the knife strapped to my leg and my leg wallet with American money. As my eyes became accustomed to the dark, I could see a woman tied with her mouth gagged. It was Mary Bertram or Suzanne Cloutier, depending on her story, but I was happy she was alive and felt somewhat better to know she also had fallen into this trap.

CHAPTER 13

The *Susie* gave another whistle, and I heard a shout the steamer was leaving. The engines increased in sound, and I felt the *Susie* pick up steam as it pushed the barge. I tried the ropes that tied my arms, but I could not move them. The thief who took my money wandered over and hissed in my ear.

"I am not allowed to hurt you until my boss has had a little discussion, then you are mine. I have not forgotten you, and I still have problems with my eyes."

"Why the gag for her and where are we headed?"

"She kept making noises, and that created problems, except that brought you to us. We are on our way to freedom land, the United States of America and the Alaskan Territory, and that is all you need to know." That was more than I expected and I needed to see if I could develop his trust.

"My name is John, and I regret hitting you so hard, but I was scared." I was spinning such a crock of nonsense, but the question was whether it was effective? When I looked at Mary, I saw her look of disgust, but if she believed me, maybe they would as well. I went on to talk about his size and strength and noticed Mary almost starting to laugh so I gave her a stare, and her face turned expressionless. The second fellow snorted.

"Eddy, he is telling a thumper and playing you for a fool. Now button your lip and don't talk to him." The man named Eddy came over and hit me so hard in the mouth I thought I would fall.

"That is playing me for a fool so be quiet, or I will knock out some teeth." I looked away and soon fell asleep and when I awoke, the engines had stopped. I did not think I could look out the window but heard distant voices on the *Susie*.

"Amazing what happens when a steamer is short of wood but we made sure of that."

"Shut up Eddy, that's enough and you two listen carefully and do what I tell you, or you will not like the consequences. We will leave silently, and we have revolvers pointed at you so you will behave." They untied us and removed Miss Bertram's gag. I tried to estimate our location and knew the Yukon River flows downstream at six miles per hour and it was now early morning, so we must either still be in the Yukon Territory, or just inside the Alaskan Territory. Eddy held a ladder, which he put across and scampered on to shore and we followed. The shadows from the barge kept us hidden on the dock as we moved towards the trees. I looked to see if they had discovered my haversack, but no one carried it. If the crew from the *Susie* searched the barge, they might find it and the book and report one illegal passenger was a sergeant in the North West Mounted Police.

Wood was piled on the middle gangway and lanterns filled the dock. It was a small town but bigger than Forty Miles in the Yukon Territory. It would take the *Susie* until the next night to arrive at Circle City in the Alaskan Territory when a proper search might occur. This town had to be Eagle, and if I was correct, an infantry fort was here.

Several of the crew stopped and looked at us. The second mate started to walk towards us and then shouted for us to stop. They shoved us on horses and men grabbed the reigns to lead us into a forest. I heard more shouting, but that soon fell behind. I did not know if the fort or Eagle had a telegraph, but I thought Circle did.

The horses traveled through the rough country for about an hour to a little river. We were pushed into a motor launch hidden by some trees. The engine started, and I noticed a sign in the front that said, "Built in 1899 by the *Marine Vapor Engine Company*, New Jersey." This boat was a long way from home. About twenty minutes later, the launch slowed as we entered a shallow river and then motored upstream. After five minutes, we came to a stop at a little dock and exited the launch onto a trail. We continued to walk for an hour to a camp with log cabins. Near the largest cabin, we stopped and I noticed at least ten armed men, who glared at us with unfriendly expressions.

A tall man with a thick beard walked up to me. He looked to be six feet with a long face, wide-set eyes and smoked a cigar. I thought of the description provided by Big Pierre, and apart from no moustache this could be Weigand. I had no concrete ideas on an escape other than a dive into frigid waters that would kill me in less than two minutes. The reception committee prevented a quick exit, and my other problem was Miss Bertram. Two men took us to the last cabin that was surrounded by thick trees and brush, and pushed us through the door to lock it from the outside. There was a small view of the outside through the boarded windows. Miss Bertram looked at me with raised eyebrows.

"Well, Sir Galahad, that rescue was a complete failure, but you did one thing right, they did not check your legs. Do you still have your knife?" What a dreadful woman but when I looked at her I could not resist her smile.

"I kept my knife but I need to confirm why I looked for you. You are the daughter of my client, Pierre Cloutier. I went to your room and found evidence of a robbery and the Westminster Hotel said you had not checked out, so I searched the barge. My name is John Caldwell, and I have a security agency in Dawson City. What is your story?"

"That depends on how much they know of me. At present, I am Mary Bertram from San Francisco interested in mining claims and that creates problems with my use of the name Suzanne Cloutier. Your story is that you showed me various mining locations and we were to have dinner last night at the Westminster restaurant, but I failed to appear. Worried, you looked for me, entered my room and assumed I was missing and you started your search." That was a lot to remember, and I needed to confirm some details.

"When did you meet me and at what hotel and which claims did I take you to?"

"July 10 at the North Star Hotel and we saw claims at Indian River and King Solomon's Dome. You know I like red wine, and you like whisky. Where are you from?"

"Toronto and I have a theory as to what you are doing here, but I think that should wait." She did not look when I buried my leg wallet and knife. She stared out the window and looked worried and I was about to speak when I heard voices outside and put my index finger to my lips. The door opened and Eddy entered with another man who held a rifle. They brought us out along a path into a larger cabin and inside was the man I assumed was Weigand, the other man from the barge and a third person. Eddy never entered the cabin and shut the door.

I now had a good look at the other man on the barge. He was about thirty, bald with a scar over his right eye, a narrow nose and not much of a jaw. He was thin, and I estimated his height to be around five foot eight. Based on Grant's description he was one of the men who helped Peters and McMillan escape from the outpost. Weigand looked at him.

"McGill, did you or Searle search him?" McGill muttered.

"I took his revolver and bayonet."

"That is not what I asked. Did you search him?" McGill answered he assumed Eddy had.

"Search him," shouted Weigand. McGill lifted my pants, felt around my arms and waist but found nothing. I thought if I escaped I had both names and a description for these two. Eddy's last name was Searle, matching E.S., the same initials on the haversack. I had the names of these culprits, but the bad news was I could do nothing. Then it struck me that they did not care what I learned about their identities since I was not going to leave this camp alive. The third man wore a type of brown uniform with epaulets on his shoulders. He was big, about six foot two and broad with a moustache, bushy eyebrows and a long nose and a square face and I wondered was he Barton? McGill and Weigand looked unhappy when this man told us to sit and asked us our names. We answered Mary Bertram and John Caldwell. He looked at me.

"Welcome to freedom country, the Alaskan Territory." They needed the minimum amount of facts and I had to act innocent as Weigand approached and asked me a question.

"Why did you search in the mining recorder and the gold commissioner offices for claims registered to Weigand and McGill?" I was surprised they knew that and my description but I remembered I was their target in the gold fields so they were in pursuit for some time.

"Do you want the quick or the lengthy version, and what name shall I use to address you?"

"You call me Bowie and I want the detailed version."

"Mr. Bowie, before I start, is the man in the uniform Crockett?" The slap to my cheek was fast and hard. The crook desires to be called Bowie, but I had a pretty good idea I had now met Cedric Barton.

"I arrived in Dawson City in early June and checked out gold properties, but they were too expensive I set up a security agency to take miners from their claims to the banks and the gold commissioner's office and also began to work with a lawyer named William Willard."

"Tell me the quick version," he muttered so I explained Pierre Cloutier hired me to escort him from his mining claims, but I was busy and used another person. They were robbed at night when they camped not far from Dawson City. The thieves took one hundred ounces of gold, and I wanted to find out more information and learned that Dalton Weigand had filed declarations at the gold commissioner's office, including one for one hundred ounces.

"Why did you care about the payments of gold by Weigand?" asked Bowie. I believed I was now in the presence of the boss, with the real name of Cedric Barton.

"The one hundred ounces was the amount stolen from Big Pierre." I told him about my conversation with Pierre Cloutier who said Weigand had a terrible mining season, so I put those facts together. I did not want to use the word evidence since the last thing I wanted was my background discovered. The three men went in a corner to whisper and then the man in the uniform returned with a malevolent stare, leaned over and growled.

"Why did you stick your nose into how much gold McGill declared?" I told him about my landlady's request for me to look for George Martin since her husband was half owner of the claims. I decided to push back since I was tired and figured I had nothing to lose.

"Those claims were registered to both Martin and Rivest. Martin told me he was forced to transfer them to McGill. It is too bad you use incompetent men because Martin has escaped and will state he was made to sign the transfer and can identify the person." I looked at McGill, who scowled and gave me an evil stare before I continued.

"I also know that the police have proof that the other transfer is a forgery since the idiot who signed it failed to check out that the owner died last year in a mining accident." Suddenly McGill spoke.

"Boss, we have heard enough from this fellow." Barton glared at McGill and said in an icy voice.

"How is it I now learn this from a stranger rather than you. McGill, you are now an enigma since before I had absolute trust in you but now I am not sure." He paused to move closer to McGill.

"When exactly would you confide in me, perhaps provide subtle hints, or did you plan to keep it a little secret and you know how much I hate disloyalty." He turned and said in a low voice he wanted the rest of my story so I continued knowing that each word would condemn McGill.

"At the mining recorder and the gold inspector's office I discovered these transfers and sales of gold." Barton glared at McGill and sarcastically hissed.

"Did you seriously create a transfer for a person who was already dead?" McGill remained quiet and looked at the floor while Weigand moved to the back of the cabin. Barton came closer to me, and I knew he was furious as he spat out.

"I still do not understand why you did this?" he asked. I told him about discovering the burnt documents at the robbery site and more documents at Weigand's cabin, which led us to those claims, but I felt it prudent not to mention the dead body. Barton's face was now scarlet and his mouth began to twitch as he suddenly marched over to Weigand and hit him in his face with his fist. He pointed his finger in Weigand's face.

"You are the most useless piece of garbage," then he stopped. I noticed Weigand looked to me and moved his hand across his neck to tell me I was dead and I really dislike those types of messages. Barton's hands went up, and I heard Weigand say he was sorry. I was in a bad state because I had now created a strong desire for Weigand and McGill to injure me. Before I spoke, they had grounds to hurt me but now they would skip that part and move to the final stage. There was also Eddy Searle, but he would have to stand in line. I had stupidly given more information than was good for me and I felt like a chained rabbit in a kennel filled with ravenous dogs and at that point, Barton walked back to me and sneered.

"That interesting story was one I knew from another source. You have interfered in my business, but I am satisfied you at least are telling the truth, unlike your lady friend. I have one final question, why did you look for her," pointing at Miss Bertram. I explained she hired me to show her some mining claims and she missed dinner with me, so I went to her room. It looked like there had been a robbery, so I searched for her. Barton gave me a quizzical look.

"You seem to be quite skilled at this," so I told him about my work as an assistant for a lawyer in Dawson City and my time as a trooper with the Strathcona's Horse in South Africa. He snorted and shook his head but what did that mean? He sat down in front of Miss Bertram and remained silent for a minute before he spoke.

"You are my bigger problem but before Barton continued, Weigand jeered.

"This soldier stumbled on gold productions and tried to link it to robberies, but he is just a Canadian and out of his depth." Barton glared at him.

"Weigand, I am so close to shooting you I am in a struggle whether to calm down or blast away. Since when do want to admit gold production tied to robberies? You keep yammering, and I will do it, so shut up and stay out of this. Your stupidity has doomed a successful operation, and we now need to make some hard decisions. Weigand slunk away while Barton examined Miss Bertram but I was still focused about his hard decision.

"You have been on my trail for some time and are persistent. You are from San Francisco and in communication with your associates. I have copies of your telegrams and my friends in San Francisco have provided me with more information. You are not Mary Bertram, a lady searching to buy gold claims and I cannot believe how stupid you thought we were." He went over and stood next to her and I knew if he put his arm around her she would punch him, and I think he knew that.

"Gentlemen, may I introduce Jane Warne of the Pinkerton's Detective Agency who works for the United States Government. You were in the gold fields and followed my people. You arrived in early July with several agents and unfortunately for you, I have had access to all your messages and the nature of your reports."

If that was true, his organization knew far more about her than the North West Mounted Police. I suspected she was in the Yukon Territory to check on the Order of the Midnight Sun, but I never thought that the Pinkerton's people could be so careless. Was that her real name or another fake one? This far from civilization I could not rely on her or her agency to help unless she had an associate in this camp. That was a hopeless wish, and we were both far from friends and help. She looked at him and in a calm voice, as a teacher addressing a student, explained.

"I know your real name is Barton, the head of the Order of the Midnight Sun. We knew you read my messages, but my agency provided false telegrams for you. Any relevant information I sent with trusted messengers." He smiled like a cat about to eat a canary.

"You would like me to believe that, but I learned valuable information from your telegraphs, which were almost always correct. You said we had Maxim machine guns and unknown numbers of men. That is true since we are assembling men and have sufficient weaponry for the task. I do use the name Barton from time to time, but it is not my real name." He laughed and walked a few feet from her and stared at me.

"How is it that the famous Pinkerton Detectives cannot even find out my real name?" as he looked at Miss Warne and me. I did not like the way this was going and if this was secret information, he had provided it to us and I could not feign ignorance. There was too much incriminating evidence, which we never could share, since it was our death warrant.

"Your name is irrelevant since your recruits will not fight," she smiled while Barton frowned, crossed his arms and remained silent while she continued.

"They will take the pay and spend it on drink. How can a few hundred men take over the Yukon Territory? There are almost three hundred members of the North West Mounted Police with another four hundred former Empire soldiers against you and their two Maxim machine guns. Once we capture you, I will have ample time to discover your name." I had no idea of how she knew about the North West Mounted Police Maxim machine guns unless they had landed in Skagway.

"We have over a thousand men and have four Maxim machine guns for the task," he answered, but now looked upset.

"I am finished with you for now." I wondered was he bluffing, or was this only the start of more interviews. Bert and his agents have no clear evidence of this army, and if this is the headquarters, it is a joke with only fourteen men. I did not know who or what to believe. Weigand told McGill to take us away. He knocked on the door, and they took us to a kitchen for water, stew, and coffee. We did not talk and when we finished Searle took us to a shed. I went in first and saw a bucket on the floor. After we both had finished in the shed, he took us back to our cabin. After Searle left, I needed to continue my questions.

"What is your name? I am on number three, not including Josephine."

"Not a bad choice but if you are my Bonaparte, it would be your escape from Corsica that gives me hope and not his disaster at Waterloo. My name is Jane Warne, and I work for the Pinkerton's Detective Agency." I nodded for her to continue.

"My great aunt, Kate Warne was Mr. Pinkerton's first female agent. You may or may not be aware of rumours of an organization called the Order of the Midnight Sun." I interrupted her.

"They want to take over the gold fields near Dawson City." I felt I could tell her a bit about the Order of the Midnight Sun, as it was common knowledge in Skagway and elsewhere, notwithstanding the government in Ottawa thinking it was a secret. I could not tell her about Bert's agents.

"You may fool Barton and his cronies, but who is your real boss," she asked?

"It depends on you telling me the truth, Miss Warne. Why did you take the evidence from the police outpost at Indian River? That resulted in the sentencing and discipline of a constable." Miss Warne apologized and said she thought I might steal it since she thought I was with the Order but later learned that she was wrong.

"Who told you that?"

"Mr. Caldwell, I cannot give you this information since I have agents working with me and I need to protect them."

"Do you think Barton has your information?"

"Money talks and we have a leak so be careful whom you trust. I should not tell you this but where would you go with this information." Receiving this advice from lady duplicitous was a bit much. I recalled *Much Ado About Nothing*, "and trust no agent, for beauty is a witch." I told her this meant we could not work together and once I escaped, I would send her help. She sat down on one of the two beds and stared at me.

"You know I cannot tell you who my associates are as I still do not know you, nor trust you. But later that may change."

"There was my attempt to rescue you."

"I appreciate that, but I still cannot tell you the names of my agents. I need to feel they are anonymous, to protect them, and let them continue their investigation. I also believe they may be coming to rescue me." Walking back and forth helped me focus.

"How do you know this will happen?"

"Stop walking back and forth; it makes me nervous. If you searched for me at the Westminster Hotel, you met Pauline Humphries at the North Star Hotel. When I missed dinner with her, she would look for me, and she may have seen something. Since she left the Yukon Territory, I can tell you her name." She became silent and whispered.

"Sit down and tell me who are you."

"I am a special constable with the North West Mounted Police and Bert is my Sergeant. When you met us, we were in the process to investigate gold robberies and the Order of the Midnight Sun. The latter is confidential because our government wants to keep it a secret, in case it is just a rumour. I take it you work for the United States Government to investigate the Order?"

"Barton got that right, and I do not know what they plan to do with us." I did not want to reveal my vision of our end.

"Our capture might be their mistake. We are in the Alaskan Territory so Ottawa cannot intervene or send a rescue party without bringing this matter to Washington and your government will refuse to help. Prominent senators and congressmen are sympathetic to the Order and their idea of taking over the gold fields, but there is a chance the police know about our capture." She looked interested.

"I carried a haversack with a book which I left on the barge. If the *Susie's* crew discovered it on the barge they might report it to the authorities. The front of the book was inscribed Sergeant Albert Raven, NWMP. If there was a telegraph office at Eagle, the crew could telegraph this information to Dawson City." But then I changed the subject.

"We need to plan our escape. It is a long shot with fourteen or more armed men in a cold wilderness and our only weapon is one knife. But I am game for it since I am damned to be captured by the bogus brothers."

"Stop swearing, and you have a terrible way of to describe our situation. There was no sugar on that disastrous prediction."

"My experience in a prison camp is that jailers become complacent, so we need to plan several different escapes. I did it before and if we are not rescued within the week that is what we will do. If you do not want to try, then stay here because I will leave soon." She sighed, shook her head and said she would come with me.

"I have difficulty in believing the Order of the Midnight Sun exists," I said. "I do not know if they have a larger group of men or just a few in the camp. Our searches have not proven the existence of this conspiracy until now. Winter is coming, and this remote camp is far away from the gold fields. Why bring us here unless they want us out of the way while they plan something. The mining season soon ends, and the steamers will stop for the winter, so this is hardly the time to do anything." She shook her head before she exclaimed.

"When steamers finish for the season; it would be impossible to send a rescue mission to Dawson City. Rescuers would travel by land and take weeks to arrive. If they are up to a surprise and have large numbers of men and equipment, to capture a steamer on its way to Dawson City is the best method. Maybe they..." I jumped in.

"They would have to block it before Dawson City and after the last telegraph station. Logs across the river or other diversions would stop the boat. We are near Eagle, less than ten miles from Canada. If they head towards Dawson City, the next Canadian settlement is at Forty Mile, with a small North West Mounted Police detachment. Once they stop the steamer, they could fill it with troops, horses, equipment, and the Maxim machine guns. It would the just be a matter of when and where to attack." Her eyes showed her irritation while she exclaimed.

"Listen, when I am speaking, you must give me the courtesy to wait until I finish my thoughts, as I was about to say that. I find your behavior to be not unlike a stable hand and you are such an annoyance." I looked down and apologized. I thought she was finished, but she continued with my admonishment.

"You have no experience talking with a lady, and I am sure you fit right in as a soldier, but to carry on a conversation you must learn to listen and wait. I think you have potential, but you must be attentive. Do I make myself clear?" I ignored her, as I was too excited about this idea.

"Are there any American troops in this part of the Alaskan Territory?"

"They are at Fort Egbert in Eagle." She grumped and gave me a disdainful look that I pretended not to see.

"John, you are intolerable. You must wait to talk, and I think that Fort has a company of the Seventh Infantry Regiment. There is also a United States revenue steamer with a small crew," and added, "I think it is called the *Nunivak*."

"Where is it based?"

"In the summer, it is at Dall River, but I believe the *Nunivak* may now be at Circle City. My reports requested assistance on this side of the border, and they told me that the *Nunivak* would be stationed there." Pacing again seemed to help.

"Maybe we have this all wrong. Is the Order of the Midnight Sun a decoy to divert us away from their real purpose? Last summer there was a major robbery on the *Casca* where they stole five thousand ounces, and escaped. From a criminal perspective, it succeeded." I stopped to observe her reaction and then continued.

"Miners are now finishing their final cleanups on various gold creeks and each steamer carries significant amounts of gold. On each Canadian boat, members of the North West Mounted Police travel with the gold, but this did not happen on the *Casca*. Miss Warne nodded, and I continued.

"Steamers in the Alaskan Territory have only private guards who could be part of this gang. I think Barton's army will rob a steamship and every one that passes by this camp might carry a million dollars of gold. That is why they want our meddling to end and it has nothing to do with a fictitious plot to take over the Yukon Territory."

"You drive me to distraction, but I think you are right," she replied. It was time to tell her our case, so I reviewed the contents of the affidavits and the court application.

"There is no way Weigand or McGill can return to Dawson City, and I believe Weigand is the tall, bearded man who smokes cigars. McGill's full name is Robert McGill, and he faces extortion and forgery charges. These crooks are a bad lot, who shot my friend and almost killed me." She looked concerned as I continued.

"We are the only ones to stop them. Tonight, I will try and cut around the window to escape. Miss Warne remained silent and looked upset and I chose not to ask her what she thought, since I did not want to ask myself that question. I knew we now lived on borrowed time and it was time to leave, otherwise death's icy breath would suck the life out of us and into his final embrace.

Chapter 14

That night Searle brought us to the kitchen, with his rifle slung over his shoulder, and sat in silence as we ate. I assumed they wanted us to be kept apart from the other men since I did not see Peters or McMillan. After our meal, Searle walked us back to our cabin. The stars were out, which meant a cold night, and a small breeze rustled some leaves. As we walked among the trees, an engine coughed and started with a roar. Why did they start the engine, was it a test or was the boat to leave on a trip? When we entered the cabin, the door locked but I was happy to have the stove lit with candles on a table.

"I keep thinking of the launch that brought us here. I assume it will be used to board a steamer, but it could be our method of escape," I said.

"Do you know anything about engines?"

"No, but they cannot be all that complicated."

"Unless you know how to start one right away, you must assume we will not have time to figure it out with armed men in pursuit. Did a horse kick you in the head in the army or are you naturally thick?"

"Well," I said, wanting to pull her along with my idea, "We might have more time than you think for the engine and at least I have in mind an escape. I did it before in South Africa," and gave her an indignant look, which was useless since she looked out the window.

"What have you got to suggest, other than ridiculing my ideas?"

"You are right. We both should think in a positive way." She giggled and added,

"Even if it involves your idiotic ideas." I was a little hurt, but seeing her smile, I laughed since she had a lovely smile.

"We may have a rescue, and if that happens, I need to prevent the engine from starting." She gave me a long look, and I tried to appear confident, but I knew we would not be rescued in a million years. We were here alone and forgotten.

"I thought you wanted to take the boat, but at least you don't let this situation get to you."

"This is strange to be sharing a room with a man, but I prefer you to be with me. Good night John," and she crawled under a blanket in one of the beds and looked at me.

"I am scared and glad you are here." Instead of hugging or reassuring her I mumbled good night and watched as she fell asleep. I was an idiot, incapable of the smallest gestures of kindness. I was overwhelmed with her beauty and froze, but I would do better tomorrow if we had another day.

I dug up my knife. Three boards covered the window, and the frame was nailed shut. My first task was to create an opening, so I cut around the bottom frame to move the boards apart. It took about two hours, and I was satisfied that one kick would knock out the window. In bed sleep did not come with a million thoughts of danger and regret. I should have waited for Bert, and I thought of my failures including my failure to hug her when she needed it? The bed suddenly moved as she crawled next to me and I heard her whisper.

"This is not a romantic gesture. The stove is out, and you are a warm body." She turned her back and went to sleep. I was now wide-awake and wanted to say or do something, but I was a furnace and nothing more. Soon my exhaustion took over. I awoke to see Jane sitting with a blanket around her shoulders and staring out the partly boarded window.

"It snowed during the night, and I found it so peaceful watching the snow blanket the trees," she said. I put my blanket around my shoulders and sat on the other chair.

"I know I am just a warm body, but I enjoyed being next to you. May I call you Jane?" She looked at me for a long time.

"John, you are handsome, and I like you, but this is not the time for anything. We must concentrate on the threat and the chance of escape, so another time perhaps. She studied my face and softly agreed that I could call her Jane." I hoped she did not see me blush. Moving closer I told her I had cut around the window frame and the window will open, and we could try it tonight.

"I hope this is not our last day alive."

"Listen we will survive and see these men charged and convicted." I was surprised that I sounded so confident when I shared her fear. Someone opened the door, and I had not heard his approach, but snow masks a sound. He was a tall man I had never seen about my size, clean-shaven with a short haircut. His face was dark with a large nose and narrow lips and had an accent that I thought was Russian. Big Pierre described this man named Victor, who was always with Weigand at the camp. We were told to follow him to another cabin and as we entered Barton sat at a desk with Weigand next to him.

"Victor, please leave us alone." We were told to sit in a couple of chairs near a desk and Barton looked at Weigand and said for him to tell us.

"It is fortunate that I will not kill you now. Barton wanted to dispose of you last night." Weigand smiled and leaned over to explain, as if he was a teacher to students.

"You are a problem we need to solve. You know about this camp, the launch, our appearances and likely have figured out our plans. In other words, you are the ingredients to take us to the hangman. We are on a tight schedule so that you will be locked in your cabin. Death will come but the question, in what way? You may freeze, starve or encounter a bear which I leave to fate," and he looked at us and then at Barton. Barton was expressionless before he spoke.

"Your penalty was left to Weigand, since he won at poker last night. A quick death might be kinder, but he is not kind. It is cold and getting colder, and I do not think you will make it through the night. We will not heat your cabin, and the freezing weather will never leave you, and I give you two days at the most." He yelled for Victor who took us to breakfast then back to our cabin. I thought it strange to feed us before we were left to die. Once we were locked in our cabin, I said.

"During the war I had a grudging respect for my enemy but not these two. They are the most reptilian creatures I have ever met."

"Welcome to detective work. You will find worse, much worse" and I hoped that was a joke but her expression remained grim. "Do you think it is time to follow them," I asked?

"If you do that now, you would be shot." I reached down, dug up my knife and wiped it. I went to a different part of the dirt floor and dug up my leg wallet and turned to her.

"I need to know which way they will go, but I will not go out the window until I am satisfied no one is there. I will follow at a distance and believe me I plan to be careful." She walked over, put her hand on my arm.

"There is no rush so that you will wait one hour. I do not have sufficient bandages for you, so you will just be patient, which I bet is a new experience for you." After twenty minutes I said.

"Wait here; I will be back soon."

"Not so fast, I am coming." I turned and stared at her.

"I have a knife and can handle myself in a fight, and I need to stay focused and not worry about you."

"John, time is wasting, so get moving." I pushed up the partly frozen window then kicked out the boards. I went out the window, helped Jane, and we followed the tracks in the snow. Did she have an agent in Barton's gang? If she did she was a top actress since her fear was real and Barton was intelligent and possessed her information and would eliminate any spy he found.

We stopped as I looked to ensure sure we were far to the rear and hoped there was no trap ahead. I looked back but saw nothing. Near the river, we knelt as we heard an engine and watched their boat glide past us downstream towards the next settlement at Circle City in the Alaskan Territory. When it was out of sight, we walked to the river to see if there were canoes or small boats.

A rowboat low in the water was tied to a tree. I leant over to see the end of that dream since one of Barton's men took an axe to the bottom and removed the boards. The Yukon River is wide and flows at a fast rate so any escape would be through the woods in bear country. We returned to the camp and I explained our next step would be to set a fire near the river and stop a steamer but we needed to search the cabins to find matches and food. We could melt snow if we had a fire and to set the warning blaze.

I was relieved that the cabins had not been burnt. I knew they did not have adequate space in the launch to carry their supplies and equipment and they would not leave them in the cabins, so they must be hidden. We checked the cabins to ensure they were empty and that no one had been left as a sentry. We followed the tracks that headed into the woods and found an area with a small mound of snow and dirt. I took out my knife and dug until I hit metal boxes and used my knife to pry open the top to see tins of food and more importantly safety matches wrapped in paper. They planned to return, and the question was when and we might not have much time.

It took several trips to take the boxes to the kitchen. We discovered papers, kindling and wood and once the fire in the stove was started, we filled pots with snow for water. We had tinned vegetables, beef, soup and tea. Once the water was boiled, we had our first tea. It was an incredible relief to be alive and uninjured and it a place of refuge and not a prison.

"Next step, we assemble wood for a fire near the water," I said. "We will light it at night which should keep animals away. We should gather anything we needed to sleep and heat them up near the stove." To climb into a frozen blanket with an icy mattress was not a desirable option so we brought two beds and grabbed as many blankets as we could find to bring to the kitchen. As we sat by the stove with tea, we talked, or more to the point I listened.

"Kate Warne was my aunt by marriage. She was twenty-three when she approached Allan Pinkerton in 1856. He had advertised for clerical help, but my aunt wanted to be a detective and after much debate, she was hired. She handled several perilous cases, including the Adams Express Company, which involved the theft of fifty thousand dollars. Kate Warne became good friends with the chief suspect and provided crucial evidence. During the Civil War, she befriended southern sympathizers, to obtain valuable information for Alan Pinkerton and the president. She died in 1868, so I never had a chance to know her." She asked if I had heard of her

"No, but perhaps she never made the news in Toronto, and I am astounded that Pinkerton's hires women detectives."

"John, you are such an ignoramus. Think of the advantages of a detective operating without notice. As my great aunt found, no one expects us to carry on that role so we can learn far more than a male detective."

"It is wrong to put a lady in such danger." Her facial expression told me she had moved from annoyance to anger, so a hasty retreat was required to soften the explosion that was about to happen.

"I am still new at this, and I agree that it makes sense." I decided not to tell her about my family situation. My mother and sister's role was to supervise servants, organize dinners and be involved in charitable causes. Jane would not fit in Toronto society, and I realized I did not want to go back to starched shirts, dinner jackets and idle talk over a port. I liked what I did, and at this moment we were alive and safe. I enjoyed Jane's company and wanted to spend some time with her but that was interrupted by a knock on the door, and I grabbed my knife to hide behind it. Jane slowly opened it and I stood back to see a short and broad Indian with a bit of a beard.

"Have that bunch of awful men gone?" We both answered, "Yes." He sighed and exclaimed.

"We prayed for that. We were forced from our fish camp, and they would not let us hunt here and warned us if they saw us around here they would kill us. We remained silent while we watched you." I told him to come in and offered tea as he introduced himself.

"My name is James, and I come from my village on the Yukon River. We have watched the cabins for the past several weeks. Have you checked all of them?" and we told him we had. The next question perplexed me when he asked about the cabin hidden in the woods.

"What cabin," I asked?

"Follow me." We walked about five minutes through dense brush and saw a small cabin. The door was locked, and I yelled but expected no response.

"Is that you John?" It was Big Pierre voice and James shouted to wait. A few minutes later he arrived back with an old rifle. He shouted stand back from the door, pointed it at the lock and fired. The lock fell apart, and we opened the door. Big Pierre needed a shave and a bath but was unhurt. He started a jig and then suddenly stopped.

"Have Weigand and his men gone?" We said yes, and he began the dance again. We returned to the kitchen and gave him tea and biscuits. I shook my head and I was relieved since I had already mourned his death with this bunch of murderers.

"I have looked for you all over the Klondike gold fields, and I assumed you were dead." Big Pierre laughed.

"Not yet but if you had not come I would have. The stove was out this morning, and I am so cold I cannot feel my hands. First I must warm up and drink and then I will tell you my story."

"Are you surprised I found you?" asked James and I said yes.

"Welcome to our land," he said. "We are three villages, one at Moosehide, my village called Johnny's village and another one downstream. My cousin Thomas told me you were forced off the barge and looked like you were captured. He works in the boiler room of the *Susie* and saw you in Dawson City when he visited Frank." He stopped to drink some tea the continued.

"My people have wood camps along the river to supply the streamers. Our grandmothers keep track of who is related and pick the persons to be married, so our villages are one big family. I interrupted him to deal with a pressing issue.

"We need to warn the next steamer to Circle City that they might be robbed and to rescue us. We thought of setting a fire by the river to stop it."

"That will not work," said James. "The steamer captains know no one lives in this part of the river, other than us Indians, and they never stop for us, even if our people had a serious problem." I asked how they dealt with someone who was sick? James said with the doctor at Fort Egbert who is responsible for the soldiers and Indians.

"How do you get there?"

"With ice floating in the river we find the waters too cold this time of year for swimming, so we use our boats until freeze up and then walk across the frozen river." He laughed and enjoyed his response to my stupid question. Fortunately, before I said something more preposterous, Big Pierre said he was ready to talk.

"It was the beginning of September when I returned to sluice gold that Weigand appeared with three other men and my troubles began. They took their horses on to my claims and dismounted. Weigand started to question me and I told him I was mining could I visit him later. He looked at me and said your mining is finished." He started to shake but continued.

"Two men grabbed me and took me to my cabin where I was shoved on a chair. Out the window, I saw a third man who checked out my sluice box for gold. Weigand entered and asked about you and why you reviewed his files at the mining recorder's office?" Big Pierre smiled at me.

"John, I think you made Weigand mad," and I answered that I was glad.

"Weigand yelled, why did Caldwell stick his nose into my business. I told him I hired you to perform an escort to protect the gold and if you stole my gold, then you caused your own problems. Weigand laughed, and said he had ways to solve his problems." This explained how Weigand had learned about my investigations, but I wondered why he had not told everything to Barton. I was also curious why Weigand had kept Big Pierre here and still alive. I realized he had also been left to die but kept silent about that.

"I was taken from my cabin and joined another five men and rode northwest. I knew we passed Dawson City and Forty Mile, but I am not sure of the name of the last town. I was taken to this camp two weeks ago." Our case before the courts needed his evidence and I asked James if there was a telegraph at Eagle or at the fort. He said he believed the fort had a telegraph.

The next morning James and his friends took us along the path to the Yukon River where they had boats. We walked the long distance to Eagle, and then said goodbye. It was sad to see them leave and I told them I would tell Frank of their kindness and protection. We found our way to Fort Egbert, and the sentry took one look at Jane and said the Major wants to see you. He glanced at me and escorted her into the fort while I followed. We walked to a large a large headquarters that overlooked the fort. The man who came from the office gave a broad smile, shook my hand and introduced himself as Major Dunphy.

"I believe you are Jane Warne and John Caldwell?" He was about forty with blond, short hair, a small moustache, intense blue eyes and a square face.

He was tall, about an inch shorter than me and looked fit. He saw Big Pierre and said he did not know who he was, so I introduced him. Major Dunphy told us the recent news.

"The telegraphs were exceedingly busy starting with a telegram from Dawson City asking about a constable named John Caldwell who might have been kidnapped and possibly on the *Susie*. Next, a lady named Pauline Humphries arrived at the fort, worried that her friend Jane Warne had disappeared. Miss Humphries showed papers that she worked for the government and asked me to send a telegram to the Revenue sternwheeler *Nunivak* for it to come here as soon as possible." He paused then continued.

"Next a telegram arrived from Circle City. The crew of the *Susie* stated that several persons had illegally travelled on a barge to Eagle and believed one of them was Sergeant Raven of the North West Mounted Police. But where is Sergeant Raven?" I said he was not with us and explained that Sergeant Raven had given me a book with his name in it, which would have been found on the barge attached to the *Susie*. He looked at us and said you both must have a story and asked us to sit and ordered coffee. I requested if I could notify Inspector MacDonald of the North West Mounted Police that I was alive and uninjured. Jane told the major that trouble was coming and we need to respond.

"We believe a robbery attempt will be made on the next steamer that heads to St. Michaels," I added. Dunphy snorted that seemed far-fetched, and I was about to disagree when a corporal arrived and asked permission to enter. He announced he had two telegrams, which he handed to the major, and left.

"You are going to have visitors. The *Nunivak* will arrive by five." He turned to me and said, "The motor launch *Spirit*, will dock about the same time. Who is on that boat?" I said it was a small launch owned by a lawyer and added.

"I think it might have my rescuers."

Chapter 15

Dunphy was an officer, and in my experience, they go by the book and have minimal imagination and could he understand the criminal mind and what Barton might do? I looked at Jane who nodded for me to start, so I provided a summary of the robberies, the path of gold into money and the court application. At first, he was skeptical but became fascinated with the use of the motor launch and my suspicion of a future riverboat robbery. Jane added that we did not believe that this was an organization that would invade the Yukon Territory.

"They are just low life criminals with a rotten leader that I want to convict," Jane exclaimed. I needed to push the major to act now and not telegraph his colonel for advice and needed to play the money card to entice him.

"We are at the end of the season, and each paddlewheel steamer could carry more than a million dollars of gold. The last thing any crew would expect would be piracy." He studied me and grunted.

"Son, I do not know what to believe, but I accept you have quite the imagination." He started to chuckle and said he was having me on, and agreed these robbers could rob a steamer.

He called for his orderly and gave instructions to send telegrams to Circle City, Dawson City and to the Northern Navigation Company for all steamships to stop at Eagle or Circle City. He sent another telegram to the North West Mounted Police that I was in Eagle, alive and uninjured. He told the orderly that Miss Warne would meet him for her messages to her superiors.

"This is bad," he said. "I do not know which Northern Navigation Company ship it might be. It could be the *Louise, Sarah,* or the *Hanna* and I need them all to come to shore. If they stop here, I can put a platoon on board with sharpshooters, and if they see this motor launch approach, they can warn it off or blow it out of the water." I preferred them alive since we needed the evidence. I knew that something would happen and fast and I wanted to be part of it so I needed to buy horses and supplies.

"Major, thank you for your assistance. We will be back at four after we find a hotel, buy clothes and have some lunch." As we left the office, Big Pierre joined us and Jane looked at me in a strange way.

"Are you crazy, they took our money, how are you going to buy horses and guns?" I told her about my leg wallet with four hundred American coins and dollars. Big Pierre took off his hat, ripped a seam and took out some gold dust.

"Mr. Caldwell, I can take care of myself, and I will see you later for dinner." We found the Hotel Heath near the water. As we checked in, I told Jane we needed to purchase clothes, toiletries, pistols, knives, and rifles but Jane refused my help.

"Jane, it is a loan. How will you feel after I take a bath, and put on new clothes and where will you stay?" She looked at me and smiled. It took a while but she enjoyed the purchases, and I was surprised she spent more time to check out weapons than clothes, but guns kept her alive while clothes did not. We had a basic lunch in a restaurant then returned to the hotel. The last time I felt normal was the morning I searched for Jane and desperately needed a hot bath and a shave. I knocked on her door and waited but soon she walked out, and I noticed she had done her hair and with her new clothes, I thought her the most beautiful lady anywhere. She took one look at me and sighed.

"John Caldwell, stop that. You appear like you have never seen a lady before. We have work to do and no fancy talk, or I will do this job alone. Is that clear?" I nodded, shut my mouth and resolved to behave. It was now four o'clock, and as we walked to Fort Egbert, we saw an American steamer travelling south from Canada and not slowing. We ran to the dock and waved our hands only to hear the whistle and with passengers waving back. It was the *Hannah*, one of the Northern Navigation Company steamers and all we could do was watch the paddlewheels churn as it disappeared down the river.

We entered Major Dunphy's office where we were given coffee and fresh bread. Major Dunphy introduced Second Lieutenant Sam Waters, who was about my age, height and build. He had brown eyes and hair, a thick moustache, a prominent nose, and looked distinctly unfriendly. Before the major spoke, I felt I needed to clarify a question to Jane.

"How could you unload a large amount of gold from the *Hannah*, and take it to Seattle, or San Francisco?"

"Would they hide it until next year, and send it out small amounts?" she said.

"This is a greedy bunch, and I expect them to start to fight amongst themselves unless they dispose of the gold quickly." I realized that we should have waited for Major Dunphy. What I didn't expect was the reaction of the Second Lieutenant.

"Son, why not start with how are we going to rescue the *Hannah*?" I ignored him and turned to the major.

"With boats that we needed several hours ago. There will be a revenue steamer that will soon arrive, and I am not sure we can use the motor launch *Spirit*. The sooner we leave, the better."

"Us, not you," Waters exclaimed. "The Navy runs the revenue cutter. We are in American territory; that involves an American ship and American criminals. What gives you any authority here?"

"The fresh pursuit of criminals, suspected of murder, forgery, kidnapping, fraud and theft and I know what they look like, and I do not think you have that knowledge," was my response. Perhaps I went too far, but I was annoyed. The Second Lieutenant raised his arm to cut me off.

"Listen, if there is any rescuing, leave it to the army, who know how to fight. We will take your evidence before we shove you back to Canada."

"Sir, since you left West Point, have you ever been in a war, even a tiny one." I succeeded in my mission to make him irritated.

"After I graduated from West Point I was not sent on active duty to a war zone." I restrained from laughing when I told him I had experience in the war in South Africa as part of a cavalry regiment, and could be useful in a fight. Major Dunphy looked like he was going to kick one of us out of the room, which would be me. He interrupted in a loud voice.

"Gentlemen, this is premature. Let us focus on our next steps. The *Nunivak* steamer has a crew of six officers, twenty sailors and can take well over a hundred passengers and horses. We need to embark horses, feed, and supplies before we leave. Miss Warne and Mr. Caldwell, you better spend money to buy horses and tackle and be back here as soon as you can." As we left, I noticed Major Dunphy in discussion with Waters and he did not look happy. After we had left the office, Jane exploded.

"You are hopeless, and I cannot believe how immature you are. You like to annoy people and I had it all planned before you opened your big mouth since I know First Lieutenant John Cantwell, the Commander of the *Nunivak*. Fortunately, Major Dunphy took a liking to you, notwithstanding Waters, who I expect will come with us so you better solve your problems with him."

"What an arrogant, loud-mouthed, idiot. Calling me son, when he is the same age." Jane smiled and then laughed.

"John, if you work undercover as a detective then you must put that enormous pride away and be humble. It is better to make friends who talk, then enemies who don't. I agree Waters is arrogant and your solution is to butter him up and compliment him. The last thing you should do is to suggest he lacks experience. It does not help a new relationship to indicate incompetence."

"That was not what I did."

"Would you like me to repeat how, and in what fashion, you insulted him?" I shook my head and she said it was for me to say I was sorry to Waters when I was alone with him. I think I mumbled that I would.

"Stop muttering and say you will." I felt like saying, yes, sergeant, but nodded, and promised I would. This lady drives me crazy, but she is right. Once again, I proved myself ignorant. I needed to overcome my pride and work with people, even if I dislike them, and Waters was right up there.

The place that sold horses and equipment was a five-minute walk from the fort. I knew horses and I wanted the best and bought three good horses, saddles and equipment. At five we returned to Major Dunphy's office. We had just sat down when we heard the whistle of a steamer and Major Dunphy said it was the *Nunivak*. I apologize for my comments to Second Lieutenant Waters, but the major smiled at me.

"Tell that to him," then paused and laughed saying, "Sometimes he invites that treatment, but do not say I said that." I started to like the major who reminded me of Inspector MacDonald. We were asked to meet the commander and officers of the *Nunivak*. I was amazed by the size of the steamer that had two decks and a pilothouse. The engines stopped as we arrived at the gangway. A sailor noticed the major, saluted and said to wait until the boat was tied, and he brought us to the pilothouse. Two officers in work clothes looked at us and saluted Major Dunphy.

"Hello Jack," Dunphy addressed the taller fellow, who wore two stripes across his shoulders with a star. He was about thirty-five and wore a pair of glasses. He was clean-shaven and about my height but thinner.

"Good to see you, Bill, how are things in Eagle since I presume not much is happening," as he winked at Jane and I thought the major was going to leap at him until he saw his smile.

"We are busy since we need to chase after bandits who might attack the *Hannah*." The other officer said he figured something had happened when Miss Warne went missing. The major introduced us and to John Cantwell, a First Lieutenant in the Navy. It was a good thing he called himself Jack otherwise confusion would result. He shook hands with Jane.

"A delight to see you again Miss Warne." I did not ask how or where she knew him from, as it was not the time. The other officer was Second Lieutenant Brian Camden, about five foot eight with a stout body, brown hair and a large moustache. He grinned as he shook my hand with a firm grip. Major Dunphy asked when the ship could leave.

"I have two problems," Cantwell said. "We need to take on wood, water and food, so the earliest will be at daybreak. Second, I need a pilot who knows this stretch of the river and the only one available is Willie Horton since we cannot find the Indian pilot, who grew up in this section of the river. I have sent a crew to the bar to get Horton and dry him out. He is both a pilot and a drinker and if you ask me he is a better boozer." Major Dunphy said to Cantwell he needed to allow his troops on board and once they were ready, to take the *Nunivak* down the river.

"When we find the right location, we will disembark and follow a trail. We will have twenty men and horses. He looked at Jane and asked if she wanted to come. She said she would join them but alone and ignored me. I walked to her and whispered.

"Could we step outside for a talk?" She smiled and said.

"John Caldwell, I love playing you, we have a need for your skills, and it might be cold at night." She asked me who else was coming and I told her I thought one or two more. She turned and told Cantwell.

"Lieutenant, there may be two or three more coming with us." He said that was fine because they had room for twenty-four horses and feed, with a few extra horses to carry supplies. I looked out the window and saw what I thought was Wade's motor launch, so I said I needed to go to the dock.

There I witnessed something I will always cherish. Sven held the wheel with Bert, Grant, George and William grinning while Bob and Jerome tied the boat to the dock. It was an emotional get together as everyone was relieved to see me. Bert quietly said he needed to talk to me, so I gave directions to the restaurant. I had American money, which I offered but Bob said for me not to worry. Big Pierre arrived, and I asked him to show them the way. After they left Bert studied me and commented that he was glad to see me, and that at least I was not a corpse and suddenly I blurted out my apology.

"I am sorry for not waiting for you, and I regret that mistake. It won't happen again."

"Good. I told the Inspector you had learned a lesson, but he was exceedingly angry and wanted to terminate you as a special constable. My instructions are you will continue as a detective unless you do such a foolish and featherbrained escapade again and these are my choice of words, since the inspector's sarcasm was much worse and extremely rude. The inspector felt my strong recommendation to hire you was an error and he felt I was at fault. Personally, I do not care what he thinks, but I do care about your life." He asked me about the situation with Barton and Weigand. Just then I saw Jane who gave a big smile as she walked with three officers to town. Bert opened his mouth in astonishment and gave me a strange look.

"I cannot wait for this story."

"Let us go to dinner, and I will tell you a tale you will not believe."

"John ever since she disarmed you and stole our documents nothing will surprise me." On the way to the restaurant, I reviewed the events over the past week and left nothing out.

"You are either the most skilled detective, or plumb lucky, and I am not sure which it is." I said I intended pursuing Weigand and Barton with some United States soldiers. He just stared and guffawed. He asked me if I was serious and realized I was.

Bert asked with a grin.

"I assume Suzanne is going along?" I smiled and said she was.

"Her name is Jane Warne. Remember my theory that she works for Pinkerton's, on behalf of the United States Government? I was correct."

"Try to remember to be careful."

"You mean with Barton and Weigand?"

"Those two as well," and he was back to normal. Bert explained his strict instructions were if I was safe he was to return with the launch and its driver to Dawson City. Inspector MacDonald grudgingly gave permission for Constable Jerome Scott to stay if the authorities agreed. As I entered the hotel's bar, William passed a half empty whisky bottle to Jerome. Once seated they all expressed relief that I had survived.

"Thank you for being here, and once I have some whisky and food I will tell my story." It took an hour for the telling and I was happy to be safe and with friends. I asked Bob if he wanted to pursue some bad guys. He grinned and said he did. Towards the end I became melancholy, and I did not think it was the whisky but the nearness of death. My friends noticed this and Grant asked me my thoughts?

"We were left to die, and I have unfinished business. I plan to go with soldiers tomorrow to capture this gang." I looked at Jerome and asked if he wanted to come. He nodded and grinned. I stood and shook hands with my friends and told them I owed them a debt I did not know I could repay.

After dinner, they went to the Heath Hotel for more rooms while Bob and I bought another a horse, equipment and a rifle. It was late as I returned to the hotel and without looking knew my spot, by the sound that rattled the door. I had forgotten Bert's capacity to keep me awake even with a pillow over my ear. Lying awake I recalled the best pilots were the local Indians and the gang had captured the Indian pilot.

When we finished breakfast, I told my friends to thank Mr. Wade for the boat and their rescue. Bob, Jerome and I took our equipment and horses to the *Nunivak* and at the docks, sailors took them and we were told to go on board. I had no idea what we would face, but I wanted to see these men captured and convicted. It was revenge I sought for locking us in an unheated room to a cold and painful death. I was not in a compassionate frame of mind as I sharpened my knife with visions of capturing snakes as my war continued and I was not in a forgiving mood.

CHAPTER 16

I found the First Lieutenant in the pilothouse in conversation with Major Dunphy. They paused when I arrived, and I apologized for the interruption.

"The missing pilot was taken by Barton's gang which could give them knowledge of this part of the Yukon River."

"You give common criminals too much intelligence," Cantwell laughed. "The Indian pilot is probably hunting, and I need to continue with my briefing. Thank you for that, and you may go." I was summarily dismissed and thought why the more senior rank the less open to common sense? Barton had an experienced pilot that knew where to hide his boat and now I needed to talk to Bob, Jerome and Jane. She was elsewhere on the ship, so I took Bob and Jerome to the front of the deck and told them I thought Barton had an experienced pilot and he could use the boat to travel back to Canada or hide the launch. Bob looked at me and told me to explain that to the major.

"Bob I did that and was effectively thrown out of the pilot house and did West Point teach logic and common sense?" Bob gave me an unpleasant look and knew I should refrain from disparaging comments about his school, even if warranted.

At seven the engines started, the steamer shuddered, and the sounds of the steady rhythm of the paddle wheels filled the ship. A sailor stopped me and asked if I was Mr. Caldwell? He escorted me to a dining room where Cantwell, Dunphy, Waters and Jane sat around a table, and I was told to sit. Cantwell explained the boat was proceeding downstream and he had posted sailors to keep watch for signs of disturbances on the banks. He advised that the distance between Dawson City and St. Michaels was around fifteen hundred miles.

"This stretch of the Yukon River flows at between five to eight miles an hour and our four boilers move the paddlewheels at around twelve miles an hour. Our speed is between seventeen to twenty miles an hour. The distance from Eagle to Circle City is one hundred and fifty-eight miles, so if we do not stop, we will arrive in eight hours." His next question was when and where did we think this gang of robbers would stop the *Hannah*? Jane looked at me, so I gave it my best thought.

"It will depend on where they stop the steamer and transfer the gold. I do not think it matters how much gold was on the *Hannah* since it is a question of how much time they thought they had, and the weight of the gold. The loss of the *Islander* amounted to three million dollars or over nine thousand pounds, but that was a coastal ship in the Inland Passage, which is far larger than any steamboat. My best guess for the maximum amount of gold on the *Hannah* is no more than twenty thousand ounces or about twelve hundred pounds." I paused to see how my idea was received and no one asked questions. So far, they were with me on my theory.

"The cargo size of the launch limits how much gold they can take from the boat. This gang will not take the gold to land since they need a significant number of horses and wagons. Where would they head this time of year? Snow leaves a trail, and the bigger question is where they would hide it? I believe they will stay on their boat and take the gold to Canada." Second Lieutenant Waters laughed and sneered.

"Sir, they will rob the *Hannah* close to Circle City and land the gold to transport it by wagons. Is there a map we can look at," and once he found one he proceeded to provide his views on where they were headed?

I might as well not have spoken since everything I said was ignored. I quietly sighed and I did not want to annoy Waters or Dunphy, but his colossal stupidity was astounding. I think the chance to prove himself was his sole objective, but it overtook solid facts. If I raised objections, they might decide to keep me on the boat, and I knew I could help. Waters did not equivocate since he was convinced, but the obvious question is how they would hide their trail when the snow fell? It would be a big arrow saying here we are or every few feet they would sweep the track. Barton is smart and to take the gold on land made no sense unless they want to entice us into a trap? Waters spent the time to review the map and worked on areas of arrival. At West Point, he must have excelled in map training. Part way through Water's lecture Major Dunphy interrupted him.

"We will divide into two sections. I would lead one section with my sergeant major and four of my men." That was a big mistake but remained silent since at least he was on to practical instructions, and not a silly geography lesson of the Yukon River. He finished by telling Jane and me that we would be part of his section. I knew if I went with Waters it would be a short time before I called him an idiot or punched him and that would have me arrested and on the boat.

Why was Jane coming, because I wanted her safe on the ship, and I thought it most inappropriate for a lady to be in danger. I needed to remind the major about the other two men with me.

"Sir, there are two other experienced men with me and could they come along?"

"I will think about that. Second Lieutenant Waters will lead the other patrol with Sergeant Oliver and seven men. They are to stay within a reasonable distance together to maintain lines of communication. If a section finds something, under no circumstances are they to attack, but to find the other one and bring us all together. You can understand that there are strengths in numbers. Are there any questions?" There were none, and we were told to go below and to explain this to the others not present. We were to check our weapons, saddle the horses and eat. As I left, I heard Major Dunphy's loud voice directed at me.

"Show me these other fellows, and I hope they are experienced" I brought him to Bob and Jerome. He ignored Jerome but stared at Bob.

"Robby, I do not believe it. Are you going to build a bridge?" He clapped him on the back.

"Bill, I had no idea you were in the Alaskan Territory. Congratulations on your promotion." I learned they were classmates at West Point, so Bob or Robby was now part of the group. The major smiled at me.

"Bring the other man and both will be in my section." It took me a few minutes before I found Waters and asked if I could speak to him privately. When we were alone, I apologized for my behavior, and he looked at me and said it was about time.

"You are from another country and here at the pleasure of the army so next time, watch yourself."

"Lieutenant, based on my experience we will be in two sections, and we need to keep in communication. Getting shot is bad and if it is by your side it is a tragedy."

"If I wanted your advice, I would ask, but I am not asking now or in the future." I tried not to show emotion, but I knew this cowboy was dangerous now and he would not change. Bob approached and took me by the arm.

"I wanted to say John, how relieved I am to have you safe and do you mind if tag along near you?" I told him that would be an honour and thought he would be much better than that fool Waters. My next question was had he retired from the Army?

"I am not on active service, but I am in the reserves, and I have my commission as a Captain."

"You are not telling me everything."

"Perhaps not, but Special Constable Caldwell, you also hold things back and in time we shall talk and explain our stories," as he smiled and then saluted. That will be an interesting revelation.

I checked the horses, saddled them and checked my weapons and returned for lunch. I must have fallen asleep when Dunphy shook my arm and asked if I wanted to be the lead scout. He said his troops were good soldiers, but not used to being on horses so I asked if Jerome and Captain Innes could ride with me. He laughed and said they can be the next two riders. Jerome came over, and I told him of the plan.

Jane was in an earnest discussion with Bob, and I wanted to listen but needed to stay away. My belief was a review of their earlier instructions and updates. I knew if I approached they would stop or talk about the weather. I moved to the front and found Jerome, and as we talked, the steamer slowed. It was after four, and we were an hour from Circle City. On shore, a couple of men had their hands in the air near overturned bushes and mud tracks. Each had a rifle pointed at the ground, and I eased out my revolver and held it by my side. Perhaps I was jumpy, but my experience with Barton was to expect the unexpected.

The steamer reversed its paddlewheels, and we stopped with the boat tied to trees. Several armed soldiers and sailors checked out the woods as the two men came on board and kept their weapons pointed downwards. They explained they were part of the *Hannah's* crew and were escorted to the dining hall to meet First Lieutenant Cantwell and Major Dunphy. I walked into the hall and sat near Bob, Jane and Waters. The major glanced at me and asked the two men for an explanation. The older man looked at the other one, nodded and started.

"Yesterday a motor launch appeared and kept pace with the *Hannah*. They shot at the pilothouse, so the captain reversed the paddlewheels and brought her to a stop. The motor launch tied up to the *Hannah* and several men came on board, pointed their weapons at passengers and told them to sit." He drank some coffee and continued.

"I heard rifle shots on the baggage deck but did not go down to investigate, and over the next two hours, this gang brought large bundles from the ship to the motor launch. Someone told me the *Hannah* carried a large shipment of gold and I saw their small boat piled high with these bags and they then headed downstream. I learned two crewmen were shot, but are expected to live. Several men were left on board and about four hours later the launch returned to take off more bags and the men." He stopped and asked if we needed more information and Dunphy told him to continue.

"When the motor launch was out of site, the *Hannah* started its engines and resumed travelling downstream. Several of our crew looked for signs where the launch had landed, and after some time I saw an area on the shore with broken twigs, muddy imprints and wagon tracks. I reported to the captain and the boat stopped and we volunteered to go ashore to warn the next steamer to stop." That seemed to be the end of his story, and they were sent below to rest.

Was he a member of the crew or was he left by Barton to make sure we stopped? I was suspicious since this man never looked directly at the major. Had I the only suspicious mind and what did Jane think. I decided to jump in since the two-crew members were out of the room.

"Sir, I still believe the gold stayed on the motor launch, and we will walk into a diversion or a potential trap." Jane gave me a smile, but I did not know if that was for my thoughtful remark or a foolish one. Bob looked interested, but Waters snorted.

"Did you not hear the crew say what happened and are you scared of a few criminals? Or is it your suggestion we give up now and go home with our tails between our legs." This nincompoop officer was not going to stop as I struggled to control myself.

"I am not suggesting we go home, but I do not know if this man is part of Barton's gang, so we need to be careful. I am going to shore, and I will exercise extreme caution, and I suggest you do the same." Waters smiled, but before he spoke, Major Dunphy spoke.

"I want to check this out. Caldwell, you may be correct, but we are going to investigate. Second Lieutenant, this man has experience and will travel with Captain Innes, who fought in Cuba. I will leave it to them to act as they see fit and I suggest you take extreme care. Otherwise, I may ask Captain Innes to lead your section. Do I make myself clear?" Waters stood and said yes sir. I could not have improved on what the Major had said.

It took about two hours to bring the horses, tents and equipment on shore. Once on land, I spoke briefly with Jerome and Bob to warn them that Waters had no experience and was an idiot. Once again, I annoyed Bob with my useless description of a West Point graduate but I was on a war footing, and I did not give a damn about the social niceties. I told him to hold judgment and bet him five dollars that Waters would make a serious blunder. He smirked and took my wager. I told them this might be a trap and to watch out for Jane, and we would proceed slowly and carefully. Jane took me aside and said for me to be careful. I told her she should stay on the steamer, but she narrowed her eyes before she took me on.

"I think not John. I was hired to do a job, and I will finish it, whether it is in accordance with your wishes," as she glared at me and continued.

"If you are correct and this was only a robbery then my time here is finished." I told her I wanted her to stay in the Yukon Territory.

"John, I like you but not now and maybe another time it will be different." I thought she was going to kiss me when she noticed soldiers looking at us. She became serious and told me she would ride with Major Dunphy. Waters rode out at a fast gallop to travel with his section on the left of the trail, while I was to lead on the right side. Our instructions were to stay not too far apart, but good luck on that one since Water's section had already disappeared. I told the major I was ready and planned to go at a slower pace than Waters with my rifle at the ready.

The mission was dangerous and increased the chance of mistaking a friend for an enemy. My section was spread out, and perhaps it would have been better to put Bob as the leader of the other section, but it was too late. It seemed strange to be back as the lead scout in a hostile land. I meant what I said to the major that Barton and Weigand were intelligent and to set a diversion away from the gold robbery would be brilliant. I wondered how many men we followed and what weapons they had in store for us. If they planned this some time ago and if it was a trap we needed to take our time and be cautious.

My horse moved at a slow walk as I took out my field glasses and looked ahead to discover tracks. Did this represent several wagons or was one wagon used multiple times? If they carried heavy loads, then they would become stuck, and I should see evidence of struggles to push them forward but I couldn't see this and reported that to the major, who agreed that this could be a false trail. He told me to continue my searches but it was late, and I was worried. If this was a well-designed plot by Barton, then they might have something devious ahead. My suspicion made me speak, whether Dunphy wanted to hear my fears.

"Sir, we may have an ambush ahead since there are thick woods that could cover dug in trenches. We will need to dismount cover ourselves and advance. As one group moves, the other would cover them." Major Dunphy scowled at me like I was a dunce.

"Caldwell, I thought you had sense so do not let me down. I did this when I served in Cuba and is it your nature to annoy people, or are you even aware of it?" It was time to calm the mess.

"Sorry sir, I was worried and spoke without thinking." I did not know he had been in Cuba, and I overreacted, but I was scared about Jane. Bob tried not to laugh, but that did not last as I heard his loud guffaw. I refused to look at him or join in his merriment since I neither could not shake my fear and did not see any humour in the situation.

Our patrol rode for another hour, and I felt it was time to stop for the night, so I put my hand up. The major rode up, and I suggested we set a defensive position. He snorted and gave me a nasty look, but after he looked at my grave expression he started to laugh.

"We are all young once and with that goes inexperience. I know you mean well Caldwell." I said I could try and find Waters and did he have any idea where they were? The major said he did not and said he was concerned. Bob rode over and whispered.

"It would be unwise to send someone out." He shook his head, reached into his pocket and gave me five dollars. We established a defensive perimeter, put up our tents but did not light fires. Where was Waters section? Was he in trouble and already captured but none of us heard any shots. What a pickle we were in and I had serious concerns about an attack. Six soldiers were in front and in my troubled state it meant Barton would infiltrate at the rear. I heard bushes break and we ran towards the sound. One of the men yelled.

"Halt, who goes there? I had not seen men in that area.

"Lieutenant Waters here."

"Advance to be recognized." Major Dunphy shouted. They walked their horses into the clearing with the last of the daylight now gone. It was a moonlit night, which meant no clouds and frigid cold. Bob and Dunphy quietly talked and when they were finished Major Dunphy announced that fires were permitted and all points of attack would have posted sentries. He took Waters out of our bivouac, and I did not know what they discussed, but my sense was that we would travel in one large section the next day.

With a hot meal, we organized shifts for sentry duties. I heard the major tell Waters he was the duty officer all night. My shift was after midnight, from one to seven, which was fine, since our tent was near the fire. Bob and Jerome shared our tent, which was a mixed blessing since Bob snored, and Jerome kicked. We were up before one and provided coffee and bread before we started our sentry duties. The night was uneventful other than extreme cold. The moon gave a gentle glow on the snow that gave the appearance of thousands of sparkling diamonds.

Morning took us west. I was the front man in the patrol while Waters was at the rear. I slowly rode with my rifle at the ready and checked every bush and tree, but I could not sense a potential threat. The tracks disappeared, along with the signs of wagon wheels, so I dismounted and walked. I became tired from pushing aside brush and branches, and I was thankful that Bob and Jerome covered me. The snow and mud showed that the wagons had turned so I signaled no danger.

Ahead I noticed a slight excavation so I dismounted, I knelt and gradually pushed branches and twigs when I saw an arm, so I dug further and found the rest. I turned him over and saw that he had not been attacked by an animal but had been shot in the chest. He was an Indian and about twenty and I wondered if Barton's men found him and eliminated a witness. Major Dunphy rode up and I told him the tracks stopped, and the wagon or wagons had turned.

"Sir, I found a body and I think someone from Barton's gang killed him to keep the operation secret."

"Caldwell, perhaps someone mistook him for an animal." I needed to refrain from a sarcastic rejoinder and explained our process.

"Give me time to search for an expired round, and I will see the distance to determine if it was an execution or an accident. Hunters always check after they shoot and if it was an accident they would never leave a body." He agreed, so I started my search, while the rest had coffee. Jerome and Bob assisted, and I told them to walk back from the front of the body. Jerome found it in some mud, and the distance from the shell to the body was thirty feet and there was no way it was a mistake, they killed him and left him for the animals. The remnants of the bullet were from a Winchester rifle, which I put in a handkerchief. I knew that the two men we took on board the boat had rifles and one of them could be a Winchester. We put the body on a hors as Dunphy checked his maps, but I did not care where we went since Barton and his gang were gone. Did he take the boat to St. Michaels or Canada? If the gold did not leave the motor launch where would it stop? If I knew that, we could find the stolen bullion.

"We are close to Circle City, so we will continue there to send telegraphs," was the decision from Dunphy. He told Waters to take two men back to the *Nunivak* and to request it proceed to Circle City. I asked the major to keep the two crew who directed us on this trail to remain on the ship as we needed to talk to them. Major Dunphy gave a scornful grimace and shook his head but refrained from calling me hopeless. Jane came over and said I should return to Canada while she would continue to St. Michaels.

"I want to go with you," I said.

"You believe they are heading to Canada and still want to follow me? Follow your hunch and not me, because it is time for you to think like a detective. You need to pursue the gang and not a lady who has no time for you." She saw how that remark affected me.

"At least not right now but maybe we will meet another time and then we can figure out us. I can take care of myself, and I agree that these robbers will return to Canada, but I still need to investigate St. Michaels." I did not say anything and just nodded, but I said I needed to find out her contact.

"If I find something, how can I send you a telegraph?"

"Contact me at Fort St. Michaels where part of the Eighth Infantry Regiment is located. My name will be…" She started to laugh, "Jane Warne or use Captain Raleigh." I wanted to ask if that someone new or was that Bob's real name.

"Can I trust the telegraph operator's confidentiality? Barton knew what you sent." Jane said not to worry as the lines that run from Fort Egbert to Fort St. Michaels are under army control. We looked at each other, and I turned and walked away as I did not want her to see my face.

Barton's gang had backtracked to somewhere near Dawson City. To handle that much gold you needed a big area to hide it and there are countless places to conceal it in the Klondike gold fields. Next season he could ship the gold in sections, but he would need to disguise himself and a few of his senior men and change names. His biggest problem was greed as I remember how fast Eddy Searle removed my money and did not offer a share to McGill. Unless Barton enforced a deadly sense of fear in his men, they might try and steal the gold. The police would place a few informants in Lousetown and evidence of a windfall would lead to a quick capture. Barton had to guard against anyone spending gold. I did not want to leave her and hated the thought of her going through another capture, so maybe Bob could go with her. She was not ready for love, and I did not think that would happen with him. I found Bob and before I spoke he announced,

"I am going to St. Michaels with Jane and I know you have to go back to Canada. Sorry, I cannot continue with you, but it has been fun."

"Bob, take care and guard her as she is important to me." He gave a knowing smile and said he would. Circle City was barely a village since the military post had closed last year. After we had dismounted, I heard the whistle of the *Nunivak*. I was informed that telegraphs were sent to Dawson City, Eagle and St. Michaels. The message was short; no gold was found and to look for a small motor launch. A separate one was to the Northern Transportation Company that asked how much gold was on the *Hannah*? I shook Bob's hand and told him to be careful. Jane and I remained silent for a while.

"There is much I want to say, but I won't. Take care and remember you have a friend who is waiting for you."

"I know John and you also have a lady who will see you again, but I just do not know when, or where." She gave me a hug and said, "Until next time detective," and waved at me as we brought our horses on to the *Nunivak*. When I would see her again was unknown but the desire I had to see her was both strong and certain.

Chapter 17

It was hard to leave Jane but I had to focus on my job. I went to find Major Dunphy because I needed to examine both crewmen and I had yet to explain that Jerome was with the police. I went to First Lieutenant Cantwell to request time to interview the crewmen in custody and to give him the remnants of the expired round. I asked that the two rifles be locked until we were sure if the two men were innocent. He knew I was with the police and this time he was gracious but wanted to know my questions. I told him I needed to find out if they were actual members of the crew and I could do this by questions about their jobs. I asked if I could be alone with each of them, but Cantwell replied not while he was in charge and Major Dunphy would be with me.

"Caldwell, I do not know you, and I do not want to report an unexplained accident to my superiors. We need this information for the judge at Eagle, and your involvement will be acting on behalf of Major Dunphy. Is that clear?" I nodded and followed him into the dining room to see the major seated with a coffee cup in his hand and a cigar in the other. He did not say much other than I would ask the questions and he would take notes. The senior crewmember was brought in. He was about forty, thin and about five foot five inches and had lost most of his teeth. He was not happy and grumbled at me.

"Why am I here?"

"Your name?"

"Smitty."

"Tell me about your job on the *Hannah*?"

"What's it to you, boy." I looked at the major and asked if I could throw him overboard?

"Sure, but make it seem like an accident," so I stood and that stopped his smile, as he examined my size. I pulled him up with my arms, shook him and started to pull him towards the door.

"Sorry sir, I worked in the engine room." I stopped and pulled him back to a chair.

"Tell me the number of boilers on the ship?" There was a pause, and he said two. I asked if he was sure? "No, there might be more."

"How many?" Smitty looked scared as he said he was not sure. My next question as to the name of the captain and he gave the answer of Jones.

"Are you sure, since the company told me it was Captain Macpherson."

"Could be," he replied. This was becoming repetitive, but I tried again, asking the distance the *Hannah* would take to St. Michaels?

"I do not know," was his answer. Finally, I questioned how stupid did he think we were?

"Enough for you to have wasted days wandering through the woods," and on that point, I agreed. I told him we had found a body and I knew American justice would move fast. I looked at him and softly whispered.

"Better do some neck exercises although I doubt that will stop a big snap. On a few occasions, it has taken the head right off so you should hope for that since sometimes you just suffer a slow strangulation." I paused to see his reaction, and that did the trick.

"Do you have a Winchester?"

"No, Keating has one." I would wait to confront him.

"Perhaps if you told us the whole story, it might go better with you."

"I never killed anyone."

"You are part of the same gang, and under the law, those who conspire together have the same sentence."

"Barton will kill me."

"No different than the hangman, you are dead either way." I looked at Major Dunphy who looked interested but remained silent and then started to hum. I liked this officer.

"Who are you," Smitty asked?

"I am your worst nightmare," I responded, "I have chased Barton and Weigand for a long time since they murdered a man in Canada and committed acts of fraud and theft. How long have you worked with Barton?" He sat there but would not look at me. I was about to start to raise my voice but forced myself to stay calm and remembered Jane's advice. This man and his evidence were the first opportunity in this case, but I was in the United States and needed to outsmart him. I gave him a long stare.

"Here is what I am going to do. When we arrive at Eagle, I will telegraph Dawson City to state I was most impressed with a little bird that told me great stories about Barton and Weigand. I will not name you, but I will make sure your description is broadcast. That person is thin, about forty, missing some teeth and has cooperated in providing evidence. I would make sure this information gets out in Lousetown and Dawson City." I paused to ascertain if this was effective before I prodded him some more.

"How many days will you last? Barton has people in the Alaskan Territory, and I am sure he has friends in jail. His people could be anywhere, and he has enough gold to bribe or influence anyone he wants. Not a pretty picture is it Smitty? Barton is not a nice man when he is annoyed, and I bet he will be extremely upset. Barton left me to die and smiled when he told me." Dunphy watched all of this while he continued to hum.

Smitty trembled, his lips quivered, and he tried to see if I was telling the truth, but he learned nothing from my expression. He was worried about Dawson City and Lousetown but not St. Michaels, so that confirmed my theory as to where they sent the gold. I needed to hear some more facts. In a very soft tone of voice, I asked if he wanted some coffee. I watched Major Dunphy, as I told him.

"This officer will do all he can to keep you in a military fort away from the civilian jails." The major nodded his head in agreement since he commanded the fort. Once Smitty had coffee, he started to talk. I knew I could not use this in court since there was a threat but I wanted this information. He explained he was hired in Dawson City last May but California was his home. Smitty said he had joined a freedom army to bring the Yukon Territory to be part of the Alaskan Territory. The name was the Order of the Midnight

Sun, and he was part of an organized force of over one thousand men. The information provided by Barton was they had sophisticated weaponry, including Maxim machine guns and plenty of money.

The first robbery was the *Casca* last July, and since then he was assigned to do work around King Solomon's Dome. He never saw an army, nor did he train with other soldiers. He became suspicious that none existed, but it was too late, and he could not leave. He was warned, like the others, that they knew too much information and Barton would kill anyone who tried to escape. Smitty resigned himself to wait for a time to run and explained the other man was Keating, who was loyal to Barton and leant over to whisper.

"Keating straps a knife to his leg, and I think he still has it unless someone took it." Major Dunphy ran to the door and shouted for me to guard Smitty.

I grabbed my revolver, heard yells and saw a couple of soldiers run past. I told Smitty to hide at the end of the dining room, and I hid behind the door. Someone fired on the deck near me, and Keating ran into the dining room to see Smitty under a table. He pointed his pistol at Smitty and whispered.

"Barton hates a rat, goodbye Smitty," but he had not seen me.

"Drop it," I shouted. Keating turned with his gun, and I shot him in the chest. He fell, and I moved to feel for a pulse, but there was nothing. I was shocked that he was dead because I truly thought he would run or drop the gun. Two soldiers raced in, and I let my weapon fall to the deck and raised my hands. Major Dunphy walked in holding a bleeding arm, followed by Cantwell. I was told to pick up my pistol as the doctor arrived to examine the body. The bullet went into his chest above his heart, and he died instantly. Soldiers removed his body out of the room followed by the doctor and Major Dunphy.

Cantwell remained and I told him what had happened and explained when I see a person with a gun and I tell them to drop it and count one second. If they don't drop it, I shoot at the chest, which was how I was trained. Smitty confirmed this. Cantwell stared at me, and I was not sure he wanted me to remain on his boat. I asked how did Keating get the gun? Cantwell said the soldiers did not search him, but they took away his rifle. He stabbed a sailor to grab his gun and knocked him and went to look for Smitty. I wondered why he was so distrustful of his partner that he wanted him dead but I guess he knew Smitty would talk.

"I am sorry we set the stage for this, but if you had not killed him he would have been tried and hung, so you saved court time," Cantwell said. I hated what I had done and wished Keating could have died without my involvement. I asked if they could send Jerome Scott to me to help me with more questions of the witness and I would pass on any information to the judge. After Cantwell left, Jerome walked into the dining hall, and I explained what had just happened.

"Jerome, help me take notes from this witness," since it is hard to ask a question to a witness and take notes at the same time. I started my next set of questions by my reminder to Smitty that Keating was going to kill him. He did not say anything at first then he thanked me. I came over and sat with him at a table and said he had not finished his story about how they were at the river.

"It started when we took the steamer *Louise* from Dawson City to Eagle. The first part of the plan was to purchase a wagon and four horses and to drive to the area by the Yukon River where the boat stopped. We filled it with rocks and created a trail, and when we finished, we set the horses free and pushed the wagon into the river." He asked for water then explained that their final job was to stand onshore to alert us but they never expected to be asked questions.

"What were you to do next?" Smitty's answer was they were to travel to Circle City and take a steamer back to Dawson City.

"How many men have you seen together with Barton's group," was my next question.

"Not more than twelve."

"Where did Barton put the gold?" Smitty looked at the ground and whispered,

"They took as much gold that could fit on the motor launch."

"Do you know how much gold?" but he did not know, only that the launch left and came back again and he estimated the total time to and from the *Hannah* to be about four hours.

"Where does Barton stay?"

"I do not know since he sends either McGill or Weigand to get us at an abandoned mining camp downstream from Dawson City." I knew from the city was almost fifty miles upstream from Forty Mile and asked if the camp was before or after Forty Mile?

"The camp is thirty miles below Dawson City and near Forty Mile." I now had a general location of the place.

"Where does Eddy Searle stay?"

"I overheard someone mention he lives in Lousetown, so I guess he likes the ladies, but you didn't hear that from me." My next question was the location of the nearest creek to his mining camp? He thought it was next to the cabins and large enough for the motor launch.

"You mentioned you did some work near the Indian River. What did you do?" Smitty did not look worried when he answered.

"We delivered supplies and some gold from the Indian River."

"Did you see Peters and McMillan at the camp?"

"Yes, but how do you know them?" I ignored his question.

"Did you spend time at a mining camp at King Solomon's Dome?"

"I was never there. One time we travelled along a trail near there when McGill and Weigand rode out to meet us."

"Do they cover the launch with branches?" Smitty gave me a stare but did not answer. I had delayed my final question but had to ask it.

"Why did you kill the Indian?" He paused and said he was at the horses when he heard a shot. He grabbed his rifle and ran towards the noise when he saw Keating standing over someone on the ground.

"One less witness was what Keating said. We tried to hide the body but obviously not well enough." Smitty began to cry and said he never wanted to hurt anyone and it was Keating that had killed him. I thanked him and said I would see about some food. Jerome said he would check on that and that I should brief him later as I needed to stay with Smitty. After Smitty ate, two sailors took him to the brig. I know it was not supposed to happen between police and criminals, but I liked him. Sleep overcame me when Jerome woke me and said Major Dunphy wanted to see me and I told Jerome to come with me. The major was on a bed, pale and in pain. He thanked me for my help, and I said it was a great privilege to be with him. Jerome summarized Smitty's evidence and Major Dunphy told us to make sure that evidence was given to the Judge in Eagle.

Our time in Eagle was busy. We found a room and purchased tickets for the next steamer to Dawson City. I told Jerome not to mention any information about Barton's camp as I did not want this information to be revealed to anyone and I did not know if the judge had a big mouth.

I was concerned about the telegraph office since I did not know the operator and whether Barton paid him. My report to the Detachment was, "Arrive next steamer. Report then. Safe." Short and simple and Bert will try and figure what I said. My mind returned to Keating. What is with my useless warnings but at least I was alive. I started to shake, and I was not sure if I could be a detective. Jerome noticed.

"When I first killed, I could not sleep for several nights," he said.

"Why was this shooting different since I killed men during the war and I could deal with that."

"You were at a distance and in war and we both knew that could happen. Here you thought Keating would drop the weapon, but he did not and you had to shoot him." I proceeded to talk it out, and I found Jerome to be a good listener, and he never said a word. We decided to go to the restaurant and have a whisky.

Our final goodbye was at Fort Egbert with Cantwell, Waters and Major Dunphy. It took some time to set out what Smitty said and my showdown with Keating. Dunphy looked a little better as he told us they had received some answers and unfortunately Barton's launch had not been found. The Northern Commercial Company advised that the *Hannah* carried two hundred thousand ounces and the remaining gold on the steamer was only fifty thousand ounces. This information was not for public knowledge since all shipments of gold are kept confidential, but the insurance company will pay a reward of ten thousand dollars for the capture of the criminals.

I estimated the total weight and calculated it was over ninety-three hundred pounds. That was a heavy load for a small launch, and a fortune, since one hundred and fifty thousand ounces was around three million dollars. Problems will start for Barton, whether to sell the gold, or send it, and criminal minds will intermingle with criminal greed. I realized I drifted and turned my attention back to our goodbyes. We told them it had been an honour to work together and they said the same as we shook hands. I reminded them to give the expired round and the Winchester to the judge as evidence. Keating was the murderer, but they might use the noose for Smitty.

The ride on the *Susie* was relaxing as I slept most of the way. I had decided to keep the horses and paid extra for the freight. I made a complete set of notes and compared them with Jerome's. I told him he was a great partner and I would discuss his help with Inspector MacDonald and arrived at Dawson City at ten in the morning. It was time to do a reconnaissance to the west of Dawson City. We would travel towards Forty Mile to find Barton's camp and the creek. I would do it by the rules and regulations of the North West Mounted Police.

I stopped at my office where Matthew showed me an envelope from my mother and inside I found her letter and a cheque from our company for three thousand dollars. With this new deposit, I had over four thousand dollars. At the Detachment, I was directed to Inspector MacDonald's office. Inside I saw the inspector, Bert, Jerome and Grant. Jerome already had provided his report, and it took time for my story. I started with my search at the docks, my capture on the barge, the boat to the camp, escape from the camp and the search with Major Dunphy. They already knew I killed Keating, so I went over the details and what Smitty had told us. Jerome had his notes to corroborate the information, and when I finished, no one asked questions.

Inspector MacDonald broke the silence and asked if I was Irish, as I seemed to have their luck, which was getting quite old and tiresome. He could not understand why Keating had not fired first and I said I thought Keating was surprised. The Inspector grunted something, but I could not hear it. It was time to reveal my plan.

"Barton knows Smitty and Keating have not returned so that he will move his camp and we need to proceed as soon as possible." I heard a snort as the inspector glared at me.

"Caldwell, we can run this Detachment in your absence. What did you think I was doing?" He had worked on orders to assemble a large patrol of twenty men with a wagon and a Maxim machine gun. I asked when could they move and he said they should be able to leave after lunch. He had spoken to a miner who knew the area and agreed to escort them. The inspector expected them to be in position for an attack at dawn.

"Sir," I said, "Can we not borrow the motor launch? When we are near, we could turn off the engine and drift to the other side of the camp where we could land and set up a defensive perimeter on the other side." The three of them discussed this, and after a few minutes I was told if I could get the launch and an operator, it would happen. Only men who served in South Africa would go on the launch, and we could take twelve. I asked if I could go and was told yes. Before I left, I told them Big Pierre has evidence to provide which prompted Inspector MacDonald to roll his eyes.

"We already took care of it, and the judge granted the application. As I said before, we can make decisions without you. Sergeant Raven can explain to you later and get moving." Frederick Wade was found at court and during an adjournment I explained the mission. He scowled at me and asked if his motor launch might be destroyed or damaged. I answered that either could happen and I asked if he wanted to sell it? He gave me a strange look.

"Caldwell, I paid over two thousand dollars to buy and ship that motor launch. However, I was thinking of buying one with a different engine, and it's a good thing you are rich," so I told him I would deliver a cheque that afternoon for fifteen hundred dollars.

"Did you not hear me," Wade curtly said, it was two thousand dollars I paid."

"It is no longer new, and you can afford a better one." He scowled at me but noticed my grin and told me it was seventeen fifty and no less. I nodded, and we had a deal and always remembered what my grandfather taught me, to strive for the middle ground.

" You have a boat, so get moving and in one hour, see me at my office to get the keys." I returned to our building and told Matthew to take a horse and find Sven. Matthew asked did I not know that Sven was in the house?

"Find him and bring him to me." I started to arrange my weapons when I heard Sven. I told him to go to Mr. Wade's office and get the keys to my new boat. I gave him the direction and instructed him to get the motor launch filled with fuel and check it out. Sven gave me a strange look but kept quiet. I told him we might be in danger and he needed weapons and warm clothes. He asked if I wanted to see the motor launch and we agreed to meet at three in the afternoon.

"Pick up more ropes and see if the engine can heat stew and tea since it will be cold tonight." Sven grinned.

"Yes, Captain Caldwell." I met him at the docks, and we checked the boat. The length was twenty-four feet, with the width of fourteen feet. We went on board and attached the extra ropes. I ducked down to examine the bow and observed extra planks for strength. Sven started the engine, and we pulled out upstream to test the maximum revolutions.

The engine ticked over as Sven discussed his inspection and the adjustment of some valves. When the engine was hot enough, we put on the kettle and soon we had hot water for tea. Sven gave me the wheel, and I practiced increasing and decreasing the engine speed to see if there would be problems in landings on shore. We took it back to the dock, and I helped land it. I gave him money to buy extra blankets, tea and food and told him to buy extra ropes to put around the edge of the boat in case someone fell into the water.

"At night time we leave," and asked if he had questions.

"No John, I am glad you are back as I was worried, and once again you head into trouble. Do you ever think of taking a rest?" I smiled and shook my head. As I left, I heard his sigh and saw his sad face examining me and wondered if he knew something I did not but decided not to ask.

Chapter 18

It took a while to obtain maps and information from a miner who knew the area. I ate at the Royal Alexandria hotel, and while there I spoke with a pilot who gave further directions. At seven I met Sven and explained the need for secrecy since we did not want anyone to hear or see us leave, untied the launch and let it drift downstream to Lousetown where we tied it to some trees and returned to the house.

At two in the morning, we walked over the bridge to Lousetown and west to the boat. Grant was already there with his eleven men and told me he would leave Corporal Peterson in charge of the launch when we went ashore. Peterson, who had served in South Africa, was about as tough as they come. The settlement of Forty Mile was about fifty miles from Dawson City, and our objective was the abandoned mining camp thirty miles away. Sven and I agreed we would shut off the engine and drift to our destination in one and a half hours.

As we left Dawson City snow began to cover the launch, and we extinguished all lanterns and other than the sound of the engine, we were almost invisible. The cold had increased, so I distributed blankets and heated up stew and tea. I moved to the front and shifted the men, so they all had time next to the engine heat. At the agreed time, I went to the rear with Sven, and we stopped the engine. The snow ended, and clouds covered the stars while the only sound was the river as I listened for the noise of men or horses. My field glasses scanned the shore to see a few cabins. Smoke escaped from the chimneys, but I did not see anyone outside the cabins. If they stood in the shadows, I hoped they did not observe us. I raised my hand, and several men paddled the boat closer to shore.

I moved to the back again and studied the cabins when I heard an engine's cough and then a steady roar. I told Sven to start our engine when Barton's boat slowly moved out of a side creek. It had several men at the back and was low in the river. I did not think they noticed us and shouted to Sven to increase our speed and ram it. Grant suddenly turned to look at me but kept quiet. I did not want to alert the camp by firing our weapons, nor did I want to lose Barton's boat. Our orders from the inspector were to be near that camp so we could not chase their boat and I wanted it stopped, so this was my way to do it. Our boat picked up speed when men in the other boat saw us and yelled. I shouted to hold on, and we hit it in the middle, and then our bow pushed their boat over. As it slipped into the water, I yelled.

"Throw out the ropes," and ordered Sven to stop the engine and slowly reverse. Their boat sank in less than a minute due to the weight of heavy gold. Several men grabbed the ropes, and I told Sven to go forward. We looked for others in the frigid water and managed to bring four on board. Grant asked how many were in Barton's boat and informed him there were five. One had disappeared into the river or went on shore. We gave our blankets to the survivors, none of whom I recognized and Grant put the prisoners next to the engine heat under guard when suddenly I thought I saw a face disappear and jumped in. The water was so cold I knew I had about a minute and swam downstream to grab the body. I was already losing sensation in my arms when a rope hit me. I grabbed it and we were pulled to the boat and were helped in. When I pulled the body in I assumed I had rescued a corpse but the man threw up water and started to cough and shiver and in the lamp I recognized Robert McGill. Sven helped him to the back and it took a while to warm up and I was given some clothes to change. I knew that I almost drowned, since the water was too cold and thanked my luck.

The boat had slowed and then stopped at the side of the river. A couple of constables grabbed the ropes and climbed the bank. Grant ordered another man to stay on board to guard the prisoners with Peterson. The remainder followed Grant and I asked Sven to check the front of the boat for damage. I waited until he called out it did not leak and told him to stay there as I jumped ashore, found Jerome and asked him to follow me to search the shore. Grant suddenly appeared, and he was not happy.

"I told Peterson to tie them and make them some tea, but were you crazy to ram that boat? You will be fired and the Inspector will convict me."

"It worked," I cheerfully replied. "Besides I bought the boat and the front appears to be strong enough, but I must remember to avoid side collisions. The good news this gang is down five men, but the bad news is that boat carried gold, which is why it sank so fast. I need to check if another man crawled ashore," when I heard his voice say stop. He would not let me escape, and now I was in for a lecture. Grant always had his way with words and this night was no exception. I told him with the weight; that boat would not drift, and we could retrieve the gold next summer. He stared at me.

"This news will hit every bar in town, and someone will get to that boat first." I said we could post guards for the winter and added that the insurance company would probably pay. I heard Grant muttering, why I always had an answer.

"Grant, you did not order Sven to ram the boat. I did." This time I heard even more rude comments.

"I do not want to talk to you until I have calmed down," which I thought prudent. I was having too much fun and would regret it later. How can anyone stomp off in the snow was beyond me while I followed and moved next to him.

"I will take the blame, after all, it was my boat, and I could do with it as I saw fit." I did not think my career was to be a policeman since my ideas conflicted with the North West Mounted Police. I was there to learn to be a detective, if it did not kill me first. I reached Grant in time for his plan.

"Caldwell has volunteered to take the lead." I slowly stepped forward, not wanting to complain or make a noise, and helped by the snow. Fifty yards from the camp I stopped, kneeled and looked around. I took out my field glasses, wiped them and scanned the camp to see around five men with rifles in a circle. One of them spoke, but I could not hear what he was said. I knew they heard the crash on the river, but I did not know if they would conduct a search. Grant had crept to me, so I whispered my observations

"I think they might explore the area. Do you want to go back to the boat, or stay here?" Grant said we would establish a defensive line and if they get too close we will order them to drop their weapons. If they refuse, we shoot them and with that we went back, and Grant relayed this order. I crawled back and used my field glasses but could not see any enemies. My first thought was they were behind me, but then I saw one man next to a cabin. I relaxed, but I was still nervous and wanted this to be over so I could get warm. I was so cold and needed to be near a stove. Why were we out in cold weather without a fire? Great plan I had suggested to the inspector.

After five minutes Grant whispered that everyone was to go back to the boat until just before dawn and the engine could keep us warm. On board, we huddled around the engine and had tea. I was amazed that the engine sound did not carry to the camp or maybe they assumed it was their boat. Just before dawn, we went back on land and again I was chosen to be in the lead. Once I returned to the same spot I saw smoke from the chimneys, but I could not see any sentries in the camp, so we sat and waited. As the sun provided the first light, a machine gun fired, accompanied by rifle shots. Inspector MacDonald yelled to the men in the camp to come out with their hands in the air. I couldn't see movement and I started to wonder what had happened when t shooting began from the cabins. Then more shots were fired at the approaching police. The Maxim had a distinct sound as it raked the cabins and several men ran out of a door towards us.

"Drop your weapons," Grant shouted, but they shot at us and we returned fire. It did not last long with a few riffraff against trained soldiers on the ground with an unobstructed view. Two men raised their hands, and we stood up and moved towards them. Three men lay on frozen snow, and I saw enough blood to assume they were dead. The firing had stopped at the camp, so we checked the bodies on the ground, but they did not need medical care. I went back to examine them and turned one over to find McMillan. I hoped Peters was still alive because we needed his testimony and as we approached the camp, Grant yelled out.

"Corporal Tupper approaching." Inspector MacDonald shouted back to approach. I followed to see one of the men who stood with his hands in the air was Peters, and as soon as he saw me, he shuddered and turned. I knew he was not happy to see his old tormentor. Grant and I searched the cabins and found no other men but an enormous number of bags. I took my knife and slit one bag to see the gold dust that spilled out. Inspector MacDonald found us and asked Grant about his part of the operation, so we went to an empty cabin, and I was permitted to stay. Grant reported the capture of seven men with three killed but no casualties from the police.

"There was a collision between our boat and what Special Constable Caldwell believes to be Barton's launch, which sank with no casualties. Caldwell believes it carried gold and we will need to protect the wreck until next year, but the insurance company may cover that expense." Good job I thought, but I know the Inspector will figure this out.

"A collision, was it? You could not see the other boat because of the poor visibility? I thought our plan was that your little cutter would drift without any noise so why could you not hear the other engine?" My problem was an alert inspector who knew something was not right.

"No sir," I said. "I told the driver to ram the boat as I believed it carried gold and we could not use our weapons, as it would alert Barton's camp. We also could not follow it because we needed to be on the other side of the cabins. I owned the boat, and I made the decision to ram it. Corporal Tupper had no previous knowledge of this, and it happened quickly. The boat sank in about one minute." These facts would come out eventually, so better to get it out now. I watched the inspector look from Grant and back to me.

"I might have known. Caldwell, you have skills as a detective, but as to patience and sober second thoughts, those qualities elude you. You could have lost my men. What were you thinking?"

"Sir, if our boat were damaged, it would take several minutes to sink. We had no weight and were within three feet of shore. The other boat went down right away because it carried a large amount of gold and I felt it was the only way to stop it. I made sure we had extra ropes to rescue the other crew. We have McGill, who is one of the key witnesses in this case. I will resign if that is your wish." That was a lot for him to take in and he stood with a grim expression.

"I do not know what I am to do with you. No one died in the water; we have the gold, which will need guarding, and we have an important witness and no police casualties. I know what Superintendent Wood would say that success is its reward. I cannot make the decision to accept your resignation since it is the superintendent who will make that decision." He looked as if he might shoot me and growled.

"You are totally unpredictable. If I invited you to join my aunt for tea in a fine restaurant with a string orchestra, you would show up with a tart, a bagpiper and offer us gin. I need predictable men under my command, and this does not include you. I preferred the story that you did not see the other boat because of the darkness and snow. To ram another boat at night will make the rounds." I hate bagpipes and gin, and I have yet to meet a tart, but I got his point. I did not comply with the rules, and regulations of the North West Mounted Police but I achieved what we needed, and I said, "Yes sir," and moved away to stand by the stove.

The prisoners from the boat were brought to warm up in one of the cabins, and Grant was ordered to return the launch to Dawson City. My orders were simple, to not to say a word to the driver or anyone else. Ten men were left to guard the gold and I did a quick look in the other buildings. There were at least eighty sacks, but it was not all the gold from the *Hannah*. I knew the sunken motor launch contained a significant amount of gold and I felt there was still more, but the question was where? I found the inspector and asked if the man in charge could estimate the amount of gold and he agreed. The remainder of the men and prisoners went to Dawson City. The Prisoners rode in the wagon escorted by the police on horses.

The motor launch arrived back at Dawson City at noon, and we helped dock and tie it. I took everyone for lunch at the Royal Alexandria Hotel. We took over the conference room where I announced that the food and drinks were on me. Part way through the meal, I had to go my bank and take out more money since the lads were on an expensive tear. I requested a bank draft for Frederick Wade, to be ready at two. The last constable left shortly before two and I sent Sven home since he had started to stagger. I showed up at Mr. Wade's office and handed the cheque to him as he looked at me and asked if I had been out of town, and I said I had.

"Get a bath and shave since you smell like a bush miner who just got to town." I said I was on my way home but wanted to deliver the cheque. I was told to show up tomorrow for the transfer with his admonition to be presentable. The next morning, I was up early to clean my weapons. Out of a sense of caution, I strapped my leg knife, my waist knife and my revolver and reported to the Detachment at eight. I was asked to go the Superintendent's home, and as I stood in the hall, I could hear a discussion. I could not hear Inspector MacDonald, but Superintendent Wood had such a loud voice that I could hear what he said.

"Let me get this correct. You want to fire Caldwell because he is unpredictable but until he came along with his research and ideas, your predictable men had come up with nothing. He came up with evidence of gold sales transferred to money and the evidence to go to court. Next, he followed Barton's men, found Pierre Cloutier, an important witness and cooperated with the United States Army. From that, he found evidence to lead us to the camp with the gold. He suggested the use of a boat to capture the men, which included a key suspect, and you want me to get rid of him?" He cleared his throat and continued.

"Ramming the boat was brilliant. Any good soldier would have done it and look at the results. We have more gold, the destruction of their boat and we hold McGill as a prisoner. Without Caldwell's ideas, none of that would have happened. That boy's antics would make a stuffed parrot laugh. He stays and I am thinking about a commendation. We need more men like him," then told the inspector to bring me in.

The superintendent smiled as he shook my hand. He explained how proud he and Inspector MacDonald were about all I had done to capture Peters and McGill. He was delighted about my discovering the camp, my efforts in the Alaskan Territory and my idea to use the boat.

"Why if I were there I would have rammed that cutter myself. That was brilliant Caldwell. Well done." Inspector MacDonald tried to smile, but he looked dreadful and I preferred his scowl. I said thank you and asked was there was anything else he would like me to do? I was told to take the day to rest, then to work with the inspector and Sergeant Raven to put together the evidence. I returned to my office to find Bert, William, Jerome and Grant. Bert asked if I was still with the police.

"Yes, although Inspector MacDonald wanted to kick me out." Grant asked if Wood liked my ramming the boat and I told him he thought it was brilliant. He looked at Bert and said pay up as they bet on what the superintendent would do and say. I told them I would like to have them for dinner tomorrow night. As they left, Grant and Jerome teased Bert but he said,

"Caldwell will do it again, so next time I will double my bet." After returning to the office, Matthews came in to give me a report on our growing business. He told me he hired a former Australian cowboy and an Irish horse racer. I had seen a couple of strangers and asked if anyone stayed in the barn. Matthew smiled,

"Only the cowboy and horse racer."

"Are you charging rent?" Matthew looked down and said he would split the profits with me.

"William and I own the place, not you."

"I forgot about him, and so I will pay him a third."

"Listen, Matthew, people who work for me live rent free. Give them back their money, and they will help with security, the chores and repairs. Is there anything else I need to know? I need to look at the books to check on income and expenses. If you ever try to make money at my expense again, I will fire you." He was pale and looked at the ground, but he understood.

I went to the boarding house to invite George to dinner, and to the hotel to arrange for meals and a server. At the docks, I searched for a carpenter, and once I found one, I arranged for a crew to bring my boat out of the water and check it for damage and arranged for a place to keep it out of the water this winter.

At the telegraph office, I leaned over the man who worked the telegraph and growled to him that this was a private message and warned him, if I heard he passed on my message, I would return and put him in both freezing rivers.

The message was brief. "Jane Warne. It was only a robbery. Look for poker player and cigar accomplice. Have third in custody. I miss you. Caldwell. A simple telegram would not bring her back. The Order of the Midnight Sun did not exist, except as a front for the real purpose of gold thefts. It was interesting that we both searched at the same time for this bunch of crooks, which had brought us together. I missed her and maybe I should travel to St. Michaels and help with their search but too many reasons stood in the way. Jane did not want my involvement in her life, and she was safe with Bob. I wanted to convict Peters and McGill and required confessions. Now I needed to search for Barton, Weigand and Searle and I had unfinished business here.

After the telegraph office, I focused on how to organize the evidence. We had a lot of witnesses, and the first witness should be Peters. I did not pay attention when I heard a voice that ordered me to walk and not to turn or yell. It was Searle who said he had a gun under his coat, which shocked me so much it drove out my fear. I was furious to be caught by one of the bad guys and of course it was Eddy. We had a long history of encounters and I was not sure why he did this when we had most of his gang and the launch. Was it revenge or just plain mischief and I knew I would have to find out the hard way since with Eddy, there was no easy way.

CHAPTER 19

Searle told me to walk to the far end of the docks.

"I thought your gang had left the Yukon Territory?" He did not say anything.

"Eddy, there are no barges and I sunk Barton's boat. What are you going to do with me?"

"Shut up and keep walking." The last shed at the east end of Dawson City faced me. Searle looked around to check that we were alone. What a morning with the end of the mining season and not a person in sight. The door was kicked open and I was shoved in. He told me to open my jacket and sneered.

"You never change, drop the knife and revolver."

"The last time it was a bayonet. Could you return them when you are finished? They cost money, and you still owe me the one hundred dollars you stole on the barge. Why are you doing this?" Our ritual was I asked questions, and he ignored them and today was no exception. He told me to stand away as he picked up my weapons then turned and walked out of the shed. Before he left, he said he would be back. The door slammed shut, and I heard a metallic sound, which I assumed to be a lock on the outside. There were cracks between the boards and some light entered. I kneeled and extracted my leg knife. I may be predictable but so is Searle who did not check my legs and I was getting tired of replacing my weapons and now he owed me over fifty dollars for my weapons.

How soon would Bert or Jerome realize I was gone? Big Pierre, George and Mrs. Rivest were also at risk as witnesses. I walked around the shed and over to the door. The lock was outside, but the door hinges were on the inside, so I bent down and examined the screw head. I used the end of my knife to start to turn one, but they were frozen, and I worried that they might break. Carefully I worked at the bottom three screws. My next challenge was the top three ones, but my height helped, and they came out.

My final test was the center hinge. I managed one screw but the second one broke, and I was lucky with the third one, and it came out. I started to pull at the door, to twist and shove it and it came loose in sections. I held my knife as I looked out, but no one was in view. My knife was ready to throw as I slowly stepped out and found I had clenched my teeth I was so angry. If Searle was there I might have killed him and damn any consequences. Snow fell as I walked up to Second Avenue and I started to calm my injured pride and to think. We needed to protect our witnesses and to find Searle, and once again I needed more weapons. If we were fast, we could place police around the shed to wait for Searle. The general store was near to buy another revolver and knife. The owner sniggered and asked me why I kept losing them. My look was not friendly as I ignored him and paid. Bert's office was my next stop and saw him in a review of some papers.

"Searle kidnapped me, and we need to guard our witnesses and see if we can capture him," as Bert asked if that was a joke.

"I wish that it was. We need to move fast, and I have now spent another fifty dollars on replacement weapons. Perhaps I should take out an insurance policy." I explained Bert what happened near the telegraph office, my imprisonment in the shed and my I escape.

"Inspector MacDonald was correct, you do have the luck."

"What about skill" but Bert just laughed and sent police for Big Pierre to the Majestic Hotel and Mrs. Rivest's boarding house. I led three constables down to the dock to set a trap.

Waiting was hard, and the cold weather made it difficult to stand. We agreed to move further away so we could move around but after three hours, we gave up and headed to the Detachment. They brought in George Martin and Mrs. Rivest but not Big Pierre remained missing. I told them to check the Mining Recorder's Office where he was found and brought to safety. A patrol was sent to check sheds at the dock while another one was sent to search Lousetown.

I went with Jerome to my house to interview the Australian cowboy and the Irish horse rider. Once there I asked Sven to grab some rifles and meet me in the barn. I told them that I did not know these two men and I needed to be satisfied they were not part of Barton's gang. The first one I wanted to interview was the Irish fellow. My memory of stories from our Irish stable hand in King City of the tricks used at Dublin races would be useful. We went to the barn and found the Irishman. He was tiny, about five foot four, thin, with wavy blond hair and a long, cauliflower nose. His name was Patrick who nervously watched our rifles.

"Tell me about the tricks used in horse racing in Dublin." He said he could not. It is easy to disprove a liar when you have right questions.

"Why not?"

"My horse racing was in Cork, in the west of Ireland and I never raced in Dublin." After some more discussions, I realized he was not a threat to me or to someone trying to break in, so we went to the Australian. He had his equipment and yelled,

"Thanks for the bunk," as he ran towards the gate. I told Frank to be careful since some enemies might try and kill or capture me. He laughed and brought out his cousin who he said was a good hunter.

"Frank, when were you going to tell me this?" He shrugged his shoulders and smiled.

"How much do I pay you?" He reminded me that it was five dollars a month so I said I would pay the same for his cousin. I suggested he keep Ben and Lucky outside as much as possible. I asked the cousin's name who answered, "Joseph." What a biblical family and they need to keep the missionaries at a distance.

No one notices the Indians in Dawson City, and they are borderline invisible. There are places they cannot go, but in the streets and alleyways they can watch and follow. I needed shadows to pursue Barton's people, so I told Frank to find some of his friends to protect me as I walked around the city. He also needed to find guards for the house, and I would also pay them. I emphasized that under no circumstances were they to hurt anyone and they were to call me if they saw someone that looked suspicious.

What a strange and peculiar day. To be imprisoned and escape was upsetting but why did they want me? It made no sense since the police captured most of Barton's men, the gold and others could seal the fate of the gang without me. Searle wanted me, but for what purpose? I took Jerome to the store to purchase more rifles and ammunition. We took them back to the house, and I left two in the dining room and gave the other two to Frank and Joseph. I asked Patrick if he knew how to use a rifle.

"No, but I have my methods," as he took out a large knife.

"This is my way to handle situations because betting on horses creates problems." I had underestimated him. Jerome and I walked and discussed potential threats and checked each street. As we approached the Detachment, I noticed an Indian with Frank, and I felt better with my protectors. I met with Bert and Inspector MacDonald in his office.

"How did you manage to be captured and escape in the morning and could you try to stay out of trouble, for at least one day?" His sarcasm had improved, and I knew he did not want an answer but appeared concerned.

"Do you know why they still want to capture you," asked the inspector? I said I did not know, but it worried me.

"I have the same fears, and I need you for the trial. I have a telegraph from Major Dunphy of the United States Infantry in Eagle. He praised you as essential in solving the robbery on the *Hannah*, and they are prepared to bring a witness named Smitty here if he will not be charged under Canadian law. He will face a trial in Eagle, and they require you as a witness. Superintendent Wood, Sergeant Raven and this major have a high opinion of you, so why am I the only one who does not share that view?" I wisely kept my mouth closed. I liked the Inspector, but his problem was not seeing the bigger picture. His focus is on my minor mistakes and not my contributions.

"Sir", I asked, "Do you agree with the proposal from Major Dunphy?" He said he wanted to hear from me and I knew he had some of these facts as I set out a summary of Smitty's and my evidence. I emphasized this was all required for a conviction. The inspector looked at Bert,

"You agree," so a message was sent that consented to the major's proposal.

"Next, I need you both to interview Peters. My notes show that Caldwell has done that before," and then he remembered and scowled at me.

"Could you kindly do it this time without scaring him half to death." This time he smiled so I gave him my most innocent look and said of course. I added that we needed to review the evidence of Pierre Cloutier, Mrs. Rivest and George Martin before we speak to McGill. We had the Court Order and the evidence from the mining recorder and gold commissioner's office. I suggested we wait until Smitty provided his testimony, so each day McGill will sit in his cell without any communication until we talked to him. My final suggestion was to erect the hangman's scaffold in view of his window, which was received without comment. The inspector shook his head, sighed, and suggested we had work to do. Once we left, Bert's gave me a mournful stare.

"Is it humanly possible for you not to upset the inspector? He will not admit it, but I sense he appreciates your intelligence and ideas, but he hates surprises and the macabre and evil approach you bring to police work. Your actions or the inability to think first drives him up a wall, which results in extra pressure on me. His irritation is now entrenched and he arrives annoyed each day, compliments of a special constable who bloody well knows better. Do you understand?" Even Bert had reached his limits with me.

"Yes, Sergeant, I understand." We went back to Bert's office and made notes for the witness questions. As he explained, the more proven facts you have in your question to a witness, the more likely they will acknowledge and agree. We divided the issues and worked until five. I asked Bert if we could bring George Martin to the dinner, but Bert said if something went wrong, Inspector MacDonald would kick his ass across the parade square, so George would remain at the Detachment. I was instructed to wait for Jerome to walk me back to my home.

"John, exercise extreme caution now and no foolhardy steps or chasing after someone. Ignore your gut feeling and think first."

"I always think first, but some events occur that are out of my control."

"Give that a rest. You will not do anything without Jerome next to you and when in doubt do not do anything and that is an order." I would have saluted, but I was not in uniform.

"Yes, Sergeant." I would give it my best effort if I could. Jerome and I headed home and at a distance I saw Frank's friend, or was it his brother or cousin? I trusted Frank and knew he would not let me down. At the house, I asked Frank if his friends had seen anything and he told me he had three in a team to check the streets.

"Thomas and John observed a man who followed you on the next street and Sam is watching him." I thanked him and saw Joseph and Patrick in conversation and asked if they had seen Matthew, but they shook their heads. Where was he and why had he disappeared. Except for George, my rescuers were at the party. After the first drink, I saw Frank motion for me.

"Two men are watching the house so follow me over the fence." Sven, Jerome, Grant and I took the rifles and headed to the side door. I requested William and Bert to watch the house. Joseph and Patrick were in the shadows as we followed Frank over the fence and went a long way around the block. We slowly walked up to the two men who stood in the shadow, and one turned to look at me.

"Hello John, I did not mean to interrupt your party since you seem to have matters under control." It was James Riley.

"How are my friends in St. Michaels?"

"They are still there, and Jane thanks you for the message," he replied.

"James, unless you think you can catch Barton's gang tonight, come in and join my dinner." He turned, spoke to another man and then said they would. He introduced his partner, Philip Fuller, who looked like a boxer as he had a tough look and was my size. I was glad he was a friend and not an enemy and as we walked to the house, James gave a history of his trip. It was a trail that led back to San Francisco in pursuit of Barton's money. James, Philip and Jane were Pinkerton agents, but he was not authorized to tell me about Bob, other than he was not with their agency. Their evidence concluded that the Order of the Midnight Sun did not exist and had issued their report to their client, but he was not authorized to tell me the name. I asked why he was outside watching my house.

"I did not appreciate Barton kidnapping my friend," so James was up to date. I asked if they wanted to stay at the house and they agreed. With drinks and food, it took time to tell my story and at the end, James said if I wanted a job with Pinkerton's, I could join. I said not now, but maybe someday. I asked if he was to return as a land surveyor, but he told me he would leave soon and for me to rent out the office. At ten we started a poker game. I held a winning hand when Patrick called me, while everyone stopped to listen.

"Joseph is over the fence, and Frank is waiting for you." Bert looked at me and told me to stay, and he would go to the Detachment to bring a patrol. As soon as he left, I asked who wanted to join me, and everyone stood. I told William to stay and Jerome told me to also to remain until the patrol returned. Grant remained quiet; I knew he loved police work and a sergeant had given an order. Jerome looked torn, but I looked at him and said he was my guard so get moving. We took four rifles and revolvers and once over the fence, Frank whispered, "Three men are on the next block watching your house." I told Frank to stay with Patrick and walked with my guests behind me. We went on a side street and circled around. They did not see us, as they were too preoccupied surveying my house. The correct method to remove potential threats was to place men in support and on the other side. At night, the chance to injure your own was possible, but we would try this, brought our rifles to our chests and moved slowly towards them. There was not much light, and we hoped they would not notice us. When we were about thirty feet from them, one looked at us, and Grant shouted.

"Put down your weapons." They started to shoot so we returned fire, and all three fell. Sven grabbed his arm and said he was hit. Once we arrived, Grant pushed them with his boot and two remained still, but the third man clutched his arm. I went closer wishing it was Searle, but it was a stranger. They were stupid or desperate, as a rifle is deadly at thirty-foot range, but a pistol is not and what had caused them to resist? Bert ran towards us with a patrol of five police, and he looked unhappy.

"Sergeant, we captured a suspect who may lead us to Barton," I said.

"I really don't care and this might be your last day as a special constable." He looked at Grant, then Jerome.

"You both are also in trouble." I told Bert I needed to talk to him once I checked on Sven. I walked back to Bert and explained that we had the advantage, and if the situation were different, we would have waited.

"We were six to three, and they did not see us. My big fear was they would notice the patrol's arrival and run." I looked at Bert's face and continued.

"It was important to capture a new prisoner who spied on my house. Jerome and Grant told me to stay, but I decided to leave, which forced them to come with me. Bert, you know me, I cannot be on the defensive, and I need to seek these people out." The darkness made it hard to gauge Bert's expression.

"John, unfortunately, I do know you, and I give up. I gave you a direct order, which you disobeyed, and you continue to ignore the danger. I do not know your family, so to send a message that you were killed will be easier, but it still will be hard on me so stop these foolish risks."

"I took a calculated risk, but the odds were in our favour." I was not sure what he muttered but it sounded like having as much sense as a mad hatter. I decided my best solution was to remain silent. Our little skirmish broke up the party, and we needed to bring Sven and the prisoner to the hospital. The unknown gang member was now under an armed guard. Bert and Grant filed their report to the officer in charge, and it was two hours before we helped Sven home.

We took turns on watch and the remainder of the night was quiet. I believe we had broken up most of Barton's gang but Searle was still at large, and there might be more in the area. Until we had them all, I had to remain cautious. That meant extra men at the house and employing Frank's extended family. It would cost extra money, but I could afford it and if the choice was death, or spending a few extra dollars, I had the money. After breakfast, Jerome and I went to the Detachment to see Bert. As I walked into his office, Bert asked Jerome to wait outside and closed the door.

"There was a time when my meetings with the inspector were routine, and he never raised his voice. Since you arrived, he has changed to the point I no longer want to meet with him. This morning he told me he did not want to hear you tempting death, and I was not to mention you unless it was a life or death emergency. The inspector is resigned to your actions, and his only request to me was for you to get the suspect to talk, and to try not to kill him since we need his evidence. John, I am tired of warning you. Be patient and wait to request assistance since you are not alone." I sat silent and realized I created these problems but questioned if I could ever change. Bert stood up and said now to business.

"We have a report on an estimate of gold in their camp. It was twenty thousand ounces or about four hundred thousand dollars." I suggested the owners of the *Casca*, and the *Hannah* should be notified of this as soon as possible. Grant said there was one more thing to do which was to interview our new prisoner from last night. He said he heard I was holding a winning hand in poker when the trouble began.

"Grant the pot was ten dollars and I had a full house."

"Well perhaps you get the honour to prod him, but please keep it gentle because he is our witness and not your favorite punch bag. Do you understand?" I nodded and went into the prisoner's area and asked the guard to let me in and for him to go for a smoke. The prisoner's cell was dark and forbidding as I entered, only to hear an unwelcome greeting.

"I don't talk to police so get the hell out of here." I was not wearing a uniform, but he recognized me from last night, and I was sure he knew why I was there. His problems were his confinement, my size and attitude. I was tired, grumpy and annoyed to be spied on during my party and wanted revenge. He was small with a shallow face, narrow eyes and compressed lips. I kept quiet as I slowly moved up to stand over him. I silently grabbed his injured arm and squeezed it which resulted in a scream.

"Help me; this man is crazy." The cells remained silent as I dropped his arm.

"The guard is out so let us begin again, shall we? My name is Special Constable Caldwell and your gang kidnapped me, hunted me, shot at me, and wounded my friend. You followed me, watched my home last night and interrupted my dinner party when I had a winning hand in poker. Congratulations, you have achieved your worst nightmare, sitting next to your enemy in a solitary cell distant from anyone who could listen." I could barely see him since he had scampered to the far side of his bunk.

"How is the arm? Would you like me to work on it some more, or are we ready to talk?" He peaked out at me but did not speak. We were like a weasel and a little mouse as I bent over the bunk to reach for his arm.

"My name is Thomas Burke and don't touch it, please."

"Are you going to answer my questions?" He nodded so fast I thought his head would fall off.

"Bert," I shouted, "I believe we are ready." Two chairs were brought in with a lamp. We settled down with pad and pens to extract as much information as we could, while he was eager to talk. I hoped he would not speak to lawyer since I had threatened him and his confession would be thrown out.

"Why did Searle kidnap me? Was it to obtain more information and to keep me to provide testimony?" I did not expect his reaction.

"You do not know, do you?"

"Know what?" Burke grinned at me.

"Robert McGill is Weigand's brother-in-law. Weigand's wife adores her baby brother Robert. If you think Weigand is tough, you should see Kitty, and if anything happened to McGill, God help Weigand. He wanted to exchange you for McGill." That startled me.

"You have to be joking. The North West Mounted Police have a prisoner, who I expect will be charged with murder, robbery, kidnapping and fraud. That would not happen. The Superintendent would write a nice letter to my next of kin but they would not exchange a lowly special constable for a prisoner who committed capital offences. Weigand has to give his head a shake, but he must be scared."

"Oh, that he is," Burke admitted. "I thought it was a stupid idea but kept my mouth shut." He explained that he was one of the few men recruited from San Francisco. He knew Kitty and said her mom was even tougher.

"That old witch is mean. They are an old time criminal family and Kitty's brothers are even tougher." The purpose was always to steal gold and the Order of the Midnight Sun was invented to obtain money and recruits. The image was to raise finances for a new American republic, like Texas and it had worked until now. I asked him where was the gold, which silenced him.

"Are you aware we captured your camp, took the gold left in the cabins and sank Barton's boat? My estimate was it carried a full load of gold." I waited for his response, but he sat there and said nothing and my impression was he was debating how much to reveal.

"Which boat?" he finally responded. That astounded me, since I always assumed there was just one boat. His answer took me back to the time when I interviewed Smitty on the *Nunivak*. He told me the launch left the *Hannah* and later came back some four hours later. When I asked him about covering the boat with branches, he did not answer so I assumed they took the gold and buried it, but I was wrong. They had placed half the gold on another launch.

"Do you know where the other launch is?"

"Ask Weigand or his brother-in-law, McGill. I am just the hired hand that follows orders, but those two know the location of the boat since it has plenty of gold." He looked nervous and said he would tell us something, but we could not repeat it.

"McGill drove the boat that we sank, but the driver of the other boat is a man named Victor, who scares the hell out of me. He is Weigand's bodyguard and learned his tricks in Russia with the secret police. He likes to torture his victims, so stay away from him."

"Where are Barton and Weigand?" Burke said he did not know where Barton was but he believed he was out of the Yukon Territory.

"He may be in Skagway or St. Michaels. I expect once he has more money and gold, he will head south." He looked at the floor and then at Bert but never looked at me.

"Weigand is still around here. Eddy Searle knows where he is so if you find Eddy, he will lead you to Weigand. I know Weigand will hang around Dawson City to get McGill out of jail. He will not go home to face his wife and her bloodthirsty family. If he returns home without McGill, he will be like a rabbit in a dog kennel." Burke looked nervous as we took turns taking notes.

"How do we find Searle?" I asked.

"If you find him, he will know I talked, and he will kill me." Bert said we would keep him in separate cells.

"No, Eddy will let everyone know, and that is my death sentence, and I will never get out of here." I told him about the statements from Smitty and Peters and I reviewed the evidence from Big Pierre and George Martin.

"We want to know who killed Albert James? We found his body in a tunnel on McGill's claims, at King Solomon's Dome." Burke said he would not talk unless we agreed not to charge him with murder. Any murder is a capital offence, so if convicted, you had a date with a hangman. Bert said he needed to speak to his superiors and I needed to talk to Peters as to what he knew of Burke. We agreed to end the session, and I gave Burke a long look as I left but he had already avoided me and I needed him to worry. I needed to talk to Frederick Wade about conspiracy and intent to murder, and I knew the act was specific to those who did it. We brought in Peters who told us the same set of facts. I offered him a cigarette since I needed to overcome my previous session with him at George's camp. Peters looked curious and asked if we had found all the gold. He started to smile as I looked at him and he shrugged.

"Was he asked about the other boat?" He laughed and continued,

"Do you know how proud Barton was of them? They cost a lot of money, and I would hate to see him when he learned you sank the one that carried the gold. The other boat is hidden, but not too far from the mining camp. The persons who know the location are Weigand and Victor but McGill might know as well. Stay away from Victor. If you think Weigand is dangerous, Victor is far worse. Burton is long gone from here and they never informed us of the location of the gold, since they knew we were too greedy."

We now had sufficient evidence for charges against Peters, Burke and McGill. There was also possession of stolen property for the prisoners captured at Barton's camp, but we had nothing for murder. I kept thinking about Albert James. There were two aspects to a murder charge. If he was killed in Dawson City and moved to the tunnel, we may have a witness. However, if he died in the mineshaft, we need to find out who was there at the time. Ownership of a mining claim was not enough and we needed a witness who could talk and was still alive.

CHAPTER 20

Eddy Searle lived in Lousetown, a mean, rough and nasty place. He had made a huge mistake by locking me in a shed and I wanted revenge. Matthew Talbot's disappearance also upset me, since Dawson City remained dangerous with Barton's hired thugs in pursuit and they could have my clerk as a hostage. I brought Sven since Jerome needed to rest. Sven's trigger hand worked, and he was delighted to accompany me. I did not know if it was the danger or the ladies, but I refrained from enquiring.

Before we started, I visited Bert to ask for help to search for Searle. The problem was the police only had a rough sketch and a general description. I told Bert that Matthew had disappeared and I would search for both. His sigh could be heard out of his office as he gave me the evil eye and ordered Jerome to accompany me. We crossed the bridge to Lousetown and at ten in the morning in October could bring snow or the sunshine but now it was clear and cold. Our plan was to check both hotels and bars and the bars were not a problem since they all used my escort service and were happy to see me. The delicate issue was the early morning activity in the hotels by enterprising ladies. They were friendly enough, but their clients would not like to see them, since it would be embarrassing to encounter a Member of the Territorial Council, a lawyer or a judge. The proprietors were also a problem since this was a good source of revenue and they made it difficult for us to conduct searches, since we did not have a warrant and we had no reasonable grounds to obtain one. As they say in court, we were on a fishing expedition, hoping to find someone or something.

Miss Agnelli owned a modest small house in a back street. She opened the curtains, smiled and invited us in. She was about forty with a black wig, flushed cheeks, and large full lips and her questions were with an accent.

"It is John, is it not?" "How tall you are and so handsome and who are these fellows? You must return tonight for my special show since the girls would love to see you." She took us into a parlour and served us tea and biscuits when Sven figured her accent and spoke to her in Italian. I listened but could not understand but recognized the names of Searle and Weigand. Miss Agnelli became suddenly serious.

"Your friend asked about Eddy and Dalton. They never are permitted in my house since I have a good reputation and deal only with gentlemen. I am sorry, but those two are fit for a garbage wagon and should crawl back to where they came. Victor and Eddy like the ladies, so hang around our houses here and follow them. If you survive an encounter with Victor he will lead you to Dalton. Your clerk Matthew is at a restaurant near here and is so sweet. Let the poor boy continue his sleep since his heart was broken." It was a relief he was alive but how did she know Weigand's and Searle's first names if they never were in her house? And how did she know I employed Mathew unless he talked more than he should. She was someone I should cultivate as a source of information and her friendly demeanor masked a more interesting background.

By noon we were hungry and went to a restaurant near her establishment, and as we sat, I noticed a body on the ground next to the bar. I stood up, but the bartender said, let him sleep, so I looked down to discover Mathew and asked the barkeeper how long he had been there.

"Since late last night. He kept crying about his sweetheart named Louise but then I noticed her boyfriend at the door, so I hid him. That man is huge and mean, and I did not want my place ruined. Do you know how difficult it is to clean up blood?" We found a wagon and as we drove I thought of the name Louise and why was it familiar. I remembered the time I bailed Matthew out of jail, and then that name came to me. He was in love with Louise, and her big boyfriend was the one who hurt him, but there was something else that bothered me about that name. We carried him into my home, and as I made coffee, I saw movement. Matthew looked at me and asked if I had fired him and I told him I had not yet decided.

"Where have you been? You disappeared two days ago, and I assumed you were dead." Matthew looked at the floor.

"Two days ago, a lady friend met me at the office and asked for my help. I told her I loved her, but she said her heart was with another man. She heard I worked with a detective and requested I look for her missing boyfriend and she gave me his description." He stopped and took some water.

"I take it her name was Louise?"

"Yes, how did you know?"

"Mathew," I answered, "You told me her name when I hired you in jail."

"I should have asked you, but I knew you would not let me do it, so I left without informing you. I spent the next day in search for him in Dawson City in the bars, hotels and the hospital. Next, I went to Lousetown and two things happened. I saw Louise again, fell apart and started to drink. When you hired me, you knew that there was a big fellow who liked Louise and seriously hurt me, just for talking to her. Yesterday he saw me with her, waited, followed me and threatened to kill me, but someone stopped him." I thought I had the connection but asked anyway,

"What was the name of Louise's boyfriend?"

"An American named Albert James."

"Can you describe the fellow who attacked you when you were around Louise?" Mathew stared at me.

"He has an accent, is about your size and height, and is clean-shaven with a short haircut. His face is quite dark and has a big nose."

"Is his name Victor?" He looked surprised and nodded.

"How do you know that as well?" I told him to eat and sleep, but I needed him to tell me where Louise worked since we needed to protect her and gave the location of her restaurant. I called Sven and said we were going to the Detachment. I knew two things we needed to do and fast. There was only one bridge to Lousetown, and a patrol could be stationed at the bridge to check for persons leaving. We needed to take Louise into protective custody and to interview her. Our assumption was the Order of the Midnight Sun murdered Albert James to prevent him from talking, but these facts proved we were wrong. The motives for my case were fraud and theft, but this cause was unexpected. It was Victor's jealousy that caused Albert James death, and I was not sure if Weigand knew this.

Bert and Inspector MacDonald heard my evidence. Victor was always with Weigand, including Barton's camp near Eagle and we had the love letter from Louise to Albert James. We had similar fact evidence, since Victor's had threatened to kill Matthew. Inspector MacDonald had the power of a Justice of the Police and based on my story he granted a search warrant. He ordered Jerome and ten men to Lousetown and I decided to go with them while other patrols would watch the bridge and the docks. Jerome and I were to find and bring Louise to the Detachment.

As I left the Detachment, I asked Sven to come. After the last few incidents, I now took precautions. I knew I should wait for the patrol to accompany us but I worried for Louise. Matthew had told me the name of her restaurant was the Gold Nugget. My problem was I was the only one who could recognize Victor and Weigand so if they saw me, they would either disappear or kill me. Mathew told me Victor was insanely jealous of Louise, who could not stand him. Another risk was he was unpredictable and dangerous. I decided we should at least check out the restaurant since it was daytime and then we could wait for the patrol. The restaurant had few customers as I asked the manager to see Louise and the lady behind the counter sighed.

"I am very anxious about her since she did not show up for work this morning, which is most unusual." Jerome was in uniform as I showed my North West Mounted Police identification. The lady looked even more worried as she gave us the address for Louise. She asked about the tall fellow who had been there a few minutes earlier, but I said I did not know him. Outside Jerome suggested we wait until the police arrived and for once I thought about my talk with Bert.

"If we waited, she could be killed or captured." Jerome gave me a long stare and shook his head.

"Caldwell, I long ago repaid my debt to you and you will take me to an early grave." I heard him mutter I would get him fired. It was about ten minutes when we arrived at her boarding house.

"We need to carry out a reconnaissance around the building." Sven kept grinning as he looked at Jerome's face but remained quiet. We were close to the building when I noticed Matthew. He had brought two of my rifles, and next to him were James Riley and Philip Fuller, both armed with rifles. I told Matthew to sit and not follow us. I took one Winchester and gave the other one to Jerome. Sven would use his revolver. It was a two-story log house. James and Philip went to the back while Jerome, Sven and I went to the front door. I listened but heard nothing as I led the way and checked each room on the main floor. I knew that once we started up the stairs, we would make a noise but after a quick search, there was no point, she was gone. As we left, I spotted Matthew in tears. I went over and told him I did not need another distraction and told him to return home, and I would let him know as soon as we had news.

We started to ask questions in nearby buildings. Two buildings down, an old miner told me that he had trouble sleeping and heard a girl crying for help, but did not hear anything else. He had gone to his window and saw a big man, struggling with a girl and heading south. He did not know what to do and knew that he would have to find a constable, but at that time of night, it could take a while, so he returned to his bed.

A primary suspect and a key witness had disappeared so could this case get any worse? The police would check steamers and soon the last one would stop for the winter and unless we caught them, they would be trapped here. It would take time and we would find the last of this gang but would Louise still be alive? As we headed into the downtown part of Lousetown, I saw the patrol. Grant was in the lead as we ran up and explained the situation. Grant said they worked in two teams of four constables each and gave me a grave look before he spoke.

"If you continue with your search be careful, since you are not part of my patrol, and you have civilians with you." I told him we would be careful and at that remark he chuckled, shook his head and walked away with his patrol. I turned to our group.

"Weigand will not wait for a search. He is smart and will do something not expected, so we should check the river for the second launch. If we see

Weigand and Victor, they will have Louise. I need to distract them so when I fall to the ground, fire at the boat as we need to stop the launch entering the river." I wondered what possessed me to offer that plan because that had all the ingredients for a disaster. I waited for someone to talk me out of it but they looked away or at the ground. Sven smiled and then winked. I guess in the French Foreign Legion they did this all the time but it was a first for me.

We walked to where the Klondike and Yukon Rivers join and on the left side, a steep hill stretched down to the Klondike River. There were large clumps of evergreen trees, which gave partial cover. We moved to take cover behind some rocks and trees. I took out my field glasses and looked to the rivers. Weigand and a woman with blond hair walked towards the Yukon River. He held her to his chest and on their right, I spotted Victor who removed lumber and bushes from a launch. My suspicion was the boat contained the remaining gold, and it seemed to be frozen on the ice since Victor pushed and rocked it. The boat began to move towards the water, so we did not have much time since the Yukon River was still open and it was an escape route to the Alaskan Territory.

"It's them," I whispered. "Weigand is holding Louise and on the right Victor is moving the launch. I need to bring Weigand and Louise away from the boat to prevent them from entering it when it is in the water. I will slowly walk to speak to Weigand, if Sven and Jerome cover me. James and Philip, wait until I drop down, and shoot at the boat. Is that clear?"

Jerome said it was too dangerous and I agreed, but what choice did we have. That girl was in their control, which meant we were limited in what we could do. I told them to try and stay hidden, or otherwise things will be risky, or worse. I gave my rifle to Jerome, and I moved my knife to rest on my back. I raised my hands as I came out of the clump of trees. Weigand saw me first and pointed his rifle. I yelled if we could talk as I had information for them. Victor shook his head, and I knew he did not like this. I could not hear their discussion, but I noticed Louise watched me and gave a small smile.

"Caldwell, I am astounded that you still are after me. You are the most persistent fool who once again interferes with my profits. Turn around, or I will kill you. Now go." I tried to smile and said I had news he needed to hear and I was unarmed. I was surprised what he next said.

"You can come within ten feet and stop. Open your coat so I can see if you have any weapons," but he kept looking behind me as I opened my coat.

"Weigand, I will slowly drop my revolver, and I will take it out with my finger on the trigger guard, nice and slow." I managed to perform this trick without being shot and started to move to the left of the boat. Victor took out his pistol and pointed it at me as Weigand stood and watched. I stopped about twenty feet from the boat. The breeze blew snow into my face as Weigand dragged Louise and came closer with his revolver aimed at my chest. Victor moved with him, still holding his gun at me. If anything went wrong, they had me in range so I had to trust nothing would happen.

"You are smart," I whispered, and Weigand moved closer.

"Speak louder," he ordered but moved again, slightly nearer. Victor followed, and I preferred his weapon further away, but this was my plan.

"Weigand, I admire what you have accomplished, the gold robberies, transferring money and…"

"What information do you have?" snapped Weigand. I continued, although I seriously questioned my plan. Was I about to be shot since I knew Weigand wanted me dead and Victor was insane.

"In Canada, four convictions make you eligible for an appointment with the hangman; rape, treason, piracy and murder. There is no evidence of rape, but I would watch Victor." That aroused Victor who threatened to kill me but Weigand told him to shut up.

"At the beginning, there was evidence of treason, a good hanging offence and we heard of armed men, machine guns and rifles, to violently overthrow the government in the Yukon Territory. Later we found this was a decoy and the Order of the Midnight Sun does not exist." Weigand smiled.

"Get on with it," he said, but appeared interested and I continued.

"Piracy is taking command of a ship to rob it, which is also a capital offence. That did happen, but it was outside of Canada, so there is no crime under Canadian law. However, there is one crime that you do not know about, which is unlawful killing and we now have new evidence that links McGill,

Victor and you to the crime of murder, which brings you three to the long drop." I watched his face, and he seemed confused, but Louise turned ashen. My problem was I could not see Victor, who was unpredictable and unbalanced. My other concern was his tendency to kill, but I could not look in his direction since this story required Weigand's full attention. I carried on and hoped I could still speak without a tremble in my voice.

"Your bodyguard has some serious flaws. Apart from a love of torture, he is a jealous man, and you know this, but there is something you do not know. He threatened to kill my clerk just for talking to Louise, and we now have proof that Victor killed another man. Louise loved him, and your bodyguard found out and killed him. Victor disposed of his body in a tunnel on McGill's claims, where you have the legal right to mine. We have the factual connections to tie you in to this. Bad luck Weigand, as you now face a murder conviction."

Louise screamed and charged Victor. Weigand took out his gun, turned and pointed at Victor. Victor held his gun in one hand, while his other hand tried to protect his face from Louise, as she cried and scratched his face. He shoved her to the ground. I ran as shots went past on my left and nearby, but I did not look back and kept running.

CHAPTER 21

I jumped into the trees and rolled when I heard Jerome shout that is was over. Victor lay on the ground while Weigand held his hands in the air. Louise staggered towards us while James and Philip crept towards Weigand. Sven gave me my rifle, and we went to comfort Louise. I had no choice, and I think she must have suspected the worst. I told Jerome to help her because I needed to check on Victor. I used my boot to turn him and saw that half his skull remained in the snow. I was numb and thanked my protector for keeping me safe. Weigand sat on the ground with two rifles directed at his chest. As I arrived, Philip whispered to him.

"It has been a long and hard year that I have looked for you. Let me refresh your memory. I have reviewed the witness statement time and time again. It was September, on the docks in San Francisco where you discovered my youngest brother and told him to drop his gun, which he did. You strolled up and shot him in the head and bragged to your buddy that is how you handle snitches." He stopped, and I was not sure he could continue, but he did.

"You never warned him. You could have tied him, but you wanted to be the tough man and impress your gang. My only wish is to see you hang and I don't care if it happens in Canada, San Francisco, or the Alaskan Territory. Justice has been a long time in coming, but it will happen when you do the long drop."

"I didn't do it." Weigand's face was ashen, and he started to tremble.

"Your buddy Laing was an undercover agent who will provide testimony," Philip said. He lifted Weigand and walloped him hard in the face. As Weigand fell, Fuller whispered, "Let's take a walk," and after yanking him, started to push him towards the river when I came over and put my arm on his.

"Philip, this is Canada, and I am a peace officer with the North West Mounted Police. This is not the time for your vigilante justice so give him to me." I noticed that James looked on impassively and realized these detectives lived by different rules. Philip shoved Weigand to me, who mouthed, "Thank you," and I told him to sit next to Sven. I looked at James and asked who shot Victor?

"We thought Weigand might kill him, but it was us," said James.

"You recall your bizarre plan. It began fine, we started to shoot at the boat when Victor suddenly pushed Louise to the ground and Weigand dropped his pistol to raise his hands. At this point, you were to fall to the ground, but your sudden decision to run left us no choice because Victor started to fire. It ended up as a shooting range, with Victor the target."

"James, give me some credit. I only ran after Victor shot at me and a moving target is better than one on the ground." I noticed his grin and realized he was pulling my leg. These detectives were from another world, to move from a death to a joke in less than five minutes was macabre. Perhaps we were almost kindred spirits, but even this was too much for me.

"Can you see if we can sit in on the interview," asked James? I explained that Inspector MacDonald would decide that. I told him that we might have an opportunity soon with the American's bringing in an important witness, since Weigand managed to upset the authorities here and in the Alaskan Territory. Sven came over, and I gave Weigand to him. I needed to move out of Weigand's hearing and walked with James to about twenty feet from Weigand when Jerome joined me.

"Why did Jane Warne not recognize Weigand?" James said she had been on a different investigation and only had a general description, and he had grown a beard. The other problem was she never heard his voice. James said Barton had started a series of robberies in California and during one theft, Weigand murdered Philip's brother, also a Pinkerton agent. I said we would talk later as now we needed to bring Weigand to the Detachment, help Louise and bring a coroner. Jerome said he would watch the body to maintain the continuity of evidence. I walked back to Weigand

"What is Victor's last name since we require it for the death certificate."

"Bolotnikov, he joined me in San Francisco, but he never talked about his past. If you want to get it right, his first name is Viktor."

"Weigand when will you stop spouting rubbish. You knew he was in the Russian Secret Police and you were aware he liked to torture." Weigand remained quiet. In a moment of time, Victor or Viktor went from breathing to an element in a court case. My body shook, and I wondered why did I take such risks? I noticed Jerome and James observed me but then Grant and his patrol arrived, and I gave a brief report. We checked the motor launch, and by my estimate, there were at least fifty bags of gold. Grant posted five men and sent a constable for wagons.

"Why do you like destroying boats? You did not sink this one, but it sure is holed."

"It can be repaired, but I did not want them to escape into the river." Grant said I certainly accomplished that. We stopped at the Gold Nugget restaurant to explain that Louise was safe. The walk to the Detachment seemed to take forever. I met Bert at the entrance and watched Jerome as he escorted Weigand to the cells. Bert looked concerned and told me to come with him to Inspector MacDonald's office. Inspector MacDonald told me to sit and went to his desk to pour me a glass of whisky and told me to drink it.

"You look dreadful, and I am not sure I want to hear your report, but I am glad you are alive, again." There were six other witnesses, so I told the facts without any explanations. When I finished, there was silence since I had nothing else to add, and did not want to talk anymore. There was a deep blackness in me. Was this how a condemned prisoner felt on the way to the scaffold? I think my expression did it and Inspector MacDonald did not lecture me. In a gentle voice, he told me to go home, and he would soon be out as a coroner. The inspector sighed and said in a soft voice that he did not agree with all that I did that day, but Louise was safe, and I helped bring in a wanted prisoner. As I was leaving, he grasped my hand.

"Caldwell, I do not understand you or why you take these risks but try to think next time." I remembered not much else other than Bert escorting me out of the office.

"I do not want to be a pallbearer at your funeral," Bert said. "I like you too much, and you have the intelligence to help me here so go home and give your blessings to the force that kept you alive. Please do not do that again John, as I need you alive." I knew they both cared for me and had kept me in the police, which I found surprising.

Could I have done it differently? Faced with Louise at the mercy of those two, I would do it again. To take these risks frightened me and something triggers this response, and I need to understand if I can stop it before something or someone ends my life. I was now both exhausted and morbid. At the house, I took another glass of whisky and went to bed. It was dark when I awoke and heard noises from the kitchen and in the kitchen I found Mrs. Rivest, George, William, Sven, James and Philip setting plates and enjoying my whisky. I was told to sit and watch as William handed me a glass and soon we ate.

Laughter, beef stew and fresh bread brought me out of my black mood, and soon I asked the story of Pinkerton's of the Yukon Territory. I was right about Jane Warne since she was never alone, as she always had at least one other Pinkerton detective with her. When she was at Big Pierre's cabin, James and Phillip hid with their rifles on top of a nearby hill. The abduction in Dawson City was unusual but she was there to meet another female agent. Barton's gang was from San Francisco, and after several successful heists, they had moved north. Barton came up with the idea of the Order of the Midnight Sun when he heard American miners complain about the taxes and royalties they had to pay. The uncertainty of the border dispute between the United States and Great Britain brought in more men and money.

Most of the men did not know the truth, and there was resentment against England and a suspicion that the Empire might take more of the Alaskan Territory. Rumours circulated that the Canadians planned to seize Skagway since no Canadian ships were permitted to dock at the port, which fed right into Barton's plan. Before he robbed the *Hannah*, he had a million dollars from the robberies and the theft from the *Hannah* was to be his last before heading south. Four million dollars was enough money to share and still live in luxury. James apologized about the documents from the North West Mounted Police outpost since Jane thought I was part of Barton's gang. When she described me to James, he said that was his friend John Caldwell, and at that time they had no idea I was with the police.

"I like you James, but hand over those documents, and we will make certified copies." He went to another room and returned with the maps and claim numbers. James thought Barton was in the United States, but he did not know where. The only other gang member they wanted was Searle, and I told them he was in Lousetown and our next task was to capture him.

The next afternoon I took my notes and the documents from James and went to the Detachment. Inspector MacDonald had left word at the front for me to meet him with Bert and Frederick Wade, the attorney for the police. They wanted to discuss potential charges, so Bert and I reviewed the evidence and I told them of what I knew from the Pinkerton's agents and Major Dunphy. Inspector MacDonald was irate that the American's did not inform us of their agents operating in the Yukon Territory. He was even more upset with the theft of police evidence. Bert looked at him and reminded him that Canada had Dominion Police in Seattle and Skagway, and our government had not told the United States government.

"We both were skating around on this one and not willing to admit our suspicions, in case we were wrong. Let us move on and work with them, as we are after the same criminal gang," was Bert's observation. This was the time for my surprise, and I took out my briefcase and handed the inspector the missing documents, as Bert gave me an evil smile.

"Sir, the documents from the outpost returned with an apology." Once that was out of the way, the next issue was the nature of the charges? I was right that the facts did not warrant piracy and treason, but were any of the suspects guilty of murder? I reviewed our finding Albert James in the mineshaft on McGill's property. How I ripped open his jacket and found a letter from Louise, who could prove Victor's jealousy. We have another witness named Matthew Talbot who can say Victor threatened to kill him for talking

THE KLONDIKE DETECTIVE

to Louise. Victor was always with Weigand and followed his orders, and we can provide Peter's evidence that McGill is Weigand's brother-in-law. Finally, there was the mining agreement between McGill and Weigand." Wade looked at us like a hungry cat amongst sparrows.

"I am sure the American's will be shocked to learn we only have six in a jury and not twelve. Six makes a conviction much easier, but we do not have adequate evidence to charge McGill or Weigand, and we cannot charge a dead culprit." He looked at me and grinned.

"Once you have finished your interviews with McGill and Weigand, the preliminary hearing will start. That is just to give the judge enough information to commit to trial, but you better move fast since the preliminary hearing will begin in six days and the *Hannah* will be here with the other witness." It was evident that Mr. Wade was up to date on this file. Bert and I went to his office to discuss lists of further evidence and we needed to bring in Louise and interview McGill and Weigand. We agreed to brief the Pinkerton agents as I said they could help us. Bert grunted, which I translated to mean, possibly.

Freeze up was coming and the cessation of shipping until next spring. There was an urgency to get the Alaskan contingent here and gone in the next few days. A blackboard was set up to list potential charges, witness statements and documents. We were interrupted and told that the *Nunivak* had docked, followed by Inspector MacDonald, who told us to join him in to greet our visitors.

First Lieutenant Cantwell and Major Dunphy came onto the dock and shook my hand, and I introduced Inspector MacDonald and Bert. Cantwell told us they were early as the local Indian pilot warned them of an early freeze up. We were invited to the dining room where were informed that they needed to leave tomorrow. Smitty could provide testimony, so long as he was back on the ship at seven in the morning and I was to give testimony in front of a judge after lunch. Dunphy apologized but said if this did not happen now we would have to wait until spring.

Second Lieutenant Waters approached with five soldiers that guarded Smitty. Poor old Smitty, who was so harmless that only one drunk soldier was required. Bert and I escorted the soldiers and prisoner to the Detachment, and Bert arranged for a Justice of the Peace and court reporter to stand by for two o'clock. We took them for coffee at the mess and when we finished, we went to Bert's office with Smitty, Waters and the five soldiers. We pushed the evidence away and asked the soldiers and Waters to wait outside. Waters was outraged.

"He is an American prisoner in our custody on foreign soil, and I will be present." Bert gave me a look that I understood to mean, what an idiot. Where could Smitty run with soldiers and dozens of police around? Bert said that was not a problem and offered him a chair and after that, we ignored him as we went through Smitty's story. His evidence was the same, he had joined a freedom army to bring the Yukon Territory into the Alaskan Territory. The first robbery was on the *Casca* steamer last July and he did work around King Solomon's Dome. He had no knowledge that Keating would kill that Indian. I told him the murder was not part of the Canadian criminal law since those offences were outside of Canadian jurisdiction.

"Who was in charge and where is Barton," I asked.

"There were three who were the bosses. Barton liked to call himself Commander and the other two senior men are Weigand and McGill. Weigand always had Victor around to do his nasty little deeds and stay away from him. Barton kept to himself, and I have no idea where he is, but I think he is in California. I cannot tell you more than that." I decided to bring some new information that Smitty might not know.

"Victor is dead, and we have McGill and Weigand in custody and the last person we want is Searle."

"Look in Lousetown but watch out for him or he will kill you." There were no more questions, so he was escorted out. When we were alone, I turned to Bert, and he did not like my expression.

"I have bad news. We need to do more work to find out where Victor Bolotnikov and Weigand stayed and search their rooms. We also need to go the camp near Forty Mile to conduct a further investigation. At the time when we sank their boat and captured the men, we left in a hurry. Only a couple of police are there with instructions to prevent anyone stealing from the sunken launch." Bert gave me a long stare and smiled.

"As your sergeant, I have translated our task to mean you. I must be ready for the preliminary hearing, and I have no time. Have fun and let me know what you find." That was disconcerting, and I realized I would have a busy few days. We filled the blackboard with lists of offences, witnesses and documents and then it was lunchtime. Bert had the Justice of the Peace and Court reporter arranged for the hearing at two when I would be on the *Nunivak*.

At one o'clock I was escorted to the dining room on the *Nunivak* and introduced to the judge. His name was James Wickersham and had combed over hair, a large moustache and eyes that looked right through you. The judge explained that before I testified, I was to hold a Bible and to swear on my oath, to tell the truth, and nothing but the truth, so help me God and did I understand the process? I said I did, and then he leaned over to study me.

"Son, you look pretty young so if you need a break, just put your hand up as this is pretty awful stuff you will tell," and I thanked the judge and waited. The hearing that required my testimony went fast, and we were finished by two o'clock. The judge thanked me and adjourned the court and the Major invited me to have coffee and bread. While we ate, he told me he had made a full recovery and we talked about our time together pursuing the fake gold thieves, and he acknowledged he should have listened to me but felt he needed to follow the trail. It was a privilege to be with the major and as he looked around, he said he had two messages. Bob Innes had followed a trail to San Francisco and would be back next spring if I took him fishing. The next message was from Jane Warne, who was in San Francisco and said she missed me.

"Of all the pleasures of the world, having friends is near the top." He then wished me good luck, and I told him the same. I arrived late for the Preliminary Hearing. The guards were members of the North West Mounted Police and soldiers of the United States Infantry. Smitty answered questions from Mr. Wade but sounded nervous, and his eyes never left Weigand. I was impressed he even spoke since he knew this would put him on Weigand's death list. At the back, the inspector whispered that Weigand and McGill each had a lawyer, but the rest of the accused did not. I knew the other men would feel betrayed and have no loyalty to their bosses. The fact that Weigand and McGill had separate lawyers indicated they might testify against each other.

Neither lawyer could shake Smitty in cross-examination although they had been given a summary of what he would say, but did not have the right to speak to him. The Preliminary Inquiry was their chance to accomplish this. The hearing adjourned at four and Smitty was escorted out of the room. Bert and I returned to his office where I was told to go home and sleep. I told Bert I needed to visit the camp tomorrow since freeze could be any day. He requested I finish all my searches and to check out Lousetown as soon as I could. An early supper was interrupted when Matthew knocked on my door. I opened it, and he told me that Louise had improved.

"Good," I said, "Since we need to interview her," which made Matthew unhappy. I told Sven to get the boat ready first thing in the morning just as James and Philip sauntered into my room. I repeated the messages I received from Bob and Jane but did not mention her missing me. I invited them on the boat to explore Barton's cabins.

The incoming freeze up was why I moved the trip to the next day. Gold miners were new to this land, but Indians have lived here thousands of years and knew the weather and the land. I checked on the dogs, saw Frank and told him I would take the boat to the camp in the morning. He asked if he could come and bring Sam, who had never been on a launch with an engine and wanted to see if moose were still in the area.

I brought Sven, Frank, and Jerome, and we met James and Philip at the dock. The first stop was at Moosehide to pick up Frank's uncle. I studied Sam who was of indeterminate age, short with a little beard and spoke broken English. He sat next to Sven and chatted away, but I had no idea if either knew what the other said. James and Philip told war stories of bank robberies and kidnapping. James wanted to come back to Dawson City since the place was home to him. The talk soon turned to theories of how Barton might send the money and the gold. We finally arrived at the area where the boat had sunk. Our boat slowed and stopped as we drifted to shore as Frank and his uncle jumped out to pull us in.

I told them to wait while I walked to the cabins with Jerome. As I approached a corporal pointed his weapon but recognized us. I explained we needed to search for evidence, starting with the ground near where the boat sunk, and then to check the camp. We carefully walked to the area where McGill came ashore. If he swam to shore with something important, where would he hide it or was it still in the sunken boat? The water was too cold and murky for an underwater search since the rain and snow had brought dirt from the shore into the blackish water.

Sam found a sealed tin partly hidden in a depression near the Yukon River. I opened the end to see if it had water in it but it was dry. The first document summarized ounces of gold and their sources. The second page had bank accounts in Dawson City, Seattle, San Francisco and New Orleans, with a total over a million dollars and the summary did not include the robbery from the *Hannah*. I was excited since we based our case on existing evidence and these new documents could make a difference. Once we finished our trial, this statement would be crucial to any American case, so we needed to maintain the integrity of these documents. They would be locked up under our control and when sent south they would require a reliable person such as myself to keep them safe.

I always wanted to see San Francisco. James and Philip looked at the papers and said that New Orleans was not part of their investigation. James said no agents worked in Louisiana since it was outside of their mandate but entered the information in his notebook. We did not find any other evidence, but we had something more valuable than gold, new and essential information. I did not know if Barton was aware McGill had left these documents in a tin. This was what Searle looked for when he searched Victor's cabin. If Weigand learned we had the list of bank accounts and amounts, he would be on Barton's death list so I believed we had a bargaining chip and the only question was whether McGill and Weigand preferred Canadian justice to that of Barton.

CHAPTER 22

Sam was dropped off at Moosehide, and when we landed at Dawson City, my crew decided it was time for a meal while Jerome and I took the tin to Bert. After he had read the documents, Bert shook his head and said that this would create problems for Barton and Weigand and my idea to search the camp was excellent detective work. Another constable was requested to assist in making three copies of the documents, which were locked in his safe. Bert looked extremely pleased and started to whistle and then suddenly stopped to look at me.

"I cannot give a copy to your American friends since I do not have anything in writing, but you can tell them we will respond once we receive an official request from the State Department." He wanted one more search of Lousetown and an interview with Louise. I said Weigand might kill his brother-in-law when he learned what we found but Bert just smiled and sent me home. Dinner at the house was a meal filled with stories, jokes and regret since I owed James and Philip a debt and had a great adventure with them. I explained we would provide the documents once we had an official request. One more trip with the boat was required. The miners took so much moose and caribou that people at Moosehide suffered from hunger and I wanted to give something to Sam. I gave Sven enough money to buy food and supplies to travel to Moosehide to distribute food to the families, elders and Sam.

Jerome stayed the night and early the next morning we went to Lousetown. It was a day where the rays of the sun sparkled on the snow, trees and the ground. The wind from the rivers prompted us to stride as this cold and cloudless days made everyone stay inside near a fire. Weigand and Victor had lived upstairs over a building that housed O'Brien Brewing & Malting Company. In the front was a bar named "The Bigger Hammer." We showed our warrants to obtain the keys to their rooms. Weigand's room was a mess. We saw clothes on the floor, cupboards open and a mattress partly off the bed.

Victor's room was clean and empty, so either he had moved or left nothing in his chambers. When we returned the keys, I asked why was the bar called the Bigger Hammer and was told if you drank too much, your head felt like that, which was not a good recommendation for a saloon. In the Gold Nugget restaurant, we saw Louise was in conversation with a customer. I asked the person at the bar if we could speak to her alone and when I showed my identification we were permitted to use the manager's office. Her last name was Cooper, and she could not provide much in the way of facts, other than Victor's jealousy. She often saw him with Weigand and others but did not know their names. I asked her if Victor had another room since we had checked his room over the brewery and found no evidence he used it. She became angry.

"I never went to his room let alone on a date with him. He would talk to me while I worked and I do remember his mentioning Eddy Searle, who Victor told me he sometimes stayed with him.

"Miss Cooper, do you know where Eddy Searle lives?" She shook her head and said she did not know since Victor had kept much of his life secret. After a few more questions, with non-responsive answers, I told her she was most helpful but did not think she would be a witness.

Coffee was at the Royal Alexander Hotel, while we warmed up. We were back at Bert's office by ten o'clock, and I asked Bert if Jerome might help. He said he would check later with his shift commander. I gave the results of my search, including the most significant finding, which was the absence of evidence.

"Bert, I think someone else is secretly in search for these documents, and I do not believe McGill told Weigand he lost these papers. We have a snitch in the jail and I am suspicious that Weigand communicates with Searle. Bert seemed distracted and said he would deal with this later but needed to itemize evidence.

"John, we need to assemble the case and do more interviews. We know Searle shot Corporal Tupper at the Grand Forks outpost and McGill, McMillan and Peters were with him. McMillan is dead but Peters will testify, and I am not sure what McGill will say. But we have enough evidence for most of the charges."

"If Weigand and McGill take the stand, how would they explain these amounts of gold," I said? I could imagine their testimony. "Your honour, that gold is not from the *Casca,* but from the big heist on the *Hannah*." That would not help them since it was possession of stolen gold found in Canada. Bert asked whether we should start to question McGill or Weigand first? I gave an evil grin, smiled and said,

"McGill as his confidence will be shaken once we show him the tin can and what it contained. If he talks, he will be like a loose board on a lumber wagon and we can use his statement against Weigand." McGill was brought in under escort to Bert's office where we had left our notes on the blackboard for his reading pleasure and placed him on a little chair.

"Special Constable Caldwell, why don't you start?" McGill was tall about six feet, but I was five inches taller and broader, so I walked over and looked down at him.

"Bert, is it nine or ten charges we have against him?" Bert replied so far, we had nine offences, and I went through the list which included, assault on a peace officer, two counts of kidnapping, fraud, forgery, extortion, two charges of theft over two hundred dollars, possession of stolen property and conspiracy. McGill paid attention.

"That was ten charges," he muttered.

"Do you know what drives a gold miner crazy," I asked? McGill answered he was not sure.

"Theft of gold is your charge," I said.

"You are charged with that indictable offence which is the most severe one, like your American felony charges. A jury in the Yukon Territory is six men, all British subjects, and not twelve like the American juries. And guess who will be on the jury?" McGill got it, if he elected to be tried by a jury, he could kiss his freedom goodbye, as he would have gold miners on his jury. I moved to a different subject.

"I find it interesting that the Criminal Code chose an amount of theft over two hundred dollars as a serious indictable offence. When the clerk reads that charge, it will state, Robert McGill, you are charged with two counts of theft over two hundred dollars between July 1, 1901 and October 10, 1901, totaling one million dollars." He looked scared.

"If I add possession of stolen property from the *Hannah*, that would bring it to another three million dollars." He glanced at Bert, who gave a big smile.

"Now Robert, why would I choose one million dollars? We need to work with conclusive evidence that is both reliable and relevant." I had the tin on the desk hidden under my hat, reached in and pulled it out. I held it near to him but out of his grasp.

"Guess where we found this?" He did not say a word, but his eyes stared at the tin.

"You were the only senior man on the launch so it would be you who had charge of that tin. Remember where we found you after your boat had an unfortunate accident and sank with a load of gold? As the boat tipped you thought what could you do with it and my guess was you threw it on shore and you hoped you could get word to Searle to get it. Or you probably know Searle to be greedy and decided to leave it but either way we have an evidence trail to you. The one thing you did not do was to tell Weigand, who would not be happy if he knew we had this information. That was before I almost drowned to rescue you and don't make me regret that." He sat, stared at me and at the tin and shook his head. I took the papers out and read the details of the various bank accounts and the notes of the ounces of gold.

"Would you like me to summarize our documents, and witnesses we have organized for the judge?" McGill just nodded so Bert, and I took turns to read the evidence, but I was not sure if he listened, as his eyes never left the can.

"If you cooperate the only concession we can offer in sentencing is for the prosecutor not to recommend the lash."

"Lash," he laughed, "Why lash a dead man?"

"Robert," I said, "We are not under American law, and there is no evidence of piracy, treason, or murder and we are satisfied that Victor Bolotnikov killed Albert James."

"It was on my property and I thought because of that I faced the death penalty." I explained that his penalty was likely years in jail and possibly the lash, but you will not be sentenced to death. He looked at me and gave the first sign of relief.

"Peters warned me about you but you saved me and now I am really confused. Are you sure?" I assured him it was true and wished the story of the scare I gave Peters would go away. Maybe the shock of seeing the tin, or relief that he would not be hung or my rescue, but he started to talk to the point he would not shut up, so we did not have to ask a lot of questions. Our challenge was keeping accurate notes and it took almost three hours interspersed with coffee and half a tin for cigarettes. There was one thing that interested me and I asked why he threw the tin on land.

"I should have left it with the boat but at the time I wasn't thinking and took it. When I was leaving the boat I did not know what to do, so I threw the can before losing consciousness."

"Why were you and Eddy Searle told to kill me?"

"It is not my fault I have idiots in my family. Weigand was annoyed that you had connected the evidence from the transfer of gold into money. After you had stopped us, we met with Barton who was furious since he learned you were a member of the North West Mounted Police and did not need any more pressure. He wanted to keep the focus on robberies, and with a large gang, a murder would get out if it happened in Canada, since that is an offence that has a death penalty. He told Weigand to capture you, but I had no idea he later left you to die. My guess was that Barton believed no one would find that remote camp in the Alaskan Territory and he assumed you would die there, alone and forgotten."

"When did you learn of this since Weigand is part of your family? He looked to the floor and said when they were on the launch after they left the camp and thought they would return to pick us up. I was not sure if that was the truth, but by now I was too preoccupied with the case to worry about his role. My next topic was Barton including when did he arrive and how long he was here.

"Just twice. Barton operates out of San Francisco and is smart and powerful. His men work with the telegraph companies and the banks and his tentacles extend into the police force and politicians. This job was short term, and his direction was to rob the gold and leave. He is brilliant and came up with the idea of the Order of the Midnight Sun." Barton's problem was he drew resources from two governments. The attempt to overthrow the Yukon Territory by armed Americans created a major crisis, bordering on a war that brought in the Dominion Police and the Pinkerton's Detective Agency. We had to review a few points, and we felt we had the case wrapped up, so we did not require Weigand as a witness, but I wanted him to see the tin. My dislike for this creature made me try to outsmart him. He was arrogant and left me with the impression that he felt superior. I knew I was young and was in my first few months as a detective, but I wanted a confession. My pride pushed me to take him on since I remembered his insult in the camp in the Alaskan Territory that I was just a Canadian and out of my depth. We decided to put Peters, Burke and McGill in separate cells to protect them. Weigand might be his brother-in-law, but once he sees the tin that might be too much. As McGill was about to return to his cell, I asked about Eddy Searle. He looked scared and shook his head.

"A rat leaves a sinking ship, and Eddy has long ago erased his trail as he is always out for number one. He is vicious and cruel so be careful if you take him on, as he is like Victor. I never asked for a share of the money Eddy took from you on the barge, as I like to live. He is in Lousetown and pays for protection, so if you go after him, bring friends and be prepared to fight.

It was late when we reviewed our notes. We would need to interview Burke again and then take on Weigand. Once we completed this, we would provide a summary to the prosecutor. There was a knock on the door and Constable Jerome Scott came in said he would work with Sergeant Raven for one week. We now had another member of the team. The next morning Burke was brought to Bert's office, and Jerome took notes. Burke said he would not talk unless we guaranteed we would not charge him with murder. I confirmed this and realized our inmates were talking.

"Why was Albert James left in the tunnel? Was it to keep him out of the way?" Burke moved his chair a few feet away as I promised I would leave his arm alone.

"Victor offered to look after him and the next thing I learned James was dead, but no one told me the reason. I later learned that Victor had stabbed him and the plan was to come back later and bury the body since they believed no one would look there. I thought this was a stupid idea, and he should be buried immediately, but things moved so fast, and we thought we had time. I had no part in that killing, and I am sorry." He was uncomfortable as his eyes darted from Bert to me.

We agreed Burke should be the first witness. It would give the Justice of the Peace the big picture. I asked about Eddy Searle and where he stays. Burke shook his head, frowned and refused to talk. There was no point asking witnesses about Searle since either they did not know where he lived or they were too scared to answer. Once he left, we discussed a strategy to deal with Weigand. He will act tough and refuse to talk, but his men told us he always wanted to be the center of attention.

Weigand reminded me of some senior students from school and adulation from other students. If we take that away, they react. At first, Weigand will not cooperate, so we need to spend days to ignore him and to treat him as an insignificant person. When I mentioned this idea, Bert and Jerome agreed to give it a try. The next morning Weigand was escorted to Bert's office with Jerome to take notes. Weigand stood and looked at us. I had managed to acquire Cuban cigars, and when offered one, he took it and after a few puffs, he thanked me.

"This is the only pleasure I have now so I can smoke and relax as I have nothing to say. When you become tired, take me back to my cell." I tried to put out of my thoughts how he left us to die. It was a tough battle, but I calmed down, and it helped not to look at him.

We avoided him and everything we did we excluded Weigand. I brought back coffee and biscuits for us, and we discussed the weather, hockey teams and politics. At twelve two constables watched Weigand while he ate and after lunch Bert and I reviewed the case in front of him. At five o'clock we asked Jerome to find a constable to take Weigand to his cell. At eight the next morning he returned to Bert's office, and we continued to ignore him and made notes for Mr. Wade. We occasionally reviewed a document or witness statement, but we never used the name Weigand, just that fellow there, or that man. At lunch, two constables were in charge, and we went to meet with Mr. Wade. We returned to Bert's office at five with Weigand still there.

"Bring that fellow back at eight," said Bert. Day three with Weigand was when I produced the tin can and papers. I read out the total of the gold profit and the bank statements. "Where did you get that?" He tried to remain calm.

"Why do you care?" was my response. "You are not here to talk to us so it is no concern of yours. You are an insignificant part of this case as you played a minor part in a brilliant scheme concocted by Cedric Barton."

"Caldwell, you are such a jackass. You have no idea of my capabilities and genius as I was the mastermind of these robberies."

"Don't steal Barton's ideas. He had the brains and created the Order of the Midnight Sun. He reversed your decisions, and you went along with everything, like a good little follower. Just accept your small part of this and do not compare yourself to a leader with ideas." I wondered if I overplayed this.

"You are too stupid to see the facts you little shit. I ran things here, no one else. I came up with the idea of the Order of the Midnight Sun and I recruited and planned the robberies and arranged the transfers to McGill. Everything was my doing, including sending the money to other bank accounts. Barton can wait until the cows come home for a penny from the gold robberies since the money went to me." I hoped Jerome got this but to call me a little shit was too much. He knew what he had done, and I thought he immediately regretted his outburst.

"I gave you nothing, and I will not talk in court and what I said to you is useless." I was pleased with our strategy and we now need to check the money trail, the bank accounts and all bank transfers from Weigand and McGill.

Some of the accounts are in San Francisco, so I hope Jane and the Pinkerton Detectives are efficient and careful.

Weigand was in the big league among crooks, but he was not a lawyer, and now he had confessed to three police officers. His exaggerated sense of importance and arrogance did him in, and he still believed we could not use his confession. I looked forward to the court when we could relate the bragging of this nitwit and the only question the magistrate would have was whether Weigand spoke freely and without threats. If our lawyer can either maximize or minimize Weigand's role, he may want to take the stand, but once we repeat his confession, what will he do? I am sure his lawyer will warn him against testifying in court, but we had a confession we could use.

He sat there and refused to talk while Bert and I took turns to ask questions but received no reply, so he went back to his cell. Jerome had it all down, and we finished that day that Weigand had played a bad hand. The next few days consisted of witnesses, testimonies, review of documents and work with our lawyer. By Saturday at noon we felt we had finished the preparations for the Preliminary Inquiry to start Monday. Security required that we hold it within the North West Mounted Police mess hall. We would have armed men around the building, and all prisoners would be shackled. After lunch, Bert sent me home.

It was strange to be free since I had worked almost every day for over a month. I changed and took Ben and Lucky along the river. Lucky was on a leash until we left town, then I let them both run. Clouds drifted and now snow covered the mountains. In this wilderness, it seemed you were the only person. The only sounds were the shuddering of the river and the wind, but to be safe I also carried my rifle as I did not know where Searle was or if he had others with him.

Today I would relax and decide my future and did I make the right choice to be a detective? There were times of extreme danger and regret and I wondered if I should return to Toronto? A raven landed in front of me, and the dogs had not seen it. It made a gurgling sound and hopped closer. Most animals will look away if you look in their eyes but this one stared at me so I asked if I should stay, or leave? It sat there, croaked and then flew over the frozen river. What was that answer? The majesty of the broad stretches of trees entranced me. I heard a wolf howl and the dogs started in that direction then Ben headed back with Lucky. This place was my home and my job was both fascinating and scary. Suddenly the sound of a rifle shot dropped me to the ground. I looked but could not see anyone. I took off my glove and worked the bolt on my rifle.

Hunting was over, so what would be the reason for the shot. I was the only one there and lay for a few minutes and then slowly stood up. I looked in the direction of the mystery shooter, then carried my rifle at the ready and jogged to Dawson City. If I was the intended target, I needed to determine who pulled the bolt on the weapon. As I walked, I became increasingly angry. I was resolved to track down Searle and needed to hire all of Frank's family, extended family and friends. It would be Searle or me that would survive, but this town could not handle both.

CHAPTER 23

After I had returned to the Detachment to file my report, I went home to think. Ben and Lucky came to my bedroom and as I scratched them, I had to determine if this was an accident or a warning. I knew if Searle were the shooter, his accuracy would kill me if that were his intent since he had the opportunity to fire several shots before I was in a position to return fire so why did he let me live? Eddy was not compassionate and had an evil streak. I was low on the list of influential people since I was neither a lawyer nor a judge. He wanted me to meet him, but that was a bizarre invitation. I wished a midnight rendezvous so I could prepare but this was a nasty and underhanded way to behave. I would take the appropriate steps but to have a phantom enemy was a dangerous distraction. The Preliminary Hearing was to start on Monday, but Mr. Wade wanted to put into evidence Weigand's confession, and his lawyer objected so a hearing was held to determine if the statement was voluntary. McWilliams was the Justice of the Police, a Scot with a sense of humour.

"So, let me understand counsel, your objection is the police conduct towards your client, but you do not complain of a threat. The objection is that the police ignored your client, who then became upset and uttered a confession. This is the biggest crock of nonsense I have ever heard, and you have no cases to back this argument. I think your esteemed client should have thought this through, as he was there for three days, and probably knew what they were up to." The impression I had was the magistrate thought Weigand to be stupid and deserved the consequences of his actions. He pronounced the words "esteemed client" in a high-pitched voice to play to the crowded courtroom that responded with laughs and jeers. Weigand and his counsel were not happy but what could they do?

Weigand's statement was ruled admissible; the case unfolded without a problem, and he did not take the stand. The men from the camp, Peters, Burke and McGill all provided testimony. We had our friendly witnesses, Big Pierre, George Martin, Mrs. Rivest, Henry Lloyd, Roland Caton and myself and all documents were ruled admissible. It finished Friday at five with all charges to proceed, and the matter was remitted to a Territorial Court for a trial to start Monday, November 25, 1901.

There was an appeal from the Justice of the Peace admitting Weigand's confession. The judge dismissed it and held Magistrate McWilliams's decision was correct. I had less than three weeks to find Searle. In the first week of November, an arctic cold front arrived. I hired four more men from Mooseide, and they stayed with Frank and his brother. The patrols increased to search Lousetown while Sven, Jerome and I spent countless hours in checking the area. I started to spend time in empty buildings that overlooked the river at Lousetown and discovered quickly I hated extreme weather.

The time I had followed Searle I helped to capture a fellow who had a bank key. His name was Joe Costello who did occasional work for Eddy Searle. He had been released to stand trial but left the Yukon Territory. We went back to ask the prisoners in custody about Costello, but no one knew him. The safety deposit key opened a box at the Bank of Commerce that held almost thirty thousand dollars. Was that money for Barton, and why was it not transferred? They had the papers to show they had obtained this amount of gold, so why keep it here?

It was on November fifteenth when Frank received definite information as to Searle's location and this time a large patrol of seven armed men would be at the building. It was four in the morning as we silently walked to our rendezvous. There was no moon, a darkened sky and falling snow to help muffle our sounds as we surrounded the building. Two men guarded the rear door, and another two men stood guard in the front.

I used a knife to pry open the front door, and we removed our boots and crept along the ground floor to search those rooms to ensure no one waited for us. I knew Searle would be upstairs, but I did not know if he heard us. I whispered to Jerome and another constable to follow as I ascended the stairs. It was the landing at the top that gave me away since I did not see the string attached to the bell. It rang and then shots came at us, and we returned fire when I felt an intense pain in my upper left arm. I continued to shoot until I needed to change revolvers and realized Searle had stopped shooting. He could be dead, out of bullets or waiting for a clear shot once I was in his view. As I reached the upper floor, the window at the end of the corridor showed the snow had stopped, and the moon was now out. I felt faint and lay on the floor to push myself with my revolver in my hand. It was cold, but sweat trickled down my face, and my heart raced. I raised my pistol and expected to die since his door was open. He sat on the bed with his revolver at his head, glanced at me and looked out the window.

"What a ridiculous end. If you can send a letter to my mother tell her, I am sorry. Her address is in the suitcase."

"Eddy there is no death penalty in Canada, so you will not be hung. Put down the weapon."

"You don't understand. I kept some of Weigand's money in my safety deposit box. That was a big mistake, and it will be only a matter of time when Barton finds this out. As you know, Barton and Weigand are unpleasant men and will not kill before they torture me. You know what makes it funny? Weigand never trusted me, so he told Victor to handle the money, but Victor wanted to impress a lady, and needed to buy clothes. He asked me to take care of the money transfers, and I paid him the one hundred dollars I stole from you. Goodbye, Caldwell, you and I share one trait, we are persistent." He never looked back as I called for him not to do it, and then there was the shot. I turned away and yelled out.

"I am fine, but Searle is dead." I felt weak, and my last thought was why that last bullet was for him and not me. I woke up in the hospital the next day. His ending was bittersweet as I did not want Searle to die that way. I sent the letter to his mother and added a separate note about his courage. What I did not mention was his choice to spare me and realized he did not trust his gang to send the letter.

There were vague memories of visitors. Mrs. Rivest was always there and sometimes snuck in Ben and Lucky. I remember Grant, Bert, William, George and Sven in the crowded room. I thought George had his eye on Mrs. Rivest. Jerome, Matthew, Frank, the superintendent and the inspector also visited. I was surprised to see Arizona Charlie Meadows without Mae. He had sold the theatre and was heading out by horse and sleigh by the winter road.

"Listen, John, I am sorry you got plugged, but I hear you will survive. I am heading down to Arizona and if ever you get to that part of the world look me up. I sold out, and I told the new owners about you. The gold rush is starting to wind down, and I hate the cold. I need the sun and heat so take care and Mae gives her regards." There was one unexpected visitor. Scotty was the miner who gave me directions and hardtack and told me he received a letter from Frank Thompson. Thompson decided to go as far away from Weigand as he could and was somewhere in northern New Brunswick. At least I knew what happened to him and I was glad that he survived since not many of Weigand's partners did. I was in the hospital for three days and released.

The trial led to the conviction of the members of the Weigand or Barton gang, depending on which liar you believed. The men at the camp received eight years for the possession of stolen gold. The cooperation of Burke and Peters offset their additional charges, and they received eleven years. McGill took the stand and provided credible testimony, so he received only thirteen years. I ended up developing a kind of friendship for those three, but that did not extend to Weigand. Weigand refused to take the stand. His lawyer again tried to object to his confession and the judge glared at him.

"Counsel, this was ruled admissible in both the magistrates court and in this court. If I hear one more mention of this I will find you in contempt, and your client can act for himself." I knew Weigand instructed his lawyer, but the lawyer should have told him those ideas would only make it worse. The judge attempted to be composed, but the evidence pushed him to find that Weigand was the mastermind of the conspiracy and fraud. The prosecutor brought into evidence the death of Albert James and added,

"The most heinous evil brought to this young Territory." I think the judge liked it because he used it in his judgment from the bench. I had wanted to use the death of Albert James, but Mr. Wade objected that this was irrelevant, since no one was charged with murder. I had some cases from England about conspiracy, so we agreed to try it. This was after the judge threatened contempt to Weigand's lawyer, so the fight had gone out of the lawyers, and in it went, as part of the record.

The court permitted for me to state that Eddy Searle took the money. This was one of the exceptions to the hearsay rule. Hearsay is simple, if another person said something to me, I could not repeat in court what they told me because the lawyers could not cross-examine the other person. Since Searle was dead there was no way he could be examined in court. One of the exceptions to the hearsay rule was a dying declaration, and there were two parts to this. I needed to convince the judge that Eddy Searle believed he was dying, which was easy since he had a gun to his head, and used it after he spoke. Second, his statement had to relate to the cause of the death. The judge got it right away when he quoted *Hamlet* "The croaking raven doth bellow for revenge." As he spoke a large raven hovered and cawed at the window and Weigand turned white. The judge paused in his deliberation and crossed himself. I was also able to tell the judge about Weigand's plan for our deaths. The court was shocked that the winner of a poker game at the camp could choose how we would die. I recounted his words.

"You will be locked in your cabin and death will come, but the question is in what way? You may freeze, starve or encounter a bear which I leave to fate." He whispered to his lawyer that it was hearsay. He was wrong since we both could be questioned, but his lawyer appeared disgusted and moved his chair away from his client. I think by this time his counsel had given up. The judge did not seem to notice, and my statement was accepted. The whole time I spoke Weigand never stopped his stare at me. The mastermind received twenty years, and my hatred for that man was equal to what I believed he felt for me.

Two things from the trial gave me satisfaction. The first was Weigand when he learned he lost most of his money. All that work and to find out it went to Eddy Searle. The second was his additional penalty. He would receive thirty lashes when he arrived at Kingston Penitentiary and thirty at the end of his years in prison. I usually forgave but not for this man. I was still too close to his evil presence. After the trial, William and I met with the lawyers for the *Casca* and *Hannah*. The gold on the *Hannah* was the property of several dredge companies on Bonanza Creek. I took us to my usual table at the Royal Alexandria Hotel where the lawyers enjoyed ample supplies of whisky. William represented Big Pierre, George Martin, and Mrs. Rivest.

Compared to the *Casca* theft of one hundred thousand dollars, or the *Hannah* of three million dollars, my friend's loss was much less, but it had hurt them more. I told the story of my searches and investigation and spent time on my kidnapping and my near-death experience. The safety deposit money was almost thirty thousand dollars and the gold from the warehouse totaled thirty-two hundred ounces, which worked out to be over sixty-four thousand dollars. The gold from the camp and the boat at Lousetown, was one hundred thousand ounces. It was hoped the remainder was on the sunken launch, so the lawyers worked an agreement to pay Big Pierre, George Martin and Mrs. Rivest each two thousand dollars. The lawyers were both interested in my escort business and recommended my services to their clients.

I made an offer for the destroyed launch which cost me two hundred dollars. It was placed on a team of wagons and hauled to my barn as a winter project. Next year I would have two boats for transporting gold. My new name was *Destiny* so *Spirit* and *Destiny* would be part of my future. Big Pierre offered me a reward, but I told him all I wanted was to see his daughter Suzanne again and looked confused, until I told him the story.

It was just before Christmas when I wrapped blankets and cooking utensils for Frank's family, and I boots for Frank, his brother and cousins. I gave Matthew a set of law books and a pen. Sven received a new revolver and a piano that I had bought from a teacher in Dawson City. I wrapped books for Grant, William and Mrs. Rivest and gave Bert the book I had lost and several more on detective work. My employees, including those who searched the streets, were given money to buy Christmas presents.

There were two special Christmas gifts that I brought me happiness. One was a letter from my father that forgave me and welcomed me to come home.

It had arrived on the last boat but I had been too busy to read it. The second was a telegraph from Jane that stated she wrote me a letter. She missed our adventures and asked me to visit her in San Francisco where she would teach me manners and detective skills. She also wanted me to have a wonderful Christmas. I telegraphed my family and Jane. To my family, I said I loved them and would visit in the spring. My telegram to Jane was that she was always on my mind and I would visit her to learn from an expert and wished her the happiest Christmas. Christmas day arrived with a dinner of all my friends and another cherished gift I received was a wood plaque.

"To John Caldwell, the Klondike Detective. May he always discover clues, criminals and be bested by a lady." I had to thank Bert for that additional part of the plaque, and I did that when he had me over for dinner. I did not care if Jane beat me if I could be with her again. You never know what can happen when you wish for it as life has a sense of humour. I just did not want it to be too cold and not too dangerous. The end of this year was peaceful and I trusted my encounters with death would soon be distant memories.

Made in the USA
Las Vegas, NV
25 August 2023

76611626R00142